Writing from the Edge of the World

Writing from the Edge of the World

The Memoirs of Darién, 1514–1527

BY GONZALO FERNÁNDEZ DE OVIEDO

Translated and with an Introduction by G. F. Dille

THE UNIVERSITY OF ALABAMA PRESS

Tuscaloosa

Typeface: ACaslon

∞

The paper on which this book is printed meets the minimum requirements of
American National Standard for Information Sciences-Permanence of Paper for
Printed Library Materials, ANSI Z39.48–1984.

Library of Congress Cataloging-in-Publication Data

Fernández de Oviedo y Valdés, Gonzalo, 1478–1557.
　[Historia general y natural de las Indias. Libro 29, capítulos 6–24. English]
　Writing from the edge of the world : the memoirs of Darién, 1514–1527 / by Gonzalo
Fernández de Oviedo ; translated and with an introduction by G. F. Dille.
　　p. cm.
　Includes bibliographical references and index.
　ISBN-13: 978-0-8173-1518-4 (cloth : alk. paper)
　ISBN-10: 0-8173-1518-7 (cloth : alk. paper)
　ISBN-13: 978-0-8173-5339-1 (pbk. : alk. paper)
　ISBN-10: 0-8173-5339-9 (pbk. : alk. paper)
　1. Darien (Panama and Colombia)—Early works to 1800. 2. America—Discovery and
exploration—Early works to 1800. 3. America—Early accounts to 1600. I. Title.
　F1569.D3F47 2006
　917.287′ 78—dc22

　　　　　　　　　　　　　　　　　　　　　　　　　　　　　　　　2006002256

Contents

Maps

Foreword

The three fundamental histories of the first half century of the Spanish presence in the New World are, in order of composition, Peter Martyr's *Decades of the New World,* Gonzalo Fernández de Oviedo's *General and Natural History of the Indies,* and Bartolomé de las Casas's *History of the Indies.* These works provide invaluable although often conflicting views of this period of the encounter between the Old and New Worlds, and each reflects the respective experiences, character, and agendas of these three quite different personalities: Martyr, the Italian humanist, courtier, and diplomat; Las Casas, the crusading priest; and Oviedo, the autodidactic colonial bureaucrat. Of the three, Martyr and Las Casas are the best known to English readers through translations of their works. Lamentably, the same cannot be said for Oviedo, whose enormous *History* and other writings form an almost inexhaustible treasury of information on every aspect of the New World of his day. Scholars have variously credited Oviedo with many firsts: first general historian, first ethnographer, first naturalist, first anthropologist, and first sociologist of the New World. If we add first autobiographer and first Spanish novelist and poet of the Americas, his importance becomes even more compelling.

Yet, if we look for English translations of Oviedo's voluminous writings we are disappointed, finding that the majority of his *General and Natural History* is not available in English and that of the few sections that have been translated, many are out of print. Unfortunately, it is likely that Oviedo's magnum opus will never be fully available in English given its monumental bulk—five volumes of double-column, small-type pages in the current Spanish edition. There is so much material in this virtual encyclopedia of three parts, fifty books, and hundreds of chapters that it is almost impossible to comprehend its totality. Considering that its writing and rewriting occupied its author more than four decades, it would take an exceptionally dedicated (and young) translator to tackle such a huge project. In general, what we have in English of Oviedo tends to be the highlights: for example, the material relating to Columbus, the accounts of North American expeditions (Hernando de Soto, Cabeza de Vaca, Ponce de León), and incidents of the exploration or settlement of specific New World areas (the Amazon, Puerto Rico). The only English translation of a complete Oviedo work is of his 1526 *Oviedo on the Natural History of the Indies*. This text is generally referred to as the *Summary* because it is a much abbreviated form of what would become his *General and Natural History of the Indies*.

With the exception of the *Summary,* existing English translations, for the most part, are of materials that were written by others and supplied to Oviedo for incorporation into his *General and Natural History* because of his imperial appointment as Chronicler of the Indies. Yet Oviedo was no armchair historian, a point he makes constantly throughout his text. From 1514 to his death in 1557 he was a resident of the New World, first in Darién, Central America, then in Nicaragua, and finally in Santo Domingo. In truth, the entire *General and Natural History* attests to his personal involvement in the affairs of the Indies but none so much as the section on Tierra Firme (the Spanish Main), the region comprising the Caribbean coast of the South American continent and including present-day Panamá. These chapters are essentially Oviedo's memoirs of the years 1514–27.

This Darién material (from Part II, Book XXIX, Chapters VI through XXIV of the *General and Natural History*) is the text of the present translation. Although only a part of Book XXIX, these chapters form a complete and fascinating narrative with a beginning, a development, and a conclusion. They recount the circumstances of Oviedo's appointment as a royal officer, the historian's first voyage to the Indies in the "Splendid Armada," his impressions of the wonders of the New World, the cruel treatment of the Native Americans, and the deadly internecine political struggles among the Spaniards. In the memoirs of these years we have perhaps the fullest account of the first viable Spanish settlement in continental America by a cast of characters (Oviedo included) who were to make their mark for good or ill from Mexico to the tip of South America. Moreover, in this section Oviedo records the decisive moment in 1514 when he determined to link the rest of his life to the New World and to make himself its interpreter to the Old through the pages of his *General and Natural History*.

Although the later spectacular conquests of Mexico and Peru have received more attention, it was this mainland colonial establishment in Darién (now for the most part in the Republic of Panamá) that opened the door to vast unknown continents. Initially the Spanish were lured to the area by exaggerated reports of gold and pearls, but the true treasure of the land soon was realized to be its strategic location. Balboa's famous discovery that the territory was an isthmus made Darién the staging point for claiming, exploring, and exploiting the entire Pacific coast of the Americas. Through this vital transit point, Spanish conquistadors, settlers, and merchants set out for Peru and then for Asia, and through Darién the fabulous wealth of Peru and Asia flowed to Spain and to Europe.

From his youthful days at the court of Queen Isabella and King Ferdinand, his travels through Italy, and then four decades of residence in the Indies, Gonzalo Fernández de Oviedo was uniquely positioned to chronicle everything related to the New World. Kings and princes, cardinals and bishops, explorers and conquistadors, bureaucrats and merchants—there was scarcely anyone connected to the enterprise of the Indies in Spain or in the Americas whom he did not know, converse with, or correspond with. From 1492, when Oviedo first saw Columbus at the siege of Granada, until his death in 1557 in the fortress guarding Santo Domingo, he painstakingly recorded and evaluated every scrap of information on the Indies he came across. Yet, of the thousands of pages filled with his neat italic script, only a small portion saw print during his lifetime. The fifty books of the *General and Natural History* were only published three centuries after his death and several thousand pages of other writings still await editing.

This translation of Oviedo's Darién years is intended for a general audience interested in early American history as well as the history of Spain during the age that catapulted that country to the position of dominant European power in an astonishingly short period of time. I have prefaced it with a brief introduction that begins with general background information on the author's life and works within the context of the political situation in Spain and the apparatus of Spanish colonial administration. Following that is an overview of the organization and contents of the entire *General and Natural History*, its printing history, and its reception. At the end of the introduction are biographical notes on the principal figures of the narrative. In addition, there is a brief guide to the variety of monetary units in the text with some examples of salaries and purchasing power. Finally, since there is much more to Oviedo than his *General and Natural History*, the bibliography begins with a list of all known Oviedo works in order of composition together with an indication of selected full or partial Spanish editions and English translations.

The present translation is not what might be termed a "critical" translation in that it does not always account for every word of Oviedo's text nor does it always strictly preserve the order of presentation of the material. Despite all their peculiar charm, Oviedo's numerous hundred-word-plus sentences have been divided and the repetitious adjectives and verbs pared down. In a few instances the order of presentation within paragraphs has been rearranged and some paragraphs have been combined, separated, or moved in the interest of a more logical organization. Additionally, from time to time, pronouns have been replaced with nouns to clarify the referent. As consistently as possible, English spellings are used for familiar names and places (e.g., Columbus, Cortez, Castile, Seville) and for non-Spanish names and places (e.g., Pliny, Peter Martyr, Ghent). Otherwise the Spanish forms are conserved. All in all, however, any meddling with the source text has been to facilitate comprehension; nothing significant has been omitted. All the translation of the text and all translations appearing in the introduction and notes are mine, unless otherwise indicated.

Acknowledgments

Several years ago I began this translation project in the lovely colonial surroundings of Querétaro, Mexico. Then I could not have imagined the amount of time and effort that would go into the preparation of even so slim a volume as this. However, not all that time and effort was solely mine, as I am deeply indebted to many colleagues and friends whose contributions I thankfully acknowledge. At the top of the list are both Claire Etaugh, Dean of the College of Arts and Sciences of Bradley University, and William J. Walker, Chair of the Department of Foreign Languages, also at Bradley. These two friends, colleagues, and bosses, through word and deed, unfailingly supported my project from its inception. If every faculty member worked for and with administrators like them, the academic world would be a better place. In the category of moral support I cannot forget my good friend Charles Dannehl of the Department of Political Sciences, who patiently heard more about Darién and Oviedo and my problems than he probably wanted to know. In the research for the introduction and the translation, as ever, the Bradley library staff and in particular Laura Corpuz and Marina Savoie were invaluable in tracking down for me even the most recondite (for central Illinois) articles and books. Certainly, without their expertise the project would have been impossible. My dear friend Myrtle Kent, late of the Bradley English Department, kindly interrupted her snug retirement to read through an early version of the text and tactfully identified its many infelicities. In Peoria, copy editing and preparation of drafts of the manuscript were ably undertaken by Kathleen Dusenbery, whose technical skills and poet's ear for language were a godsend. Also, special thanks are due to Kathy Cum-

mins of Naperville, Illinois, for an expert and essential final copy editing. Finally, to the staff at the University of Alabama Press, my most
sincere gratitude for not giving up on this project even when I had my
doubts.

Writing from the Edge of the World

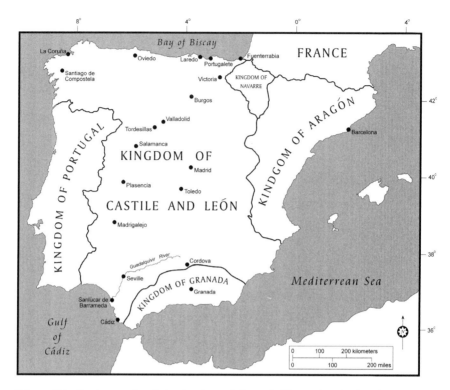

Map 1. The Iberian peninsula in the time of Gonzalo Fernández de Oviedo.

Introduction

Gonzalo Fernández de Oviedo y Valdés (1478–1557)

Oviedo in the Old World

When Gonzalo Fernández de Oviedo y Valdés was born, the Iberian peninsula was divided into five independent kingdoms. The largest was Castile-León, stretching from the Cantabrian coast through the central plateau to Andalusia. To the east and running along the Mediterranean Sea coast and including the Balearic Islands was Aragón. Between Castile and Aragón and on the border with France was the much smaller but strategically located kingdom of Navarre. To the west lay Portugal. Finally, in southern Spain, centered about the city of Granada, was the Islamic kingdom of the same name, the last vestige of the once mighty Muslim presence in the peninsula that dated from A.D. 709. Four years prior to Oviedo's birth, King Enrique IV (called the Impotent) of Castile died, leaving two women as claimants to the throne: his half-sister Isabella, married in 1469 to Ferdinand II, heir to Aragón, and Enrique's daughter Juana. Juana is known in Spanish history as the Beltraneja, because she was popularly alleged to have been the illegitimate daughter of Enrique's queen and a court favorite, Beltrán de la Cueva. Immediately upon Enrique's death, Isabella, acting with characteristic decisiveness, had herself proclaimed queen of Castile, but her control of that kingdom was consolidated only after a period of civil war with Juana's supporters.

Isabella and Ferdinand, generally referred to as the Catholic Monarchs, had just begun their campaign to recover Granada when Gonzalo Fernández de Oviedo was born in Madrid to parents originally from the area of Oviedo in the ancient kingdom of Asturias in the northern part of the peninsula. At about age twelve, and certainly through important connections, Oviedo joined the household of the young duke of Villaher-mosa, King Ferdinand's nephew. The duke and his suite traveled constantly from region to region following the court of the monarchs, which, in those times, had no fixed capital. A good deal of Oviedo's time was spent in Andalusia, the staging area for the campaign to recover Granada. In that busy year of 1492, Oviedo was present at three seminal events in Spanish history—the fall of the last Muslim kingdom of Granada, the commissioning of Christopher Columbus to sail west, and the expulsion of the Jews. A year later, in Barcelona, Oviedo witnessed the admiral's triumphant return from his first voyage of discovery to the Indies. It was during these momentous times that the young Oviedo began his lifelong practice of recording what he experienced. When Crown Prince Juan was established in his own household in 1496, Oviedo ascended to a position with that illustrious but unfortunately short-lived heir. In Prince Juan's court Oviedo shared duties with Diego and Ferdinand Columbus, the admiral's sons, and cultivated other important connections that were to serve him well in later years.

Unfortunately, after only a year, the prince suddenly died and his suite was disbanded. Oviedo remained at court for a while but, like many young, ambitious Spaniards with limited possibilities at home, he soon set out for Italy, where he remained from 1499 to 1502.[1] Renaissance Italy was a patchwork of competing city states and foreign interests. During those troubled but fascinating times, Oviedo traveled the length of the peninsula, finding service in noble houses in Genoa, Milan, Mantua, and Rome, and ultimately with the man he viewed as the incarnation of the chivalrous spirit, the king of Naples, Frederick of Aragón. Notwithstanding the corruption of the time and its deadly intrigues, Oviedo reveled in the refinements of Italian art, literature, and culture. For him it was a golden period he was to recall frequently in his writings. Unfortunately, as with his position with Prince Juan, his Neapolitan days were too few. King Frederick was deposed in the complicated political struggles between the French and Spanish for the hegemony of Italy and Oviedo had to return to Spain.

Two years later, the much venerated Queen Isabella died. Her daughter Juana (the Mad) came to the Castilian throne with her husband, king-consort Philip (the Fair) of Burgundy, son of Emperor Maximilian I of Austria. Shortly after their return to Castile from Flanders, where they resided, Philip died unexpectedly in 1506. When it became apparent that

Juana was too mentally unstable to govern, her father, Ferdinand, was called to assume the regency of Castile. Juana was confined at Tordesillas for the rest of her long and unfortunate life until her death in 1555, but as long as she was alive state papers continued to be signed with the names of Queen Juana and King Ferdinand and, after Ferdinand's death, that of her son Charles.

After Oviedo's return to Spain, there is little information on his life for the next ten years. He seems to have spent most of that period on the fringes of the peripatetic court seeking preferment on the basis of his previous royal service. While he may have seen some military service in Italy, once back in Spain, Oviedo's life was permanently linked to the pen. In 1505, Oviedo initiated his authorial career by beginning a lengthy chronicle of the Castilian monarchy, supposedly at the behest of King Ferdinand. But, to earn his living, he became one of the notaries of the Council of the Inquisition. In 1506, he returned home to Madrid, where he eked out a living exercising the functions of notary public, a profession not held in high esteem and a definite step down from his earlier days at court. Nevertheless, notary public experience would serve him well later in the Indies. About a year later, Oviedo married Margarita Vergara. Their first child was stillborn and some time later Margarita died giving birth to Oviedo's only son to survive to manhood, Francisco González de Valdés.[2]

Oviedo married again in 1512 to Isabel de Aguilar, with whom he had two children. Soon afterward he rejoined Ferdinand's court, then in Valladolid, where he was offered a secretarial position in the expedition the king was outfitting to send General Gonzalo Fernández de Córdoba, known as the Great Captain, to oppose French designs on the Spanish possessions in Italy. However, at the last minute, the expedition was canceled and Oviedo, along with many others including the Great Captain, was left disillusioned and deeply in debt. Although Oviedo would no doubt have preferred to return to Italy, at this juncture his future would lie in the west, in the Indies.

Oviedo in the New World

The natural and historic areas of Castilian expansion were to the south and west while Aragón's were eastward into the Mediterranean and in Italy. Thus it is not surprising that from the beginning the New World

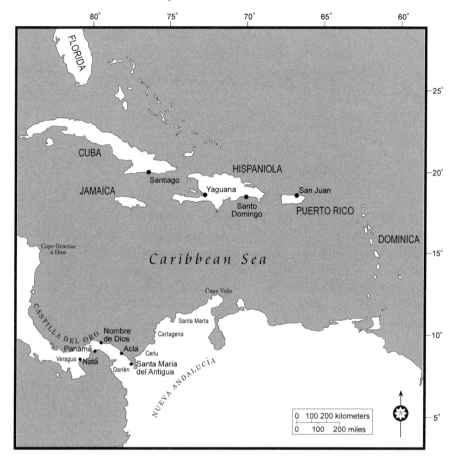

Map 2. The Caribbean region and Tierra Firme at the beginning of the sixteenth century.

territories were appended to the Crown of Castile, reflecting Queen Isabella's interest and support of Columbus's novel project. After the success of Columbus's first voyage with its promise of marvelous wealth, the monarchs ordered a larger fleet for a second expedition to be quickly put together. The complex logistics of organizing a fleet of fifteen ships in five months' time were entrusted to Bishop Juan Rodríguez de Fonseca, a man of proven loyalty to the Catholic Monarchs and of exceptional administrative ability. Because of his successful handling of this undertaking, Fonseca's talents continued to be employed in organizing subsequent voyages. Eventually, administration of the burgeoning New World affairs was vested in a subcommittee of the Council of Castile headed by the bishop. As the vast nature of the New World became apparent and more and more expeditions were sent out, the need to standardize and centralize matters pertaining to the Indies led Bishop Fonseca to develop a new bureaucracy on par with the other councils of state. Consequently, Fonseca established the powerful Council of the Indies, which was to endure until 1812. Another Fonseca creation was the all-important House of Trade for the Indies, established in Seville in 1503, with responsibility for an enormous number of functions.[3] Bishop Fonseca's trusted and very competent secretary Lope Conchillos was charged with the day-to-day operations of the bureaucracy of the Indies and so became an important person to cultivate with regard to New World affairs.

Soon after Columbus found what he imagined were the fabled East Indies, it became apparent that it was in fact terra incognita, even though Columbus himself never fully admitted it. The very generous capitulations he had negotiated with the Catholic Monarchs before his first voyage awarded him and his heirs in perpetuity all newly discovered territories with the titles of admiral of the ocean seas, viceroy, and governor and with a multitude of emoluments. Inevitably, the crown repented of the concentration of such extraordinary power and potential wealth in one person so far away from effective state control, and thus began the erosion of Columbus's monopoly over the New World. In contravention of Columbus's contract, expeditions of exploration and settlement not subject to the admiral's mandate were licensed by King Ferdinand and Bishop Fonseca. Bishop Fonseca's actions set off a blizzard of litigation with the admiral and, after his death, with his heirs over the unfulfilled terms of the capitulations that was not settled until 1536.

Since all expeditions that set out for the Indies had to be licensed by the crown, an individual wanting the governorship of some unclaimed New World territory needed the backing of some influential person to facilitate the commission, which generally came at a price. The expenses of outfitting a fleet from Spain to the Indies were enormous—ships had to be bought or leased, tons of provisions purchased, and officials, sailors, and men contracted. Although the crown would occasionally pay the costs of an expedition or buy shares in the venture, usually the financing was up to the grantee, who often formed a company of investors, soldiers, and officials with rights to share in the profits from the expected exploitation of the territory. Another problem was that, as the mainland American geography was very imperfectly known in Spain, the governors' territories often were found to overlap, setting off endless litigation in Spain and frequently bloody conflict in the Indies between the Spanish claimants.

After the Antilles were explored, the next promising area was Tierra Firme.[4] The Gulf of Urabá was first visited by Rodrigo de Bastidas's expedition in 1501 or 1502. Preliminary reports on that area as a potential source of gold, pearls, and slaves were so optimistic that a section of the coast running from the Gulf of Urabá (in present-day Colombia) to the Caribbean coast of Panamá was given the promising name of Golden Castile (Castilla del Oro).

Columbus sailed down the eastern coast of Honduras to Panamá on his fourth and final voyage in 1502 and attempted to found a settlement at Santa María de Belén in Veragua, but it was soon abandoned. The admiral continued to the region of Darién but there the deterioration of his ships forced a return to Hispaniola in 1503. In 1509, Bishop Fonseca licensed two expeditions, one directed by Alonso de Hojeda (or Ojeda) and the other by Diego de Nicuesa, to explore and settle the territory east and west of the Gulf of Urabá, respectively. Nicuesa established a settlement called Nombre de Dios on the northern coast of Panamá, but the colony was beset by the twin demons of those early outposts—starvation and dissension. Hojeda's expedition was likewise a disaster and he ultimately returned to Santo Domingo a failure. The starving remnants of Hojeda's expedition in Tierra Firme were rescued by Martín Fernández de Enciso, who had come to the area with additional provisions for Hojeda, unaware that he had gone back to Santo Domingo. Enciso's group encountered fierce indigenous resistance along the coast but was finally guided to a more promising site on the western coast of the Gulf of Urabá by one of its members, Vasco Núñez de Balboa, who had sailed that coast with Bastidas seven years before. There on the Gulf of Urabá, Enciso founded in 1510 the first Spanish settlement on mainland America to endure beyond a couple of years. This primitive frontier settlement on the very edge of the known world was christened Santa María del Antigua del Darién after a much-venerated image still to be seen in the Cathedral of Seville.[5]

The loss of their lawful leader, Hojeda, ignited factionalism among the settlers of Santa María. Enciso, as Hojeda's lieutenant, naturally thought he should be in charge, but there was another group who supported the very personable and capable Balboa. Finally, since Santa María was situated in the territory assigned to Nicuesa, it was agreed that a committee should be sent to locate Nicuesa and offer him command. Nicuesa was only too happy to accept the offer, as conditions were very bad in Nombre de Dios compared with those in the thriving community of Santa María. However, by the time Nicuesa got to Santa María, the opposition gathered strength and, to his great surprise, when the would-be governor arrived he was refused admittance. Ultimately, he was placed in a leaky boat and pushed off in the direction of Santo Domingo. The governor and his small party of faithful adherents were never seen again and were presumed drowned or killed by natives. Oviedo details this disgraceful affair in Book XXVIII of the *General and Natural History* and then summarizes it again in the prologue to Book XXIX, not hesitating to name the principal authors of this treachery for all to see, the first name on his list being Balboa's.

Balboa (or more properly Vasco Núñez, as Oviedo always refers to him) assumed command of Santa María after the Nicuesa affair. An excellent administrator and well-regarded captain, Balboa managed to control the opposing factions, the most dangerous of which was headed by Enciso, whom he eventually expelled to Spain. Balboa began a systematic exploration of the territory and, in marked contrast to what was to happen later, he established peaceful relations with the numerous and contending indigenous tribes. Through his contacts with the Native Americans he learned that that part of Tierra Firme was, in fact, an isthmus, and in 1513 Balboa became immortalized as the first European to see the Pacific Ocean from the Americas.[6]

His great accomplishments notwithstanding, as far as the king was concerned, Balboa's possession of Darién was a usurpation of Nicuesa's grant. Moreover, he was rightly suspected of having engineered the governor's death. Thus Balboa's chief concern was to persuade King Ferdinand to legitimize his de facto position with a governorship in recognition of his service. But, while his agents in Spain worked toward that goal, other representatives of the Darién factions and especially Enciso worked ceaselessly to blacken his name and procure his replacement. Unfortunately for Balboa, his lengthy report detailing the discovery and act of possession for the crown of the immense territories washed by the Pacific did not arrive in Spain until after King Ferdinand had appointed a new governor, Pedro Arias de Avila (Pedrarias Dávila), at the behest of Bishop Fonseca.

The funds that were to have taken Oviedo with the Great Captain's expedition to Italy were diverted to the formation of the so-called Splendid Armada.[7] This fleet of sixteen ships and some twelve hundred fifty men was the first large-scale, crown-financed expedition to the New World, testifying to the crown's expectation for profit from the region. The fleet was to bring Governor Pedro Arias de Avila to the newly founded settlement of Santa María del Antigua del Darién to replace Vasco Núñez de Balboa. The governor's charge was to explore, colonize, and exploit this area reputed to be so rich in gold that it could be collected in nets from the rivers. Moreover, he was to search for a passage on the isthmus giving access to the Pacific Ocean.[8]

While the fleet was being readied in Seville, the royal official who was to be inspector of mines and smelting died. Oviedo, through a relative who was a subordinate of Secretary Conchillos and through his friendship with the secretary's brother, got the long-sought position as a royal official in the governor's suite and passage paid to the Indies. Although his inspectorship was a minor office, Oviedo, as was common, also had other duties that greatly increased his income and his influence. Conchillos had reserved for himself the lucrative notary generalship for the colony, which appointed and supervised all the many notaries in the territory. Conchillos subcontracted the actual duties to Oviedo for a share of the proceeds. Oviedo also received a fee for each slave branded and fees for the registration of each expedition into the interior. In addition, Oviedo, like most officials, colonists, and clergy, acted as agent for private individuals and merchant companies in Spain engaging in commerce with the Indies. Oviedo constantly complained about his expenses, but it appears that he did very well. After a little less than a year there he may have returned to Spain with as much as a quarter million maravedís, even though his base salary as inspector was only seventy thousand (see the Money and Purchasing Power section, below).

In 1514, Santa María was a modest settlement of some five hundred Spaniards and fifteen hundred Indian slaves or servants. The Spaniards there were hardy veterans of life in the Indies; they were the survivors of shipwreck, Indian attack, disease, and starvation. They had adjusted to the tropical climate, lived in thatched huts, had learned to eat indigenous food, and had taken native women (often several) as concubines with whom they had children. One can imagine the reaction of both parties when Pedrarias's huge expedition, with its elegant gentlemen sweating in silks and brocades, made its ceremonial entry into primitive multiethnic Santa María to be greeted by the scruffy colonials. In short order the strain of so many inexperienced, unacclimated Europeans on the area's scarce resources resulted in the death by starvation and disease of some five hundred of the newcomers. Also, it was not too long before those who had swallowed tales of gold lying about for the taking were disillusioned. Many of the surviving newcomers returned to Santo Domingo, Cuba, or Spain and, according to Oviedo, even the governor thought of abandoning the project but was stopped by the opposition of the town council.[9]

The year Oviedo spent in the outpost on the very edge of civilization, or, as he put it, "the farthest part west that is presently known,"[10] was definitive in a number of ways. Despite the many hardships, he was immediately taken with the exoticism of the Indies and the possibilities the New World offered for the fame and fortune that had escaped him in Europe. At the same time, steeped as he was all his life with the chivalrous spirit and reverence for authority, he was appalled by how easily and quickly gentlemen and clergy far from royal scrutiny were compromised by the promise of easy wealth. As the official in charge of all notarial functions for the colony, including Pedrarias's confidential affairs, Oviedo was fully informed of all the intrigue and corruption that transpired there.

After a year of witnessing the colonial government's gross mismanagement and the decimation of the Native Americans, Oviedo had enough. He returned to Spain in 1515 to denounce Pedrarias directly to the king and to seek the governor's replacement. That Oviedo (a minor official who owed his position to Fonseca and Conchillos, who backed Pedrarias) would seek to overthrow so well connected a person as the governor testifies to his courage and self-assurance as well as to his ambition to try his hand at governing a territory of his own. Regardless of this difficult year spent in primitive and dangerous circumstances, from this time forward Oviedo was to consider himself a citizen of the Indies.

In Spain, Oviedo was briefly received by the aged King Ferdinand with the promise of a further hearing of his complaints, but that was not to be. The king died shortly thereafter in 1516, bringing the government to a standstill. Ferdinand's death marked the end of a dynasty. The several kingdoms that made up Spain, Philip the Fair's possessions in the Low Countries, and all the American, African, and Italian territories passed to Ferdinand's grandson, Charles of Ghent, the incapacitated Juana's eldest son. Leaving aside Philip the Fair's very brief reign in Castile, Charles was the first of the Spanish Hapsburg dynasty that would rule the Spanish empire for the next two centuries. This radical change of government to that of a sixteen-year-old king who was born and raised in the Low Countries and who did not speak Spanish provoked an administrative crisis in the peninsula that likewise impacted the Indies. Characteristically undaunted, Oviedo, at considerable personal expense, joined the general stampede of Spanish office seekers to Flanders to press his case with the new king. Oviedo's costly mission did not immediately bear fruit, as Charles and his Flemish counselors were entirely occupied with his transition to the Spanish throne. Alleging that the affairs of the Indies were too little understood by the new Flemish administration, they referred Oviedo back to Spain to the two regents, Cardinals Jiménez de Cisneros and Adrian. Unfortunately, the regents were too busy keeping the kingdom together in the absence of the new monarch to listen to Oviedo's complaints about the far-off Indies.

Oviedo was not the first to denounce conditions in the Indies. The year Oviedo arrived in Darién, Friar Bartolomé de las Casas began his lifelong crusade to ameliorate the sufferings of the Native Americans. When King Charles arrived in Spain to assume his throne in 1517, his new chancellor Jean le Sauvage and other Flemish officials were inclined to the reforms so forcefully advocated by the energetic Las Casas.[11] For a time, Bishop Fonseca, viewed as corrupt and anti-Indian, was obliged to relinquish his control over the bureaucracy of the Indies but, because of his influence, talent, and experience in New World affairs, he managed to keep his seat on the important Council of the Indies. However, Fonseca's secretary and Oviedo's chief patron, Lope Conchillos, was forced from office in disgrace and died soon thereafter.

The years of Oviedo's first return to Spain, 1515–20, were difficult. He was closely associated with Conchillos and Fonseca but an opponent of Pedrarias Dávila; moreover, Oviedo advocated reforms of the colonial system but did not agree with the more influential Las Casas concerning the remedy. Despite these incongruities, the indefatigable Oviedo pressed his grievances against Pedrarias at court, cultivated important personages, and generally worked to establish his credentials as *the* New World expert even though he had spent less than a year there. In the ongoing controversies over the "just war" (Spain's right to possess the Indies) and over the nature of the Indians and their role vis-à-vis the Spaniards, Fonseca made use of Oviedo's expertise on at least two occasions to testify concerning the capacity of the Indians and against Las Casas's campaign to abolish the *encomienda* system in the New World.[12] The mutual hostility between Las Casas and Oviedo, which lasted until each died, dates from this period. Early on, both men vied for a governorship in the territory of Santa Marta (in present-day Colombia) with quite different plans for the protection of the Indians. Las Casas prevailed, but his efforts to establish a settlement in 1519 were a resounding failure and provoked some ironic comments in Oviedo's *General and Natural History* that Las Casas never forgot or forgave.

By all accounts, in addition to his tenaciousness and abundant self-confidence, Oviedo was a man of lively wit and charm and a great raconteur.[13] Despite the powerful opposition of Las Casas and Pedrarias's agents at court, by 1519 Oviedo was able to obtain a series of royal appointments and decrees benefiting himself. In addition, he was appointed crown receiver of the embargoed estate of Balboa, whom Pedrarias had executed in 1517. Finally, with some typical exaggeration, Oviedo took personal credit for Pedrarias's replacement with a new governor, Lope de Sosa.

During these years, even with all the turmoil in Spain and all the time he must have devoted to his political maneuvering, Oviedo continued work on his projected genealogy of the Castilian monarchs started ten years before. Moreover, he found the time to finish the first Spanish novel written in the New World, the *Claribalte*. This very European romance of chivalry, which Oviedo began writing in the wilds of an American jungle, was published in Valencia in 1519. The novel was dedicated to the Duke of Calabria, King Frederick of Aragón's son, in remembrance of the author's happy Neapolitan days.

With these accomplishments in hand, Oviedo gathered up his wife and two children and sailed for Darién, no doubt thinking his fortune assured. However, it is a curious irony of Oviedo's life that often, just as things seemed to be going his way, his hopes were frustrated by the death of a potential benefactor. And so it was that on the very evening of his arrival at Darién in 1520 he was stunned to learn that the new governor, upon whom he had pinned his hopes, had died suddenly on board his ship the night before he was to disembark in the New World. Oviedo thus returned to Darién to face Pedrarias, who was still very much in control and well aware of how Oviedo had played an active role in procuring his replacement.

Oviedo's second residence in Darién lasted until 1523. In the narrative of those years he portrays himself as Pedrarias's principal opponent now that Balboa was removed, but it is difficult to know whether the governor considered him a prime threat or merely an annoyance. The major source of contention between them was Pedrarias's plan to move the seat of government from Santa María to the new settlement of Panamá, which he founded on the Pacific coast in 1519. Oviedo contended that Pedrarias's motivation for the move was to punish him for his continued opposition by ruining the city in which Oviedo had considerable investments. Pedrarias, no doubt, was pleased to discomfit one of his most severe critics but, in point of fact, there were reasons to establish the first Spanish settlement on the Pacific shore that went beyond merely getting even with Oviedo. As we have seen, the population of Santa María had grown too large to be sustained in that site and therefore needed to be distributed throughout the territory in other more viable settlements. More important, the focus of the colonial enterprise had shifted from the Caribbean coast to the Pacific and the city of Panamá offered an ideal location as a terminus of a transisthmian route and for exploration of the Pacific coast.[14]

In 1522, the astute governor, well aware of Oviedo's nature and knowing that he would fail, maneuvered Oviedo into assuming the lieutenancy of the dwindling city of Santa María. From the start, Oviedo's intransigent, self-righteous, and class-bound governance style ensured opposition among the citizenry, who had adopted much more relaxed colonial ways. A particularly bitter opponent of Oviedo was Diego de Corral, a wealthy and influential resident, whom Oviedo finally had exiled to Spain. Compounding his problems were poor relations with the local clergy headed by Dean Juan Pérez Zalduendo and Pedrarias's constant undermining of his authority. Eventually his position in Santa María became untenable. After the deaths of Oviedo's second wife and young son and after surviving a terrible wound in an assassination attempt he suspected was orchestrated by Pedrarias, Oviedo returned clandestinely to Spain to present his complaints to King Charles (since 1519, Emperor-elect Charles V of the Holy Roman Empire). En route to Spain, Oviedo stopped at Santo Domingo, where he contracted an advantageous third marriage with Catalina de Ribafrecha y Burguillos. Although his official duties and personal affairs required him to return to Tierra Firme for several years more, from this time on he considered himself a resident of Santo Domingo.

During his second return to court (1523–26), Oviedo continued to campaign for Pedrarias's replacement and sought redress for his financial losses resulting from the removal of the territorial capital to Panamá. On another front, he continued to press for the governorship of the territory around Santa Marta. As ever, even with all his political and personal activity, in the space of these three years he always found time to write. There is some documentation that suggests Oviedo translated Boccaccio's *Il corbaccio*, with the title *Labyrinth of Love*, but no trace of it exists today.

Much more important to his career was the publication of a small work that was decisive in establishing his reputation. From 1514 on Oviedo had worked ceaselessly to fashion himself as the expert on all topics American. His authority was immensely enhanced by the 1526 publication (at his own expense) of the small volume entitled *Oviedo on the Natural History of the Indies* (the *Summary*). This work, supposedly produced at the emperor's request for New World information, is a hastily compiled selection from memory of materials that Oviedo had been accumulating since 1514 for a projected comprehensive history of the Indies. The enormously successful *Summary* was one of the first of its type to be published in Spanish on the Indies. To Oviedo's great delight it was eventually translated into French, English, Latin, and, best of all, Italian by the famous Venetian humanist-diplomat Andrea Navagero, through whom it gained wide diffusion among the famous Renaissance scholars of the day.

Another success for which Oviedo gave himself credit was finally the replacement of Pedrarias with a new governor, Pedro de los Ríos, who this time arrived alive in Castilla del Oro. With that Oviedo returned to Darién in 1526 to wind up his affairs. There was still pending litigation with Diego de Corral, each party suing the other for their considerable financial losses because of the abandonment of Santa María. This was finally settled by arbitration to neither party's advantage. Also, before Oviedo could leave Castilla del Oro for good, he had to undergo "residency," a formal inquiry into the conduct of an official upon leaving office. To direct the proceeding, a residency judge might be sent from Spain or else appointed from within the colonial administration. A proclamation was issued inviting all aggrieved persons to come forward and present their civil and criminal claims against the outgoing administrator. These claims needed to be settled, dismissed, or referred to Spain before the official could leave. For example, in Pedrarias's residency, Oviedo brought multiple claims against him for losses suffered when the governor moved the territorial capital as well as claims concerning his attempted assassination, which Oviedo suspected Pedrarias had orchestrated or at the very least encouraged.

After he came to a less-than-satisfactory agreement with the ever slippery Pedrarias over damages, Oviedo moved north to León, Nicaragua, where his wife's cousin, López de Salcedo, was governor. There, as he had in Santa María, Oviedo constructed a fine house, obviously with the hope of establishing himself in a high official capacity. In León he found the time to start another of his typically ambitious projects, a proposed eleven-volume work on heraldry that was apparently never completed in full. Once again, however, his nemesis Pedrarias appeared on the scene to depose Salcedo and ruin those plans. There was nothing for Oviedo to do but to return to Panamá.

In 1530, Oviedo again sailed to Spain as representative of the Panamanian citizenry, now as unhappy with their new governor as they had been with Pedrarias. Also, he went as representative of Santo Domingo, anxious about the decline of its population, economy, and status because of the attraction of new and richer mainland discoveries, particularly in Mexico. As before, Oviedo also had a personal agenda: his long-sought governorship and support for a projected history of the New World. In both, Oviedo was successful. On the strength of his New World expertise and the success of his *Summary,* the emperor appointed him Official Chronicler of the Indies in 1532.[15] The position was poorly compensated but the commission bore with it the historian's key to the true treasure of the Indies—the right to demand of all New World authorities any information and documentation he might require for his now officially sanctioned project. As for a governorship, he finally was offered one on the northern coast of present-day Colombia but later had to renounce it for lack of the financial resources necessary to outfit an expedition to take possession.

When Oviedo returned from this mission to Spain it was not to

Panamá but to establish himself definitively in Santo Domingo. To augment his small salary as official chronicler, he was given the wardenship of the fort that protected the harbor of Santo Domingo in 1533, a post he maintained until his death. Additionally, he was made a permanent member of the city council. About this time, at the request of the emperor's son, Prince Philip, Oviedo started work on a memorial describing the court ceremonial of his early days in the household of Prince Juan. However, he concentrated on his major work, the *General and Natural History of the Indies*.[16] In 1534, Oviedo made his fourth voyage to Spain, again with the dual purpose of representing the city of Santo Domingo before the Council of the Indies and of preparing the printing of the first nineteen books of his *History* in Seville in 1535. Its publication was a great moment for Oviedo and he returned immediately to Santo Domingo to continue work on that project as well as others. For the next ten years he worked on various writing projects, tended to the fortifications in his charge, participated in city governance, and managed his considerable estates and investments.

In August 1546, at the age of sixty-eight, Oviedo once again undertook the hazards of the voyage to Spain, ostensibly to represent his city in high-level litigation. Undoubtedly, however, Oviedo's main interest was to gather additional material for the *General and Natural History*. The manuscripts for parts two and three and a revised part one were left in Spain to await the funds to print them. Before Oviedo's departure for the Indies in 1548 or 1549 he did publish a translation from the Italian of a work entitled *Rule for the Spiritual Life and Secret Theology*, which he stated was not a success.

Back in Santo Domingo, despite increasing ill health, he continued to write. Oviedo added nothing more to his *History* after 1548 or 1549, turning his attention to two other multivolume projects that are often confused, the *Battles and Quincuagenas* and the *Quincuagenas*.[17] As for the publication of his greatest work, the *General and Natural History*, only the first book of the second part was printed in the last year of his life. Gonzalo Fernández de Oviedo y Valdés died in Santo Domingo on June 25, 1557, clutching the keys to his fortress, according to the official notification:

In the very noble and loyal city of Santo Domingo, on the island of Hispaniola on the twenty-sixth day of June in the year one thousand five hundred fifty-seven, having died the previous night and passed on from this life Gonzalo Fernández de Oviedo, His Majesty's Warden of the fortress of this city, the illustrious Licentiate Alonso Maldonado, his Majesty's President of the Royal Court and Chancellery . . . went to the fortress of the said city where he found dead the said Gonzalo Fernández de Oviedo and took possession of the keys of the said fortress which the said deceased . . . held in his hand.[18]

General and Natural History of the Indies

Although without the advantage of a formal Latin-based education, then the hallmark of the educated man, Oviedo was throughout his long life compelled to read and, above all, to write, as José de la Peña observes: "He filled thousands and thousands of folio pages with his elegant, angular penmanship, shaping letters which were generally small, often miniscule . . . Oviedo was, above all, a man of the pen . . . whether as an author, a correspondent, a memorialist, a litigator, a bureaucrat, a notary, whatever it was, his joy was the act of writing itself."[19] Certainly Oviedo the bureaucrat and notary wrote for a living but his real calling was as a chronicler. From his youth in the royal courts and then from his travels in Italy there was in him a desire to make his mark as an author on a grand scale. His first typically ambitious project, begun in 1505, was to chronicle the kings of Castile, and so the idea of producing a similar chronicle of the Indies was inevitable for a man who habitually made extensive notes on everything he saw or experienced. A chronicle of the Indies was an especially attractive project since, even though the Spanish had been in the Indies for almost two decades before Oviedo arrived, there was very little published information about the New World circulating in Spanish. There were Peter Martyr's celebrated *Decades,* but these were Latin letters written over a period of thirty years compiled from reports and interviews with persons returning from the New World and addressed to aristocratic and scholarly correspondents. Although the first of what were to be the eight decades of Martyr's complete work was published in Spain in 1511, clearly Martyr had no thought to inform the average Spaniard of the great events in which their country was involved.

Because of Martyr's intellectual status, his court connections, and, above all, the fame accruing from his *Decades,* he was appointed to the powerful Council of the Indies. For Oviedo, the Italian Martyr was a model for the respect and position to which a chronicler could aspire but also an authority to be challenged by a Spaniard writing in Spanish with firsthand experience of the Indies. However, Oviedo was not merely motivated to his great work by a xenophobic disdain for the Italian armchair historian. His prologue to the *General and Natural History* directed to Emperor Charles V reflects the historian's pride in the immensity of the hitherto unknown world now appended to the Spanish crown: "in this empire of the Indies that Your Caesarean Majesty and King of Castile possesses there are such great kingdoms and provinces and such strange peoples, diversities, customs, ceremonies, and idolatries alien to everything that was written from the beginning to our times, so much so that a man's life is too short to see it, all much less ponder or understand it."[20] For Oviedo, this God-given discovery is part of the emperor's and Spain's mission to assume the leadership of the Catholic faith not only in Europe but now also in the vast and wonderful Indies and then in the whole world: "not only will the Christian faithful serve Your Caesarean Majesty but the infidels and idolaters of the whole world, hearing of these marvels, will be obligated to serve you, blessing their creator."[21]

Just as it was Charles's calling to be the "universal monarch" and Spain's providential mission to possess the New World,[22] it was Oviedo's to become the one to reveal the New World to the Old, to be its interpreter and chronicler. It was an irresistible opportunity for a writer to record Spain's greatest undertaking and make his own mark doing so. The intrusion of the historian into the pages of his history, whether in the part concerning Darién in which he assumes a somewhat exaggerated role or later on in the interjection of his comments and critiques on situations and events in which he did not take part, indicates a conscious effort of Oviedo to position himself in the grand adventure alongside the famous explorers and conquistadores and, moreover, to "own" the Indies on a symbolic intellectual level.[23]

As previously mentioned, before the *General and Natural History* came a sort of prospectus for it generally called the *Summary,* published in Toledo in 1526. Certainly it was conceived to draw the attention of the twenty-six-year-old foreign monarch, attuned primarily to the more immediate problems of his known world than to his vast but imperfectly known possessions thousands of miles away. In its brief introduction,

Oviedo presents himself to the emperor as a longtime royal servitor and chronicler of the monarchy and as an expert observer of the Indies. Oviedo's stated intention is to entertain—"I desire to give your majesty a little pleasure"—and to pique the emperor's interest in realms other than Europe—"I should like you to observe the new things"—with the hope of securing imperial backing for the much larger study he announces that he has undertaken.[24] The *Summary's* eighty-six chapters, varying in length from a paragraph to several pages, present information on all manner of topics ranging through the voyage to the Indies, the natives, the fauna and flora, the geography, gold mining, and pearl fishing, among others. Here and there it is illustrated with woodcuts produced from Oviedo's drawings, which may be the first graphic representations of the New World.[25] The immediate popularity of the *Summary* had the desired result of gaining for Oviedo an international reputation for expertise with regard to the Indies and led to his appointment as official chronicler with the royal mandate to produce the *General and Natural History*.

Oviedo's plan was for a comprehensive history in three parts: nineteen books in part one, another nineteen in part two, and twelve in part three, for a total of fifty books, each book consisting of a varying number of chapters. Oviedo worked on his history from 1514 to 1548, writing and rewriting as new material became available. In 1549, he took the finished manuscript to Seville, where he deposited it in a monastery for safekeeping. However, he was never able to find financial backing for the publication of a work he projected to be more than a thousand pages long. After his death, the four volumes containing the three parts of the manuscript passed through several hands and over the years became separated and many chapters were lost. There were various attempts made to reconstruct and publish Oviedo's history in its entirety by the Royal Academy of History, but that was not to be until the mid-nineteenth century.[26]

During his lifetime, Oviedo was able to publish only a small portion of what was to be the complete *General and Natural History*. The first part, entitled *The General History of the Indies (La historia general de las Indias),* was published by Juan Cromberger in Seville in 1535. This volume contains nineteen books plus the prologue and ten chapters of what was later to be the thirty chapters of Book L (the last) of the third part known as "Shipwrecks and Misfortunes" ("*Naufragios e infortunios*"). Another edition of the first part was issued from the press of Juan de Junta in Salamanca in 1547, with the expanded title *Chronicle of the Indies. The His-*

tory of the Indies Now Newly Printed, Corrected and Revised (Crónica de las Indias. La historia de las Indias ahora nuevamente empresa, corregida y enmendada). This title is deceptive as, according to Turner, the edition is essentially the same as the first printing and, for that reason, he believes that the 1547 work was unauthorized.[27] Ten years later, in 1557, thirty-five chapters of the first book (Book XX) of the second part of Oviedo's history were published with the title *Book XX of the Second Part of the General History of the Indies (Libro XX, de la segunda parte de la general historia de las Indias)* by Francisco Fernández de Córdoba in Valladolid. The remaining eighteen books of the second part and the twelve books of the third and final part of the *History* were not published in his lifetime, although Oviedo delivered them to Spain on his last visit there and the materials appear to have circulated in manuscript.[28]

The fifty books of all three parts were not printed until almost three centuries later when José Amador de los Ríos edited the work under the title *General and Natural History of the Indies, Islands and Mainland of the Ocean Sea (Historia general y natural de las Indias, islas y tierra firme del mar océano),* published by the Royal Academy of History, Madrid, in 1851–55.[29] Amador de los Ríos's text with modernized orthography and punctuation and his notes were reprinted with the same title by J. Natalicio González in Asunción, Paraguay, in 1944–45, and then again reedited and prefaced with a lengthy biography and introduction by Juan Pérez de Tudela Bueso with the shortened title most often used today, *General and Natural History of the Indies (Historia general y natural de las Indias).* This printing, contained in volumes 117–21 of the collection *Biblioteca de autores españoles* (Madrid: Ediciones Atlas, 1959), is the most accessible edition available today and the one from which the present translation was made.

Oviedo's *History* begins with a dedicatory letter addressed to Cardinal García Jofre de Loaysa, president of the Council of the Indies, followed by a general introduction to the first part of the history directed to Emperor Charles. Thereafter each book is preceded by its own prologue that contains a summary of the materials to be covered and often includes Oviedo's comments, frequently censorious, on the topics and persons involved. In line with the work's promise of a general and natural history, the subject matter of the chapters may be geography, botany, zoology, ethnography, or the chronicle of the Spanish presence in the Indies and related events in Spain.

Given the encyclopedic nature of its contents, Oviedo's work has been faulted for its digressiveness and often chaotic jumbling of subject matter.[30] However, there is an overall chronological and geographical plan beginning with Columbus and the Antilles in Books I to XIX. Books XX to XXXII follow the voyage of Magellan to the Moluccas and then the explorations of the southern tip of South America. From the Río de la Plata region the narrative returns to the southern Caribbean area with the expeditions to Trinidad and the areas now Venezuela and Colombia, then moves up through Panamá and Central America to the Yucatan. Books XXXIII to XL are devoted to the Mexican conquest and North American explorations. Book XLI doubles back to Guatemala then moves south through Honduras, Nicaragua, and Panamá and into the Andean region. Books XLVI through XLIX relate the explorations and conquest of Peru and Chile. The first twenty-nine chapters of the final, fiftieth book, "Shipwrecks and Misfortunes," really form a work apart. In Oviedo's words it is a collection of "some unfortunate cases, shipwrecks and things which happened at sea" that he gathered over the years.[31] As previously noted, ten of these chapters were already included at the end of the 1535 edition of the first part. The majority of the stories relate the miraculous rescue of someone through the intercession of a particular virgin or saint. The longest of these fascinating reports is Chapter XXIV, which incorporates Friar Gaspar de Carvajal's journal of Captain Francisco de Orellana's company and their grueling eight-month trip down the Marañón (Amazon) River. The thirtieth and final chapter of Book L is a sort of epilogue dated 1549 in which Oviedo responds to his detractors, presenting a lengthy and vigorous defense of having written in Spanish rather than Latin, and promises a fourth part, which was never completed.

The Reception of Oviedo's *History*

With the publication of his *Summary*, his appointment as Official Chronicler of the Indies, and then the appearance of the first parts of the *General and Natural History*, Oviedo attained the authority and fame he so desired. These works were very successful and were soon translated and disseminated throughout Europe, to the author's immense pleasure. As one would expect, given his self-confident nature, Oviedo was his own best panegyrist, but Spain being Spain and Spaniards being Spaniards, his works almost immediately provoked two influential detractors—

Ferdinand Columbus, son of the admiral, and Oviedo's most vociferous critic, Bartolomé de Las Casas.[32]

Although Oviedo had written admiringly of Christopher Columbus, his history was not well received by the admiral's heirs. Oviedo made certain statements that tended to lessen Columbus's achievement and that weakened the Columbus family's suit with the government for failure to live up to the terms of the capitulations Columbus had negotiated with the Catholic Monarchs. The erudite, bibliophile son of the admiral, Ferdinand Columbus (with whom Oviedo had served years before in Prince Juan's household), was moved to write his celebrated biography of his father after the first publication of Oviedo's history. In Ferdinand's well-known *Life of the Admiral,* Chapter X, "In Which Is Shown the Falsity of the Claim that the Spaniards Once Before Had Possession of the Indies, as Gonzalo de Oviedo Attempts to Prove in His History," is given over to disproving Oviedo's contention that the Indies were the ancient Hesperides and thus Spanish possessions from the time of the legendary King Hesperus and therefore Columbus was simply claiming back what had been Spain's long ago.[33]

Of the two critics, however, the one to do the most lasting damage to Oviedo's reputation was Las Casas. As Oviedo had denigrated Martyr, Las Casas was to take even more violent issue with Oviedo. The personal and professional rivalry between the bureaucrat and the friar dating back many years was such that neither had a good word for anything the other wrote, said, or did. Las Casas's own *History of the Indies* was apparently undertaken as a rebuttal to Oviedo's and, although it was not published until after both were long dead, like Oviedo's manuscripts, it circulated in numerous copies.[34] Two charges that Las Casas made against Oviedo have continued to obscure the worth of Oviedo's contribution even to the present day: first, that Oviedo's work was not a real history by a real historian, and second, the more serious and more resonant, that Oviedo was an enemy of the Native Americans.

Las Casas was scornful of Oviedo's temerity in writing a historical work without any formal educational preparation and, in particular, Oviedo's lack of a solid foundation in Latin. One of Las Casas's many jibes speaks of Oviedo's "presumption and arrogance in thinking that he knew anything when he had no inkling of Latin even though he cites authorities in that language."[35] The spirited and sustained defense Oviedo makes of his use of the vernacular demonstrates his sensitivity on this point. In his prologue-dedication to the multilingual Emperor Charles, Oviedo proudly refers to Castilian as "the best of the vulgar languages."[36] Thereafter the subject comes up in various passages throughout the work but Oviedo returns to respond at length in the last chapter of the history. He closes his magnum opus with a ringing defense of Spain, whose deeds are worthy of being known and being told in their own language now "so widely communicated throughout so many kingdoms . . . [that] those who write in it ought not to be held in low esteem."[37]

For the general reader, the scholarly debate over whether Oviedo's work is a real history or chronicle or encyclopedia or miscellany or farrago (as some have unkindly called it) is of little importance and the fact that it was produced in Spanish rather than Latin is more positive than negative. The *General and Natural History of the Indies* simply is what it is, a compilation of notes, memoirs, interviews, and received reports on everything related to the Indies accumulated over a period of four decades, all organized, interpreted, and commented upon by a self-acknowledged expert and directed to the Spanish public (and, he hoped, to the European public through translations). It is a unique text that describes, interprets, and fixes the dimensions and contents of an immense new land as well as chronicles the Spanish presence there.

Ironically, the criticism of his anti-indigenism, which did not seem to preoccupy Oviedo at all, is the one that has done his reputation and work the most lasting damage and caused the most controversy. Again, it was the implacable Las Casas who originated this critique—"where ever in his *History* he treats of the Indians, he never opens his mouth except to blaspheme and annihilate them as much as he can" is but a sample of what Las Casas had to say.[38] For the cleric Las Casas, a one-issue polemicist, everything regarding the Indies was subordinate to the Indian question and his laudable crusade to ameliorate their dreadful treatment by the Spaniards. Anyone who did not entirely support his position and program was his enemy and the enemy of the Native Americans. For the secular bureaucrat Oviedo, however, the Native American was but one aspect of his panorama of the New World. While he could and did appreciate their cultures, he was skeptical about their capacity to become good Catholics or to be civilized according to European notions of the term, and so the possibility of freeing them from Spanish tutelage was unthinkable.

Oviedo, as did the majority of Spaniards, Las Casas included, had little doubt about Spain's right to intrude into and to own the New World. After all, Pope Alexander VI had given the majority of it to Spain by the bull *Inter caetera* of 1493, which declared:

> We, by the Authority of Almighty God, granted unto us in Saint Peter, and by the Vicarship of Jesus Christ which we bear on the Earth, do forever, by the tenor of these presents, give, grant, assign, unto you [Isabella and Ferdinand], your heirs and successors . . . all those Lands and Islands, with their Dominions, Territories, Cities, Castles, Towers, Places and Villages, with all the Rights and Jurisdictions thereunto pertaining; constituting, assigning, and deputing you, your heirs and successors, the Lords thereof, with full and free Power, Authority, and Jurisdiction.[39]

The papal bull confirmed the Spaniards' widely held belief that Spain's discovery of the New World was providential. How else to explain that a handful of Spaniards had subjugated so many millions of Indians in so vast a territory in so short a time if not that God had ordained it? That being the case, it was Spain's God-given mission to civilize and to evangelize the Indies. In recompense for their hard-fought contributions to the extension and enrichment of the empire and of Christendom, the Spaniards who won the lands had the right to the tribute and services of its inhabitants. However, if the natives were obligated to work for the Spanish, their masters in turn had the obligation to treat them well and especially to see to their religious conversion. The nature of this relationship was the subject of much discussion in Spain and produced a mass of instructions and laws designed to protect the Native Americans. Unfortunately, it was one thing to legislate in Spain but quite another to put it into effect in the distant Indies, as Oviedo was to discover from his experience in Darién.

Oviedo possessed a secular, aristocratic, and stern moral view of how things ought to be, a view grounded in the legendary chivalrousness of the centuries-long Spanish battle to recover the Iberian peninsula from the Spanish Muslims. Although he was as interested as any other in finding the fame and fortune that had eluded him in the Old World, he was appalled by the savage conduct of his countrymen who came to Tierra Firme with the sole purpose of quickly appropriating indigenous gold by whatever means possible. The alacrity with which gentlemen and, worse, the clergy were corrupted by the promise of easy riches and the impunity with which they stole, enslaved, and murdered was, for Oviedo, a subversion of the Spanish chivalrous tradition. Worse, it was a disservice to the universal monarchy of the Catholic emperor and a desecration of Spain's God-given mission in the New World.[40] The mayhem and destruction he witnessed during his first year in Darién ostensibly prompted his return to Spain to denounce the governor's conduct against the Indians and Spanish alike and to work for his replacement. As the reader of his Darién memoirs will see, Oviedo is unflinching in documenting the atrocities inflicted by the Spanish captains on the numerous expeditions that went out from Santa María. To his credit, Oviedo's firm denunciations concerning the devastation of the Indian population that he witnessed in 1514 antedate by many years Las Casas's most famous tract *A Short Account of the Destruction of the Indies,* written in 1542 but not published until 1552.

Bartolomé de las Casas has come down through history consecrated as the "Apostle of the Indians," an anticolonialist and anti-imperialist icon. His transcendence is attested by the coinage of the term *lascasismo* (Lascasianism), which has set the agenda for the evaluation of worth of colonial writers by the touchstone of indigenism, to the exclusion of anything else. Inevitably, the person Las Casas excoriated in his own *History of the Indies,* his enemy Oviedo, has been discredited as anti-indigenist and imperialist. While it is true that the secular bureaucrat Oviedo gloried in the Spanish imperial enterprise, his anti-indigenism has been greatly exaggerated, as more recent scholarship has shown.[41]

In Santa María del Antigua del Darién Oviedo imagines his potential for fortune and fame. Here he begins his forty-year campaign to appropriate everyone and everything relating to the Indies by controlling the transmission and interpretation of the New World. One of the most intriguing features of his history is that, not content with merely being the unseen chronicler of the Americas, the bureaucrat-historian Oviedo writes himself into the enterprise of the Indies along with the Native Americans, explorers, captains, governors, bishops, and kings and queens who populate the story of the settlement of the mainland. For this period he becomes the protagonist of his own chronicle—the first citizen, defender, and leader of Santa María and ultimately, he allows, the cause of its abandonment as a result of his decisive opposition to the governor. The attempt on his life places him on par with Nicuesa and Balboa before him and attests to his importance. Oviedo rather immodestly compares his trials and tribulations to those of Job, Saint Paul, and even Christ. The chronicler's stormy journey to Brussels to see King Charles and his defense of his town against hostile Indians are as vital to his narrative as are the accounts of the captains' hazardous expeditions to the interior. Oviedo's skillful negotiations at court single-handedly benefit the entire "republic." He is better informed on the Indies than anyone else because he has access to all official and unofficial documents. His cartographic observations correct those of the first explorers of the Pacific coast and emend the master chart of the official cosmographers in Seville. Nevertheless, however much Oviedo may have exaggerated his centrality in the colonization of the Indies, there is no denying the greatness of his *General and Natural History of the Indies,* which Ricardo Padrón calls "one of the most important pieces of historical literature in the attempt of sixteenth-century Europe to apprehend the New World."[42] The present translation of the nineteen chapters of Book XXIX takes us to the genesis of what would become the first comprehensive history of the Americas.

In these chapters the reader samples Oviedo's unique narrative style, which despite its digressions, repetitions, and sermonizing has a charm all its own. Because of Oviedo's obsession with recording and interpreting all he experiences, the text shifts from discussion of an Indian woman's hairdo to Semiramis and Babylon, from the court to indigenous villages, from strange fish to bedbugs, from extreme privation to sapphires as big as eggs, from examples of incredible valor and resourcefulness to those of obscene cruelty and cynical self-interest. The memoirs of Darién give us a sample of why Oviedo has been credited with so many New World firsts—first ethnographer, geographer, sociologist, botanist, zoologist, mineralogist, comprehensive historian, and autobiographer. As if these accomplishments were not enough, we should add to the list first novelist and poet and first to propagate visual representations of the Indies.

Oviedo's biographer, Pérez de Tudela, familiar as no one else with the history and historians of the period, has concluded that for Oviedo's experiences in Spain, Italy, and the Indies; for his firsthand knowledge of the personages associated with the enterprise of the Indies; and for his zeal in recording it all, if anyone were to be selected the epitome of the "moment of the flourishing of imperial Spain it would have to be Oviedo."[43] The *General and Natural History of the Indies,* whatever its faults and shortcomings, is undeniably the most complete source of information for a seminal period in the history of Western civilization. In the events of the era that Oviedo both chronicles and takes part in, 1493–1549, there occurs the rapid formation of the Spanish New World empire that would change forever the course of the Americas and Europe.

Money and Purchasing Power

Because it would be useless to try to translate to dollars and cents the various monetary units employed throughout the text, I have retained the antique Spanish terminology. The basic unit with which to compare values is the maravedí, which was originally an actual coin but by Oviedo's day was a money of account. The following represent approximate values for the period:

The real = 34 maravedís.
The castellano = a gold coin approximately the equivalent of the peso.
The ducat = 375 maravedís, a money of account rather than actual coinage.
The mark = an old weight of eight ounces used to measure precious metals and especially pearls. In Spain and the Americas it was the equivalent of 230 grams.
The peso = 15 reales or 450 maravedís. The gold peso is the most frequently mentioned unit in Oviedo's *History* and was a weight rather than an actual coin. Since there were no New World mints until the establishment of the one in Mexico City in 1535, gold and silver were transported to Spain in the form of ingots.[44] One of Oviedo's important functions as inspector of mines and smelting was to be present when gold was melted down and to certify its purity and weight.

To have some idea of the worth of these antique units we need to examine their purchasing power and contemporary salaries. Oviedo frequently complains of the high cost of items in the Indies, but one must bear in mind that the price of European foodstuffs and manufactured goods varied from place to place in the Indies, where they were inflated by transportation expenses and price gouging. Mena García's research into the records of provisioning the 1514 armada to Tierra Firme offers detailed information concerning what foods and equipment were necessary for a lengthy sea voyage at the time as well as the prices paid in Spain.[45] Another valuable source on prices and salaries is Pérez-Mallaína, whose lists of goods and services note that a chicken cost 20 maravedís, a liter of red wine 6, a loaf of bread 2.5, a doctor's visit 136, a gentleman's outfit from shoes to cap and sword almost 15,000, and a caravel 500 ducats or about 190,000 maravedís.[46]

In the first third of the sixteenth century a seaman's daily wage plus rations was 35–45 maravedís per day or about 13,000 per year, assuming steady employment.[47] Skilled workers and officials, of course, commanded more. When Oviedo first traveled to the Indies his annual salary as a minor crown official was 70,000 maravedís, which was considerably augmented by a number of fees to which he had the rights and by his personal business dealings. His commander, Pedrarias, was granted a salary of some 360,000 maravedís, which he, like most successful New World officials, supplemented with "gifts" from Indians and Spaniards alike. At the high end of the pay scale, Oviedo's patron, Secretary Lope Conchillos, was reputed to have an annual income from his multiple offices of some 4,000,000 maravedís at the peak of his career.[48] Finally, Las Casas estimates the total cost of sending the twenty-two ships and two thousand–plus men of the "Splendid Armada" that brought Oviedo to Darién in 1514 at between 52,000 and 54,000 ducats, or about 20,000,000 maravedís.[49] Despite Spain's poverty, that the normally frugal King Ferdinand would dedicate such a sum to the undertaking attests to the expectation of great profit from this new-found territory. These expectations were, in fact, realized—Ramón Carande estimates gold shipments to Spain from the Indies for the years 1511–20 at 2,626,499 ducats.[50]

In the first few decades of the Spanish presence in the Indies most of the gold exported to Spain was looted from the indigenous people or panned from the rivers. As these sources gradually dried up, huge deposits of silver were discovered at Potosí, Peru, and then at Zacatecas, Mexico, around 1545. According to Timothy Walton, "mining, rather than pillage, was to become the main method of deriving precious metals from the Indies, and the focus shifted from gold to silver."[51] The total production of gold and silver increased throughout the sixteenth century to about 17,000,000 pesos annually by the 1590s.[52] The inevitable consequence of this flood of wealth into Spain was 107 percent inflation from 1510 to 1550.[53]

Biographical Notes on the Major Figures in the Text and the Introduction

Adrian of Utrecht (1459–1523). Although of humble birth, Adrian rose steadily through the ranks of the church and university to attain important positions. In 1506 he became tutor to the future Charles V. When Charles inherited the kingdom of Spain, Adrian, by then a cardinal, was sent ahead to form with Cardinal Jiménez de Cisneros a dual regency until the king's arrival. Soon after the elevation of Charles to the imperial dignity, Pope Leo X died (1522) and Adrian of Utrecht was elected to replace him as Pope Adrian VI. In spite of Charles's expectations of favorable treatment from the new pope, Adrian refused to be the emperor's tool. Adrian's short papacy was not a success. He faced opposition from all sides but particularly from the Romans, who despised him for being a foreigner. All his efforts to reform the corruption of the Church were stymied. The final blow was the disastrous loss of the Island of Rhodes to the Turks in October 1522. In September 1523, after about a year and a half in office, Pope Adrian died.

Almagro, Diego de (1475?–1538). Little is known of Almagro's early life. Probably he was the illegitimate son of a gentleman from Almagro. In 1514, he came to Castilla del Oro with Pedrarias's armada. When reports of a rich land to the south began circulating, Almagro, Francisco Pizarro, and Father Fernando de Luque formed a company that after many hardships and several expeditions resulted in the discovery and conquest of the Incan empire with its fabulous riches. Gradually Almagro began to feel that Pizarro had taken the lion's share of the territory and loot and their relationship soured. Almagro attempted to establish himself in present-day Chile but the expedition there met with furious indigenous opposition and he was forced to retreat to Peru. In 1537, Almagro seized the city of Cuzco, provoking armed conflict with the supporters of Pizarro, which culminated in the Battle of las Salinas in which Almagro was defeated; he was executed in 1538.

Balboa, Vasco Núñez de (1475–1517). Born in Jerez de los Caballeros, Balboa abandoned Spain to accompany Rodrigo de Bastidas's expedition to Tierra Firme in 1501. Afterward he settled in Hispaniola until, reportedly escaping his creditors, he stowed away on a ship that was part of Alonso de Hojeda's disastrous expedition to Tierra Firme. Because of his previous experience along that coast, Balboa was able to guide survivors to the Gulf of Urabá, where they founded the first viable settlement on the American continent, Santa María del Antigua del Darién. Balboa gradually assumed control of the settlement and began exploration of the territory, leading to his famous discovery of the South Sea in 1513. A year later a new governor arrived, Pedrarias Dávila, and, after a protracted struggle between them for territorial control, Pedrarias executed Balboa at Acla in 1517 on fabricated charges of treason.

Bastidas, Rodrigo de (1460–1527). Bastidas, a wealthy and educated notary from Seville, accompanied Columbus on the second voyage and also participated in Alonso de Hojeda's 1499 expedition to the Indies. Bastidas received a license from the crown in 1500 to explore at his own expense lands in Tierra Firme not previously discovered by Columbus. After landing on the coast of present-day Venezuela, Bastidas proceeded west, exploring what is now the coast of Colombia, discovering the Gulf of Urabá, and then continuing past the eastern part of Panamá perhaps as far as Portobelo. Bastidas returned to Spain in 1502, surviving a hurricane that destroyed most of the accompanying fleet, but two years later he settled in Santo Domingo. In 1524, Bastidas received a grant of land in Tierra Firme and established the important city of Santa Marta. Three years later he was mortally wounded in a rebellion of some of his settlers. Bastidas died in Cuba on his way to Santo Domingo for medical treatment. Bastidas's son became bishop of Santo Domingo and a friend of Oviedo. Oviedo's daughter married into the Bastidas family.

Catholic Monarchs: Isabella I of Castile (1451–1504) and Ferdinand II of Aragón (1452–1516). Isabella and Ferdinand were two of the ablest and most famous rulers in the history of Spain. In spite of the opposition of her half brother, Enrique IV, Isabella secretly married Prince Ferdinand, the heir to the throne of Aragón, in 1469. When Enrique IV died in 1474, Isabella ascended to the Castilian throne, but only after a four-year-long civil war with the supporters of Juana (called the Beltraneja because of her supposed illegitimacy), the daughter of Enrique IV. The marriage of Isabella and Ferdinand opened the way for a confederation of the two largest kingdoms of the peninsula and the eventual reconquest of the kingdom of Granada from the Muslims in 1492. Ferdinand of Aragón was one of the most politically astute monarchs of his day. In 1512 he incorporated the kingdom of Navarre in his realms and was very actively involved against the French incursions into Italy, which threatened his Neapolitan and Sicilian possessions. The only son and heir of the Catholic Monarchs, Prince Juan, died in 1497. A daughter, Isabella, married to the king of Portugal, died in childbirth in 1498. Another daughter, Catherine of Aragón, became the ill-fated first wife of Henry VIII of England. The third daughter was the unfortunate Juana the Mad, married to Philip the Fair of Burgundy. Two years after Queen Isabella's death in 1504, King Ferdinand remarried for political reasons and also a desire to sire a male heir. His new wife was the younger Germaine de Foix, niece of the king of France; however, this union produced no offspring. After Philip the Fair died in 1506, Juana became too unstable to rule and Ferdinand was recalled to act as regent of Castile until his death in 1516.

Charles of Ghent, King Charles I of Spain and Emperor Charles V of the Holy Roman Empire (1500–58). The eldest son of Juana the Mad and Philip the Fair, Charles established the Hapsburg dynasty (known in Spain as the House of Austria), becoming king of Spain in 1516 and Holy Roman Emperor by election in 1519. He married Isabel of Portugal (1503–39). As a result of various inheritances he was sovereign of immense territories all over the globe. His imperial duties frequently called him away from Spain, especially during the disturbances and wars surrounding the Reformation in Germany. Worn out by years of travel and conflicts, in 1556 he abdicated, ceding the throne of Spain and all its possessions to his eldest son Philip II and the imperial crown to his brother Ferdinand in Vienna. Charles spent his final years in retirement at the isolated monastery of San Jerónimo in Yuste, Spain.

Cisneros, Francisco Jiménez de (1436–1517). Cisneros, the son of an impoverished gentleman, opted for a career in the church. After studying at Salamanca and taking holy orders, he spent some years in Rome before returning to Spain. In 1484 he joined the Franciscan order. On the strength of his character and ability he became Queen Isabella's confessor and then archbishop of Toledo, the primate of Spain. After the sudden death of Philip the Fair and faced with Queen Juana's mental incapacity, in 1506 Cisneros assumed the regency of Castile until King Ferdinand could return from Naples. For this valuable service Ferdinand named him grand inquisitor and procured for him a cardinal's hat. With missionary zeal, Cisneros backed the forced conversion of the Islamic population of Granada and led and financed Spanish incursions in North Africa. As part of his campaign at home to improve the moral and intellectual level of the clergy, Cisneros founded the new university at Alcalá de Henares, which opened in 1508. After the death of King Ferdinand, from 1516 to 1517 Cisneros once more served as co-regent of Spain along with Cardinal Adrian of Utrecht, managing to control the rebellious nobles who were opposed to the foreigner, King Charles. Some have written that Cisneros died of humiliation shortly after Charles arrived in the peninsula because of the new king's refusal to receive him.

Columbus, Christopher (Cristoforo Colombo in Italian; Cristóbal Colón in Spanish) (1451–1506). Very little is known of Columbus's early life. Apparently he was born in 1451 in Genoese territory to a family engaged in the wool business. In his teens, Columbus began training as a mariner and after some years exercising his profession, he developed his great project for a faster route to the East Indies. By 1471, Columbus was in Portugal with his brother Bartholomew trying to interest the Portuguese in a westward route, to no avail. Bartholomew and Christopher then approached the Spanish, the English, and the French with the plan, again with no success. Finally in 1491, back in Spain, the Catholic Monarchs, but particularly Queen Isabella, agreed to finance the historic first voyage of discovery. In all, Columbus made four voyages to the New World (1492–93, 1493–96, 1498–1500, and 1502–4). On the fourth voyage, Columbus explored the coast of Honduras, Nicaragua, Costa Rica, and Panamá to the area of the San Blas Islands. The admiral attempted to found a settlement at Santa María de Belén in Veragua but it was quickly abandoned. Poor sailing conditions and the bad state of the ships forced a return to Cuba, where Columbus was marooned for a time. The expedition endured sickness, starvation, and mutiny but finally returned to Spain in 1504, the same year that the admiral's greatest patron, Queen Isabella, died.

Columbus, Diego (1476–1526). Diego was Christopher Columbus's son by Felipa Moniz. He married María Alvarez de Toledo, a cousin to King Ferdinand. On the death of his father, Diego inherited all his titles to become the second admiral mentioned in Oviedo's text. In 1509, he went to Santo Domingo as the second admiral and viceroy but his authority was constantly challenged by royal administrators and undermined by the monarchy. He was recalled to Spain in 1523, after which he continued the protracted struggle to maintain the family inheritance. The Columbus litigation with the crown was finally settled by Diego's son Luis in 1536 through a compromise that awarded him an annuity of 10,000 ducats, the island of Jamaica, and the province of Veragua in Panamá with the titles of Duke of Veragua and Marquis of Jamaica.

Columbus, Ferdinand (1488–1539). Ferdinand was the first admiral's illegitimate son by Beatriz Enríquez de Arana (or Harana). Perhaps the old admiral's favorite son, Ferdinand accompanied his father on the disastrous fourth voyage. Ferdinand received an excellent education and used his considerable inherited wealth to accumulate a library of reportedly twenty thousand volumes, which he left to the cathedral of Seville. The remains of that priceless collection form the Biblioteca Columbina (or Fernandina), still housed at the cathedral. Ferdinand wrote several works, of which the best known is a biography of his father, *The Life of the Admiral Christopher Columbus,* which remains a valuable reference for the period.

Conchillos, Lope (?–1521). As secretary and gatekeeper to Bishop Fonseca, the much-reviled Conchillos was in charge of the day-to-day activities of colonial administration. Certainly an able man but widely thought of as corrupt, he was part of the Aragonese *converso* (i.e., of Jewish heritage) "mafia" that surrounded King Ferdinand. After the king's death, Conchillos was imprisoned and then forced from office in disgrace by Chancellor Sauvage, largely as a result of charges made by Bartolomé de las Casas.

Corral, Diego de (1480?–1532?). Corral was a gentleman (probably from Castile), evidently a university graduate, since he is always referred to with the title of bachelor. It appears he came to the Indies with Diego de Nicuesa in 1509. Corral arrived in Darién with Nicuesa's lieutenant Rodrigo Enríquez de Colmenares, bringing relief supplies. Obviously Corral was a man of some presence as he formed part of the committee to escort Nicuesa to Santa María to assume the governorship, which was then denied him. After Nicuesa was sent off to his death, Corral remained to develop his considerable ranching interests and to sire a second family through his liaison with an Indian woman baptized Elvira. Corral resisted Balboa's leadership and became an active supporter of Pedrarias upon his arrival in 1514. Later, Corral played a prominent role in Balboa's trial and execution. When Oviedo was given charge of Santa María by Pedrarias, Corral worked ceaselessly to undermine his authority to the point that Oviedo had him sent to Spain in chains in 1523. Three years later both Oviedo and Corral returned to Santa María on the same ship but, by then, the governor had moved the capital to Panamá and both adversaries lost considerable money when Santa María was abandoned. Corral then returned to Seville where, Oviedo notes with some satisfaction, the bachelor died penniless.

Dávila, Pedrarias (Pedro Arias de Avila) (1440?–1531). Pedrarias, from an important Segovian *converso* family, was in his seventies when he came to the Indies in 1514. In an age when court connections were decisive, Pedrarias was highly regarded by the Catholic Monarchs, a friend of Peter Martyr, and strongly backed for the governorship by Bishop Fonseca when others thought him too old for the task. Pedrarias was married to Isabel de Bobadilla y de Peñalosa, the grandniece of the Marchioness de Moya, Queen Isabella's friend and confidant. The no less redoubtable Isabel de Bobadilla left her six children in Spain to accompany her husband to the primitive settlement of Darién and proved invaluable to him there and again at court when she returned to look after the governor's interests. Although Pedrarias was finally replaced as governor of Castilla del Oro, he then obtained the governorship of the territory of Nicaragua, where he died in León. Pedrarias was a ruthless, cunning, but effective governor whom both Oviedo and Las Casas denounced as the principal agent of the genocide of the indigenous Panamanian population. Las Casas referred to him as the Wrath of God.

Enciso, Martín Fernández de (?–1525?). Enciso, established in Santo Domingo by 1508, was a wealthy lawyer who financed Alonso de Hojeda's expedition to Tierra Firme. Enciso's supply ship arrived on that coast to find that Hojeda had returned to Santo Domingo for help, leaving behind at the settlement of San Sebastián the starving remnants of his fleet under the command of Francisco Pizarro. In 1510, guided by Balboa, Enciso and the survivors of Hojeda's group reached the western side of the Gulf of Urabá and founded Santa María del Antigua del Darién. Enciso was soon deposed as the leader of the colony by the machinations of Balboa and exiled to Spain in chains, where he filed suit for damages and worked to have Balboa replaced with a new governor. Enciso returned as an official with Pedrarias's armada but within a year left permanently for Spain. Enciso's *Suma de geografía*, published in Seville in 1519 and reprinted in 1530 and 1549, was apparently the first work concerning the Indies printed in Spanish.

Fonseca, Bishop Juan Rodríguez de (1451–1524). The Fonsecas, originally from Portugal, settled in Segovia, producing a powerful dynasty of churchmen and high officials. Juan Rodríguez de Fonseca was an intimate friend and loyal supporter of Queen Isabella and King Ferdinand during the civil war that brought Isabella to the throne. This loyalty continued throughout the protracted struggle to conquer the last Muslim kingdom of Granada. The royal favor Fonseca enjoyed is evidenced in the progression of important ecclesiastical offices he held—successively, archdeacon of Seville and bishop of Badajoz, of Córdoba, of Palencia, of Burgos, and of Rossano (Italy). Despite his ecclesiastical positions, Fonseca was mainly to be found at court, where his administrative abilities were highly prized. Fonseca was given the task of organizing the fifteen-ship fleet of Columbus's second voyage in only five months. As a result of his success, Fonseca became the official charged with everything relating to the newly discovered Indies. He created the House of Trade of the Indies (*Casa de Contratación de las Indias*) in Seville in 1503 and established the all-powerful Council of the Indies (*Consejo de Indias*). Fonseca's supremacy is attested by the number of New World locales named for him, for example, the Bay of Fonseca. After Ferdinand's death, Fonseca lost influence with King Charles's Flemish officials for a short period. However, as a result of Fonseca's large bribes, he survived to control affairs of the Indies until his demise. Columbus, Columbus's heirs, Las

Casas, and even Oviedo all contributed to a negative view of the bishop as arrogant, self-interested, and corrupt. Surprisingly, there is no recent biography of this key figure in the enterprise of the Indies, but a monograph by Sagarra Gamazo presents a more objective assessment of Fonseca's talents and accomplishments based on an exhaustive study of contemporary documents.

Hojeda, Alonso de (1466?–1506?). In his youth Hojeda secured a position in the household of the Duke of Medina Sidonia and, through Bishop Fonseca's patronage, participated in Columbus's second voyage. Three years later he led his own fleet to the New World, exploring the coast of Tierra Firme near the mouth of the Orinoco River. He returned to that area in 1502 but his attempt to start a colony there failed. On his third and final voyage to the mainland between Cape Vela and the Gulf of Urabá he founded San Sebastián, but the settlement was constantly under attack by the indigenous inhabitants and his men were decimated by hunger and disease. Leaving Francisco Pizarro in charge, Hojeda returned to Santo Domingo for supplies and reinforcements but was not able to raise more funds. He died soon thereafter. The survivors of San Sebastián were picked up by Martín Fernández de Enciso, Hojeda's lieutenant, and went on to the Gulf of Urabá, where they founded the town of Santa María del Antigua del Darién.

Las Casas, Bartolomé de (1484–1566). After studying in Seville and Salamanca and taking minor orders, in 1502 at the age of eighteen Las Casas sailed to Santo Domingo to manage the estates that had been established by his father and uncle, who had come over on Columbus's second voyage. This was the first of many trips between the Old World and New in his lifelong mission to seek humane treatment of the Native Americans. Eventually, Las Casas became a priest and later joined the Dominican order in 1522. Las Casas was an intelligent, tenacious, and aggressive promoter of the indigenous people. He faced fierce opposition in the Americas from Spanish landowners who held grants of Indians and from their agents and government officials in Spain who profited from the system. He was a harsh critic of Bishop Fonseca and as such enjoyed the support of King Charles's Flemish coterie. Appointed bishop of Chiapas, Mexico, Las Casas's reforming efforts ultimately failed because of local opposition, but he was partially successful in securing reform legislation, in particular the New Laws of 1542. At Valladolid in 1550–51, Las Casas sustained a moral victory in the famous debate with the eminent humanist Juan Ginés Sepúlveda over the topic of the "just war" to Christianize the Native Americans. Las Casas wrote constantly throughout his long life in Latin and Spanish but, without doubt, his most famous work was the tract *A Short Account of the Destruction of the Indies* (1542). This exposé of Spanish atrocities was widely translated and distributed throughout Europe and contributed greatly to the development of the so-called Black Legend of Spain. Las Casas's *History of the Indies* was begun in 1527 as a rebuttal to the success of Oviedo's *Summary,* to which Las Casas violently objected. The *History* was completed toward the end of his life but, according to the author's instructions, was not to be printed until forty years after his death. In fact, it was not printed until three hundred years later although copies of it circulated in manuscript.

Martyr, Peter (Pietro Martire D'Anghiera in Italian; Pedro Mártir de Anglería in Spanish) (1455–1526). Educated in humanistic studies in Italy, Martyr served for a while in the Milanese army before joining the Spanish ambassador's household on its return to Spain. Martyr participated in the siege of Granada but afterward entered the church. Because of his excellent education he was taken into the court by the Catholic Monarchs, who wished to found a school for sons of noble houses based on the new Italian humanistic model. Martyr was also sent on diplomatic missions, most notably one to the sultan of Egypt in 1501. Throughout his life, Martyr wrote hundreds of Latin letters to highly placed friends and important Italians (including the pope) concerning events in Spain. To satisfy his correspondents' curiosity for details of the New World, Martyr interviewed everyone he could who had returned from the Indies (including Oviedo) and summarized their information for his readers in Italy. The letters were eventually collected and published as the famous *Decades of the New World (De orbe novo decades).* The *Decades* was the first chronicle of the Americas and made Martyr an authority on the New World, even though he never set foot in the Indies. For his education, his court position, and his expertise, Martyr was appointed a member of the Council of the Indies, the ruling authority of the colonies. Although in old age Martyr hoped to retire to his birthplace, Arona, Italy, with a comfortable ecclesiastical position from his friend Cardinal Adrian (now pope), that did not happen. Martyr instead returned to Granada, where he died in 1526.

Nicuesa, Diego de (1464–1511). Both Hojeda and Nicuesa received territories in Tierra Firme from King Ferdinand. Nicuesa's was Castilla del Oro, which ran from the Gulf of Urabá to Veragua in present-day Panamá. Nicuesa, because of his connections and wealth, was better able to finance his expedition than was Hojeda. Both men set sail from Santo Domingo for their respective territories in 1509 and both expeditions were doomed from the start. Nicuesa, stubbornly rejecting the advice of veteran mariners, became lost off the coast of Panamá en route to his assigned territory and was marooned on an island until help arrived. Finally, after trying to establish a colony in several places along the coast, Nicuesa and his remaining men arrived at Nombre de Dios. Of some seven hundred men who set out with him from Santo Domingo, six hundred died. In the meantime, the colony of Santa María founded by the Hojeda survivors was thriving. Since the settlement was in territory assigned to Nicuesa and because Hojeda had not returned, it was decided that Nicuesa should be offered the governorship, which he gladly accepted. Unfortunately, reports came back to Santa María concerning Nicuesa's lack of judgment and harsh disciplinary practices. Upon his arrival, instead of a welcome, Nicuesa was greeted with hostility. Ultimately, Nicuesa and a few loyal followers were placed in a leaky boat and forced to sail for Santo Domingo. They were never heard from or seen again.

Pizarro, Francisco (1471?–1541). Born in Trujillo, Pizarro was the illiterate and illegitimate son of a gentleman who had fought with General Gonzalo Fernández de Córdoba (the Great Captain) in the Neapolitan wars. Pizarro joined Hojeda's disastrous 1509 expedition to Tierra Firme and was rescued by Enciso's fleet, which went on to found Santa María del Antigua del Darién in the following year. He accompanied Balboa to the Pacific coast but, in the struggle between Balboa and Governor Pedrarias Dávila, Pizarro took the side of the governor and was the officer sent to arrest Balboa. Later, Pizarro explored the Pacific coast and, with Pedrarias's backing, contracted with Diego de Almagro and Father Fernando de Luque to form an exploration company to search for the reported riches of the Indians to the south. Six hard years later, after several expeditions to Peru and a voyage to Spain, Pizarro captured the Incan Emperor Atahualpa at Cajamarca and became master of the greatest treasure ever gained by one man in the Indies, estimated at some five million ducats worth of gold and silver. Inevitably there was a falling out between Pizarro and Almagro over the spoils. In the open warfare that followed, Almagro was captured and executed. Three years later a conspiracy organized by Almagro's son and ex-followers resulted in the assassination of Pizarro in Lima.

General and Natural History of the Indies
Part II
Book XXIX

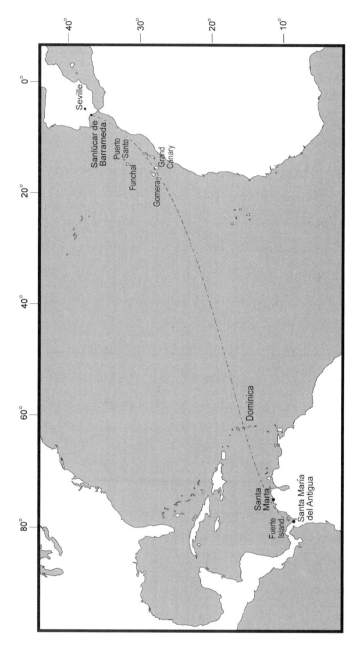

Map 3. The route of the Splendid Armada from Seville to Darién (1514).

Chapter VI—Of Governor Pedrarias Dávila's voyage to Castilla del Oro in Tierra Firme where Vasco Núñez de Balboa was captain.

Because of Bachelor Enciso's complaints against Vasco Núñez to His Most Serene Catholic Majesty King Ferdinand concerning his unjust imprisonment and exile and Vasco Núñez's cruel treatment of Diego de Nicuesa; and because of a subsequent report made by the agents of Darién, Inspector Juan de Quicedo and Captain Rodrigo de Colmenares; and because of letters against Vasco Núñez from Bachelor Diego de Corral, Gonzalo de Badajoz (Diego de Nicuesa's ex-lieutenant), Luis de Mercado, and Alonso Perez de la Rúa, all imprisoned by Vasco Núñez, the king decided to send Pedrarias Dávila with a splendid fleet to examine the charges against Vasco Núñez de Balboa and to govern Castilla del Oro in Tierra Firme.

About three thousand men assembled in Seville for this expedition. The royal officials included Alonso de la Puente as treasurer, Diego Márquez as comptroller, Juan de Tavira as factor, Juan de Quicedo as inspector of mines and smelting (the latter died in Seville and I, the chronicler, Gonzalo Fernández de Oviedo y Valdés, was appointed by his Catholic majesty in his place), Bachelor Gaspar de Espinosa from Medina de Rioseco (who later styled himself licentiate) as chief justice, and a Cordovan gentleman, Juan de Ayora (brother of the chronicler Gonzalo de Ayora),[1] as lieutenant to Captain-General Pedrarias. The captains of one-hundred-man companies were Luis Carrillo, Francisco Dávila, Antonio Téllez de Guzmán, Diego de Bustamante, Contreras, Francisco Vásquez Coronado de Valdés, Juan de Zorita, Gamarra, Villafañe, Atienza, Gonzalo Fernández de Llago, Meneses, Gaspar de Morales (the governor's cousin), and Pedrarias the younger (the governor's nephew) as captain of the artillery. I have recorded these names because most of them, as well as others already in Castilla del Oro and those who styled themselves captains later were notable in the history of the region.

Representing the spiritual realm was Bishop Don Juan de Quevedo, friar of the Order of Saint Francis. He was the first prelate to cross over to Tierra Firme with the title of bishop of Santa María del Antigua and of Castilla del Oro. The bishop's seat was the town of Santa María del Antigua del Darién, won from the Indians by Vasco Núñez and the remnants of Captain Alonso de Hojeda's expedition. After the establishment of the bishopric and because of its noble citizenry, the town was elevated to city status by the pope and the Catholic king as diocesan seat of Castilla del Oro.

Before I proceed I should tell you that among his Catholic majesty's ordinances and provisions given to Governor Pedrarias,[2] four were to be his special concern:

- First, that he should see to the conversion and good treatment of the Indians with much attention and vigilance.
- Second, that no lawyers or legal experts be allowed there because in this Island of Hispaniola[3] and in other parts experience shows how prejudicial they are to the land and masters at inventing excessive litigation and contention, so that without their malicious nitpicking, suits would be settled quickly and justly for all parties.
- Third, that before warring on the Indians they are to be read a certain Requirement, which will be discussed farther on.
- Fourth, that in all important matters the bishop and the officials should have a say and their opinions taken into account.

In all these things one sees the good and holy intentions of the prince who ordered them, thinking that the governor and prelate would always conform to the service of God and King in the governance of the state, the pacification of the Indians, and the colonization of the land. But what happened was the opposite. Instead of acting for the common good, two opposing parties formed, causing much harm, some passionately supporting the governor, others the bishop. Thus, the officials who should have sought to calm and mediate the differences became enmeshed in those very conflicts, as will be more fully explained later on.

The fleet's departure was delayed by weather. In the meantime, on the basis of dispatches from Tierra Firme, the king ordered the force reduced by half to fifteen hundred men. After an impressive muster in Seville,[4] half the men were dismissed and the rest left with the governor for Sanlúcar de Barrameda. Nevertheless, because of reports of great New World wealth, the expedition grew to well over two thousand men. This was one of the best and most select groups to come to the Indies and even if there had only been five hundred they would have been up to the task as events proved.

The fleet sailed with twenty-two ships and caravels.[5] Its chief pilot was

Juan Serrano, who was later killed along with Captain Ferdinand Magellan on the expedition discovering the great strait and the journey to the Spice Islands (as recounted in Book XX, Chapter I).[6] The fleet sailed with fine weather from the port of Sanlúcar de Barrameda on Shrove Sunday 1514,[7] but after proceeding four or five leagues a storm blew up and it had to return. I was on the last ship to leave port. Another ship carrying Comptroller Diego Márquez was still at anchor, as its pilot, Pedro Miguel, with better sense than others, refused to cast off because he saw that the weather was not good. The river pilots had left the ships at sea and returned in their boats to Sanlúcar before the sea turned bad, forcing the fleet to return to the river. Since my ship was the last to leave we were the first to return. Entering the river with no pilot, we almost sank. We struck the sand bar several times and almost capsized, but with God's mercy managed to anchor in the Guadalquivir River.[8] Then, one by one, the other ships and caravels came back to port, but for two days we could not disembark because of the foul weather as the ships were tossed about, some dragging their anchors, others drifting crosswise in the river. Finally the winds died down and everyone went ashore so as not to consume the provisions while we waited for favorable sailing weather. Because we had waited a long time for the fleet to sail, our money was low and most were in debt, especially those who persevered until the second departure. In the interval many changed their minds and went home or to some other place, and those were not the worse off. We who stayed spent the entire Lent in voluntary penance, many pawning their capes for food and others their capes and the rest of their clothing. Finally during Holy Week God sent the fair weather we were awaiting and on Holy Tuesday, April 11, 1514, the fleet again set sail.

After eight or nine days we arrived at Gomera, where we stayed twenty days taking on supplies of meat, fish, cheese, water, firewood, and all that was needed.[9] From there we proceeded in very good sailing weather. On a Saturday, the third of June and the eve of the Feast of the Holy Spirit, the flotilla anchored at Dominica, where we camped for three days near a good river.[10] The day after our arrival was the Sunday of the Feast of the Holy Spirit and a solemn mass was said to the delight of all. As if he were the first to discover it, Captain-General Pedrarias ordered the inlet named Fonseca Bay.

This naming is a practice that always makes me and others laugh and that I have criticized in various places in these histories. I will never speak well of anyone who does it unless he were a prince having good reason to erase the original name. That bay had been discovered years before, many pilots and sailors having seen and entered it. Nevertheless, governors and captains newly arrived in these parts freely change the names of harbors, rivers, mountains, promontories, and whatever they please to inflate their own deeds and obscure those of the people who came before them. I will not permit this renaming in my histories that detracts from someone's merits. Juan Rodríguez de Fonseca, Bishop of Palencia, and at that time president of the Royal Council of the Indies, procured the governor's appointment and so, to ingratiate himself, Pedrarias planted Fonseca's name on that bay. I, however, will never stop writing the truth and will denounce those unjustly changed names wherever they appear. So that anchorage and harbor is called El Aguada and is in the western part of Dominica, fourteen degrees this side of the equator.[11]

There the governor held a council on how to proceed with the bishop, officials, and the pilots and with Bachelor Enciso, the chief justice, and Captain Rodrigo de Colmenares's men, who said they were familiar with the Tierra Firme coast. The king had ordered Pedrarias that, if he could on his way to Darién, he should stop at certain islands and harbors of the Caribs,[12] such as Santa Cruz, Gaira, Cartagena, Caramari, Codego, and the islands of Barú, San Bernardo, Arenas, and Fuerte. Many years before, the Caribs had been declared slaves because they eat human flesh and because of the harm they had done to Christians and the king's Indian vassals. Frequently they had killed Spaniards who had stopped in those areas. Further, the expedition council agreed to reconnoiter Cape Aguja at Santa Marta on the coast of Tierra Firme.[13] The purpose was to ascertain whether the eleven Christians were still alive whom Captain Rodrigo de Colmenares said remained there after an attack that killed more than thirty others and also to scout out a fortress site to protect future shipping. Then the fleet would proceed to Cartagena and Codego and to the islands of Barú and Fuerte as they were on the direct route to Darién. They agreed to skip Santa Cruz because it was too out of the way to be worth the trip.

Often in subsequent years, reminiscing about this council with others who were there, we agreed on how laughable it was to give any credence to Captain Rodrigo de Colmenares. He himself confessed that in stopping at Gaira on his voyage from this city of Santo Domingo to Darién the Caribs killed thirty of his men and that, because he did not want to be accused of alienating the Indians, he did not deny that he had hurried back to the ship and departed. Imagine under what safe conduct and word of honor were the eleven Christians left behind whom he thought were still alive! In Castile many stories like these have been spread about by some ill-informed persons because they see their audiences have no idea how little they really know.

With that plan of action decided, the next day the general ordered everyone aboard ship in the harbor of Dominica (or Aguada, as it is properly called). Because some of the company were missing, cannons were fired to summon those who had gone inland to come back to the shore, and that night Lieutenant Juan de Ayora with a detail of soldiers stayed on land sounding trumpets from time to time. In this fashion the stragglers gathered and among the last to appear was a certain San Martín, who had served the governor for many years. When the lieutenant cursed him for being late, San Martín became angry, saying that he refused to embark and that he would rather stay on that beach. Of course he had no intention of doing so; he was simply angry at being verbally abused. Juan de Ayora, mindful that San Martín was the governor's retainer, went to report to Pedrarias what San Martín said. Pedrarias was enraged and there and then sent his cousin, Captain Gaspar de Morales, with orders to hang San Martín immediately from the nearest tree. And so the captain with some halberdiers of the governor's guard executed the order and the poor soul was hanged. It is true that five or six months later in Darién there was a posthumous trial for insubordination but many suspected that this summary execution resulted from an old grudge the governor had against San Martín.

An hour later, while I was with the governor on his ship, an honorable cleric named Cantado, the bishop's chaplain, came with the bishop's request that the man be given a Christian burial and not be left hanging there for the Indians to eat, and so the governor gave permission. Then Cantado and others accompanied by soldiers returned and buried him at the foot of the tree on which he was hanged on the shore of the bay. Such cruel and hasty justice frightened many. They suspected that our governor would not be overly concerned with rights and due process and that each man should watch his step since how Pedrarias punished one of his own men showed what he would do to others.

Let us return to our voyage. We left Dominica a day after the Feast of the Holy Spirit. Then on Monday, June 12, the fleet put in to the harbor of Santa Marta on the Gaira coast of Castilla del Oro where Pedrarias's territory began. By ten o'clock that day all the ships and caravels were anchored in the harbor. The beach was swarming with aggressive-looking Indians in feather headdresses and war paint and armed with bows and arrows. In council, the governor, bishop, officials, and captains agreed that Lieutenant Juan de Ayora and other captains should put to shore with as many well-armed men as would fit in three launches. They were to demand that the Indians submit to the Holy Mother Church and, in the temporal sphere, recognize the king and queen our lords and the Royal Crown and Scepter of Castile as their monarchs and natural lords. To interpret this Requirement they were to take with them an Indian from Cueva Province in Tierra Firme who had been in Spain and Captain Rodrigo de Colmenares as a person knowledgeable about the area since he said he understood something of the language of those Caribs. They were to assure the Indians that they had not come to harm them or make war on them and that if they wished peace they would be treated as their majesties' good vassals and be rewarded; if not, they would be dealt with according to their actions. The general ordered his lieutenant and men not to be the aggressors and not harm them but rather endure their taunts until it was not reasonable to allow the Christians to be offended or mistreated.

The governor selected me and other notable persons to put to shore from the flagship in three launches. I commanded the launch closest to the beach with about twenty men. Lieutenant Juan de Ayora was in the next launch with twenty-five men and in the one farthest to sea was Captain Rodrigo de Colmenares with fifteen men and the Indian interpreter. All the launches were side by side, not very far apart. As we approached, about one hundred Indians wearing feather headdresses, their bodies and faces painted blood red, and carrying bows and arrows ran the length of the beach to the place we were making for. With brave and gallant gestures they indicated they would resist our landing. Drawing close enough to them to make ourselves understood (as if we could), the Indian and Colmenares shouted many words at them and for a little while the Caribs were quiet. But in truth they did not understand them any more than a Basque understands a German or Arab or any other exotic language. Finally the Caribs gave up on the words and signs that Rodrigo de Colmenares and the Indian made in vain and with much shouting they advanced rapidly to the water's edge, discharging many arrows that reached the launches or flew overhead, some of the Indians wading out waist deep in the water to shoot. Juan de Ayora ordered the Spaniards not to respond with their crossbows and harquebuses but to cover themselves with their shields and await orders. He called aloud for witnesses that neither he nor the Christians were the aggressors, that we offered the Indians peace and they refused and in fact started the war and tried to kill our men regardless of the Requirements that were made to them in discharge of the royal consciences of our princes and their captains and soldiers, and that any subsequent harm would be on their heads and not on the Christians'.

The lieutenant saw that his admonitions were disregarded or not understood and that, sitting there, we were in great danger from the very poisonous arrows raining down on us. Nevertheless, since to withdraw would be dishonorable, he sent a skiff that had joined us to inform the governor of the situation. In the meantime, to wait any longer was both dangerous and shameful and so the lieutenant ordered two small powder shots fired over their heads and the launches to land. As quickly as we jumped onto the beach the Indians fled to safety. The governor and others were already making for the shore, where we awaited him, as they had signaled us not to pursue the Indians.

After the general landed we went to a nearby Indian dwelling,[14] where he cut branches from the trees with his sword and pronounced the formal acts of possession.[15] As captain-general, in the name of their highnesses and the Royal Crown and Scepter of Castile, he affirmed the right of royal possession that the Castilian monarchs had of these Indies, islands, and Tierra Firme of the Ocean Sea,[16] if necessary retaking them as lands of their dominion and royal patrimony. He promised that the indigenous peoples of those lands who obeyed our Holy Catholic faith and the crown of Castile, their majesties, our lords, and their successors, would be as well treated and justly governed as all their other vassals. But, those who refused to comply would be punished as rebels, disobedient, and contumacious under the laws and as ordered by their highnesses. He ordered all this formally written down and witnessed.

Seeing the Indians' disobedience, the governor ordered the lieutenant to take three hundred men and proceed one or two leagues inland to capture some Indians and return to the coast, where he would wait for them. And so they set out. A half league or less from the harbor they came on two small deserted settlements of fifteen to twenty dwellings. Along the beach they picked up four or five fishnets nicely fashioned of cotton cord that were spread out to dry. Inland among the bushes and trees they found some hammocks (beds the Indians used for sleeping) thrown aside as the Indians fled to the mountains.

The governor waited three or four hours before recalling the lieutenant and his men to the beach by trumpets and powder shots. When they came back, everyone returned to the ships and that day no Christian was wounded nor any Indian killed or captured.

CHAPTER VII—CONCERNING THE SECOND SALLY OF
GENERAL PEDRARIAS DÁVILA THREE LEAGUES INTO
THE INTERIOR FROM THE HARBOR OF SANTA MARTA
DURING WHICH SOME INDIAN MEN AND WOMEN WERE
KILLED AND CAPTURED; AND OF WHAT HAPPENED IN
THAT HARBOR AND OF THE PROVISIONS OF THE RE-
QUIREMENT THAT WAS READ TO THE INDIANS BEFORE
COMMENCING HOSTILITIES AGAINST THEM; AND OF
OTHER ITEMS PERTINENT TO THE COURSE OF THE
HISTORY.

After the events of the preceding chapter, on Tuesday, June 13, the governor in agreement with the bishop and officials ordered me, the chronicler, as inspector of mines and gold smelting, together with some experts
in those areas to go ashore with the necessary equipment and explore the
river entering that harbor for gold deposits. We were to follow the river
three or four leagues inland to its supposed source in the sierras. The
governor's nephew, Artillery Captain Pedrarias Dávila, was to accompany
us with three hundred men. If we came upon Indians we were to notify
them of the Requirement as their majesties ordered and, if possible, we
were to procure some Indian interpreters without harming them. As simply showing them the paper on which the Requirement was written
seemed pointless, the governor ordered me to carry it, *in scriptis,* to be
presented to the Indians. He himself handed it to me to read to them as
if I or anyone else could understand their language, even assuming they
would want to hear it.

Since the Requirement is frequently mentioned, it would be well here
to let you know what the injunctions were. The following is a verbatim
transcription.

The Requirement Ordered Made to the Indians
I.   On behalf of the very high, powerful, and Catholic defender of
        the Church, the ever victorious great King Ferdinand (fifth of
        that name), King of the Realms of Spain, of the Two Sicilies,
        of Jerusalem, of the Indies, Islands, and Tierra Firme of the
        Ocean Sea, etc., subjugator of barbarians, and on behalf of the
        very high, powerful, Lady Queen Doña Juana, his dear and
        beloved daughter, our lords: I, Pedrarias Dávila, their servant,

messenger, and captain, notify you and make known to the best of my abilities that God, Our Lord, three in one, created heaven and earth, and one man and one woman, of whom you, we, and all persons on earth were and are descended and procreated, as well as all those who will come after us. But because of the multitude generated since the world was created some five thousand years ago, it was necessary that some men went one way and others went another and were divided into various kingdoms and provinces because in one they could not sustain or conserve themselves.

II.   Over all these people God, Our Lord, gave dominion to one who was called Saint Peter and who was named to be prince, lord, and superior of all men on earth, whom all were to obey and who was to be head of all human lineage wherever they may live and of whatever sect or belief; and He gave him the whole world as his kingdom, realm, and jurisdiction.

III.   And even though Saint Peter was ordered to place his throne in Rome as the site most suitable to rule the world, he was also permitted to place his seat in any other part of the world and to judge and govern all people, Christians, Moors, Jews, Gentiles, and of whatever sect or belief they may be.

IV.   This man they called pope, which means "admirable," "great father," and "protector," because he is father and protector of all men.

V.   This Saint Peter was obeyed and held as lord and king and universal superior by those who lived in that time and likewise all the others after him elected to the pontificate; and so it has continued until now and will continue until the end of the world.

VI.   One of the previous pontiffs who succeeded to the aforementioned seat and dignity as prince or lord of the world made a donation of these islands and Tierra Firme of the Ocean Sea as well as all they contain to our lords the said king and queen and to their successors in these kingdoms according to certain documents that you may examine if you wish.[1] Thus, their highnesses are monarchs and lords of these islands and Tierra Firme by virtue of the said donation. Almost all those who have been notified of this have received their highnesses as monarchs and lords of these islands and Tierra Firme and have obeyed and do obey them and have served and do serve as befits a subject. With good will and without resistance or delay, as soon as they were informed of the aforesaid, they obeyed and received the men and clerics whom their highnesses sent to preach and teach our Holy Catholic faith and of their free will without condition or reward became and remain Christians; and their highnesses received them happily and kindly and ordered them treated like their other subjects and vassals and you are obliged to do the same.

VII.   Therefore, to the best of my abilities, I beg and require you to understand well what I have said and to take a reasonable amount of time to understand and deliberate the matter; and to recognize the Church as Lord and Superior of the universe and the Holy Pontiff, the pope, in its name, and the king and queen as lords, superiors, and monarchs of these islands and Tierra Firme by virtue of the said donation; and that you consent and permit these clerics to explain and preach to you concerning the aforesaid.

VIII.   You will do well if you comply with what you are obliged and required and their majesties and I, in their names, will receive you with all love and charity. You will not be enslaved but be allowed your wives, children, and possessions to enjoy and to use as you see fit. You will not be compelled to become Christian unless, on receiving instruction in the truth, you wish to receive our Holy Catholic faith as have practically all the inhabitants of the other islands. In addition, their highnesses will grant you many privileges, exemptions, and rewards.

IX.   If you do not comply or maliciously delay complying, I declare that with God's help I will move fiercely against you and will make war on you with all available resources at my command. I will subject you to the yoke and obedience of the Church and to their highnesses. I will enslave you, your wives, and children and will sell or dispose of you as their highnesses order. I will confiscate your goods and do all the damage and harm that I am able as to vassals who do not obey and do not accept their lord but resist and contradict him. I declare that

whatever deaths and damages that may ensue will be your fault
and not that of their highnesses, of mine, or of any of these
knights of my company. To attest to all that I have said and
required I request a signed affidavit from the notary present.

Signed: *Episcopus Palentinus, comes. F. Bernardus, Trinopolitanus
episcopus. F. Tomás de Matienzo. F. Al. Bustillo, magister. Licenciatus de
Sanctiago. El doctor Palacios Rubios. Licenciatus de Sosa. Gregorius,
licenciatus.*[2]

These are the contents of the Requirement, which we carried the following Wednesday, June 14, 1514. As the governor ordered, at daybreak
more than three hundred well-armed men left the beach for the interior
under the command of Captain Pedrarias, the governor's nephew, and of
the Captains Villafañe, Gaspar de Morales, me, and others. To effect the
Requirement, God willing (since the preaching fathers referred to in the
Requirement remained on board ship awaiting the outcome), we moved
two leagues inland. En route we found three small towns deserted by
the Indians, who had fled to the woods and sierras. They left behind
some hammocks, blankets, and even some gold ornaments hidden in the
underbrush. In the town nearest the coast we found many beautiful
parrot-feather headdresses of various colors. We proceeded in a very dis-
organized fashion, the fault of the captains. The Christians were strung
out as if they were rabbit hunting, searching for the things the Indians
scattered as they fled. I was on one flank in charge of some miners, silver-
smiths, and prospectors, along with fifteen other friends and servants,
about thirty persons in all.

At a narrow spot on the path up a large bare hill we were suddenly
attacked by some screaming Indians. As everyone was widely dispersed,
each man ran off in a different direction. Pedrarias the younger, like a
good soldier, with a few troops joined quickly with Captain Villafañe and,
with the few soldiers who managed to make their way to them, they began to fight on one side of the hill. My little band was on the other flank.
As we were more tightly grouped than the others, more Indians attacked
us. Because the slope was steep and smooth, the Indians who held the
heights rolled down on us great pieces of rock and, since there was no
shelter from them, several soldiers were struck. Considering the numbers
of Indians, it was certainly the work of God that no Christians were
killed, although many were wounded.

Initially the other troops pulled back but seeing how bravely Pedrarias's, Villafañe's, and my group were facing the enemy they were ashamed and hastened to aid us. We moved forward up the mountain. Halfway up, the Indians ran out of rocks to roll down but now we were in arrow range and many rained down on us. With great shouts some Indians began to descend toward us shooting arrows. An arrow grazed the calf of one of my men standing next to me, Hernando de Arroyo, a valiant native of Santander (of whom I wrote in Book XXVI, Chapter X). Though the wound was just a scratch, the poison on the arrow was so strong that he immediately fell down unconscious and it was obvious he was done for. I had two men carry him to the safety of the ship, where they tried all possible remedies but on the third day he died raving.[3]

Returning to the battle: finally we took the hill by force of arms. Three Indians were killed by musket shot and ten women including a chief's wife were taken prisoner. We pressed ahead on our march and the Indians followed us off the road, showing their faces from time to time. Descending the other side of that hill we saw a beautiful river in the plain below toward which we hastened because the sun was hot and we were very thirsty. The Indians were retreating to the river bank, where there were some nice-looking maize fields. We had stopped to eat and rest on top of the hill and then continued on in better formation than before the attack. Two of the general's messengers reached us close to the river to say that he was on the way and that we should await him there. He caught up with us at the river with more troops and now our numbers totaled more than thirteen hundred men.

After crossing the river we entered a town of about twenty thatched dwellings, which was completely abandoned. There the governor, all the captains, the comptroller, factor, Chief Justice Licenciate Espinosa, and Lieutenant Juan de Ayora went into one of those houses. In the presence of all, I said to the governor: "Sir, it seems to me that the Indians do not want to listen to the theology of this Requirement, nor do you have anyone about to explain it to them. Your Grace should order it put away until we have one of these Indians in a cage so that he can learn it at leisure and the reverend bishop can explain it to him." With that I returned the Requirement to him, much to his mirth and that of all present.

Everyone rested in those houses, waiting for the sun to go down a bit. Around two in the afternoon the alarm was given because more than a thousand Indian bowmen were advancing toward us on a nice broad road bordered by many trees planted there to adorn it. Wearing their head-dresses and war paint they came in well-organized squadrons, shouting and sounding large seashells (called *cobos*), which could be heard a long way off. The beautiful vermilion-colored paint they use is applied to their faces and entire body, making them look as though they were made of pure crimson. They mix the paint with certain gums so that it remains on them for many days. They wear this paint for several reasons: one, it firms and invigorates the skin; two, they think they are handsome and fierce painted that way; and three, even if they are wounded and lose a lot of blood, it does not seem as bad as it is against the red paint.

The general quickly left the town to face the Indians on the same road. He positioned his men in a battalion at a little less than two hundred paces from the Indians with orders that the musketeers and crossbowmen hold their fire. A small bronze two-hundred-pound cannon was set up. Two greyhounds, highly praised by their owners as being able to outrun the swiftest Indian, were placed on the flanks. When the general gave the signal, the cannon was to be fired and then all together the dogs were to be released and everyone was to shout and close with the enemy and fight bravely.

I would have liked the Requirement explained to them first but, whether as useless or unnecessary, it was not done. The way the governor dealt with the Catholic obligations he was ordered to observe before making war on the Indians became the model for subsequent incursions by individual captains, who did the same or worse, as my history will record. Later in 1516 I asked Doctor Palacios Rubios, the Requirement's compiler, if it satisfied Christian conscience and he told me yes, providing it were delivered as specified. Nevertheless, it seemed to me that he laughed many times when I recounted how it was administered on this expedition and on those of other captains afterward. But, far more laugh-able were he and his "learning" (he being reputed a great man and for that had a seat on the Royal Council of Castile) if he thought that the Indians would understand the Requirement without years of explanation. Since in Clause VII they are to be given or promised all the necessary time to understand and deliberate its contents, I would like to see the time specified. Whether or not the Indians would comply with that time limit, I could not say. Later on we will see the time the captains gave them—reading them the entire document while tying them up after having at-tacked them. However, let us return to the history.

I have described the general's battle plan when the Indians came to dislodge us from the town and how everything was in readiness. But when the signal was fired it passed over them without killing anyone and when the dogs were released, instead of attacking the Indians, they attacked each other. Two hundred paces away from us the Indians instantly fled from the main road into the dense woods alongside and, since they knew all the paths, no Indian was killed or captured.

We went on a league and, as we advanced, we flushed out many deer. The several good greyhounds we had with us recognized that game better than they did the Indians and that night, camped by a river, we feasted on five or six deer. While we were there it was reported that the Pilot Pedro de Ledesma had been wounded that day by the Indians so I went to see him. He was vomiting and had a small wound on his hip that looked more like a scratch than a poisoned arrow wound. Later it was suspected that his "sickness" was due to having finished off some wine that he took from the ship that day. Nevertheless, because he was a good pilot and knowledgeable about that coast, the general took pity on him. He was fat and heavy and it took a lot of work to get him back to the harbor the next day.

That night we kept careful watch. The next day, Thursday, Corpus Christi Day, the sailors and especially Pilot Pedro de Ledesma (whose "poison" was wearing off) informed the governor that the weather was favorable for sailing and that we ought to embark. The general agreed and gave permission for the captains and their men to return to the harbor on their own but to be sure to be back by a certain hour to set sail. On the way back were found some clothing, hammocks, and some gold ornaments worth a little more than seven thousand pesos hidden in the brush in *havas* or baskets in five or six places. That day I entered an abandoned town of some forty dwellings. One of them I ordered burned was full of bows, arrows, and bundles of herbs and I supposed it to be their armory. In that town was found a large clear sapphire and a mantel adorned with emerald-colored agates and other stones. But I reported that and other items about that harbor in Book XXVI concerning this province of Santa Marta and I will not repeat it here.[4]

So, that day, Thursday, June 15, the general had everyone back on board ship and we set sail that very night. The general did not escape criticism for having left Santa Marta with so little to show for it and justly so. Later that portion of his territory was taken from him, seeing as how he could easily have colonized it because he had more than enough people. That night the flagship led the way out of the harbor, all other ships and caravels following its lantern. A strong wind blew up and the sea became so rough toward dawn that we found ourselves in imminent danger of running aground below the harbor of Gaira. Without doubt, if daylight had been two hours later, it would have been a miracle if anyone escaped alive. However, with much effort and mainly by God's goodness and clemency we were able to put out from the shore and continue our voyage.

The fleet sailed to Fuerte Island about two and one half leagues from Cenú.[5] There the general ordered several captains and their troops to go ashore, where they seized much salt in hampers about the size of those they use to transport sea bream from the Bay of Biscay to Castile through Burgos. However, these baskets or hampers were much better made and the sea salt was fine and white. When the Indians there saw so many ships approaching they took to their canoes and fled to the mainland. That island is flat and low, probably some eight leagues around, and is a little less than ten degrees this side of the equator. On the third day we left for Darién, arriving at its anchorage in the Gulf of Urabá June 29, 1514.

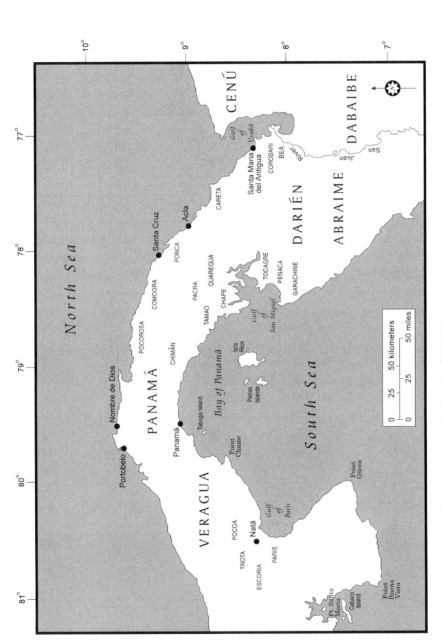

Map 4. The principal indigenous areas and places in Oviedo's text.

CHAPTER VIII—How Governor Pedrarias Dávila
arrived at the city of Santa María del Antigua
del Darién, where Captain Vasco Núñez de
Balboa was governor; how he took possession
of that office; how he set about taking Vasco
Núñez's residency; and how he sent Lieutenant
Juan de Ayora and other captains and soldiers
to settle the other coast on the South Sea.

On June 30 in the year 1514 of the nativity of our Redeemer, Pedrarias
came ashore and entered the city of Santa María del Antigua del Darién
with all the people of the fleet, some two thousand or more smartly
dressed and well-armed men and the bishop, officials, and captains, all in
as good an order as would be seen anywhere. Vasco Núñez, who governed
there (as noted previously), received him with the five hundred fifteen
men settled there. They had built more than one hundred *bohíos,* forming
a pleasant settlement through which close to the houses ran a beautiful
river of good water abounding with fish. This is the Darién River that
flows from the west and not the one that the Licentiate Vadillo called the
Darién, which is a branch of the San Juan River entering the bottom of
the Gulf of Urabá, as this history has previously shown in Book XXVII.
But let us return to the narrative.

Pedrarias presented his credentials and was received as governor to the
great delight of the settlers and newcomers except for Vasco Núñez and
his supporters. They only feigned pleasure at our coming since they
feared the accounting of their actions. The governor took possession of
the staffs of justice and distributed them as they had been assigned and
each person commenced his duties.[1] The governor also named the officials he was empowered to designate.

Living among those first settlers were more than fifteen hundred Indian men and women *naborías* who served the Christians on their plantations and in their homes. As the term *naborías* will be frequently used,
it needs to be explained. A naboría is an Indian who is assigned to serve
a master until the death of either. A naboría cannot be sold or traded
without the governor's permission. If the naboría dies, his captivity is
over; if his master dies, the naboría passes to the governor, who gives him
or her to whomever he wishes. Such Indians are called forced naborías
and not slaves. Nevertheless, I would call them slaves as they are not free.

Pedrarias's people were divided and billeted with Vasco Núñez's company. For a month after the fleet's arrival, food rations were diligently given to all and still there remained many barrels of wine, flour, and other provisions in the royal stores that should have been used up as well, as will be explained farther on.

The day after he arrived, the first thing the governor did was to confer privately with Vasco Núñez. I was present because Secretary Lope Conchillos had delegated to me his rights as notary general. As such, I had a royal commission to oversee for him all the notaries of the governor's and chief justice's tribunals and of the other courts. The governor told Vasco Núñez that the king had ordered him to be well treated for his services in that land and be gratified and favored as much as possible. Further, the governor was ordered to find out from Vasco Núñez the state of the land and which Indians were peaceful and which warlike and the governor said he intended to seek Vasco Núñez's opinion in everything. Vasco Núñez displayed contentment at all the governor's flattering words and responded that he kissed the feet of our lord king and was gratified by the goodwill shown him. Vasco Núñez said that he would truly and happily render advice or service to their highnesses and therefore would search his memory concerning the information the governor required and present it in writing since that was an official meeting and everything was being recorded.

Two days later, July 2, Vasco Núñez sent his written response containing many well-expressed and appropriate things. Among other information, he revealed the rivers, ravines, and other sites where Christians had discovered gold up to that time. He declared that three years before Pedrarias's arrival he had made peace with the following chiefs—Careta, Ponca, Careca, Chape, Cuquera, Juanaga, Bonanimana, Tecra, Comogre, Pocorosa, Pucheribuca, Chuirica, Otoque, Chorita, Pacra, Teaoca, Tenoca, Tamao, Tamaca, Tubanamá, and others;[2] that he had discovered the South Sea in 1513; that he had discovered Rica Island and its pearls;[3] that in person he had crossed that land from sea to sea; and that in everything he spoke the truth.

Within a few days the residency of Vasco Núñez and his officials was publicly announced, to be directed by the chief justice, Licentiate Gaspar de Espinosa. At the same time the governor with a lengthy interrogatory secretly began an investigation against Vasco Núñez unbeknownst to the chief justice. Perhaps it was that he did not trust the chief justice, or because the chief justice had no judicial experience (this being his first office, having only recently graduated from the University of Salamanca), or perhaps it suited the governor's purpose. Pedrarias did this investigation despite the royal order from King Ferdinand requiring Pedrarias to use no other judge in the administration of justice than Licentiate Espinosa, his chief justice. Before Licentiate Espinosa found out, statements were taken from those first settlers who remained of the expeditions of Governors Alonso de Hojeda and Diego de Nicuesa. These men well knew the truth of what had happened and Vasco Núñez's history. Meanwhile, in the public residency, many came forward to accuse Vasco Núñez of having taken things from them and Vasco Núñez settled with some of them. At first it seemed that the chief justice wished to satisfy all of their claims, but after a few days he clearly favored Vasco Núñez. It was thought that the chief justice wanted to please Bishop Juan de Quevedo, who also favored Vasco Núñez. The bishop frequently praised his services, for being the first Christian to see the South Sea and for the discovery of the isthmus, which he personally explored. The bishop declared publicly that Vasco Núñez was worthy of great rewards.

The governor was unhappy at the bishop's praise of Vasco Núñez, which he did not share, but the governor, the bishop, and the royal officials were coadministrators. When the governor's secret investigation became known, the chief justice was greatly offended and many harsh words not fitting for inclusion in this history were exchanged. As it turned out, the chief justice demanded a part in the governor's investigation in order to subvert it. Among other charges, the report proved Vasco Núñez's culpability in Diego de Nicuesa's merciless exile and his death. Finally the governor handed over the written report revealing the names of those hostile witnesses and enemies of Vasco Núñez and did nothing more than what the bishop and Licentiate Espinosa wished. Nevertheless, the governor wanted to send Vasco Núñez back to Spain in chains and all were in agreement. But the bishop was clever and delayed indefinitely Vasco Núñez's departure because they were partners in several plantations and in the ownership of naborías and Indians and the prelate intended to enrich himself through Vasco Núñez's industry. The bishop gave the governor to understand that if he sent Vasco Núñez to Castile, as soon as he returned to court, the king would learn how he had discovered the other sea and the isthmus between the two seas, where he found many deposits of gold and had personally explored the territory and pacified many chiefs. Moreover, the bishop told the governor that Miguel de Pasamonte, royal treasurer of this city of Santo Domingo and the man the king most trusted in these parts, was on Vasco Núñez's side. The result would be that Vasco Núñez would be sent back to Tierra Firme honored and gratified with whatever part of the territory of Castilla del Oro he would choose and, knowing the land so well, he would select the best. The bishop's advice to the governor was to dissimulate and occupy Vasco Núñez with litigation, promises, and constant vexations until time would tell what he should do. The chief justice concurred.

Pedrarias realized he could not disregard this advice and in a few days restored to Vasco Núñez his confiscated assets and, at the bishop's urging, gave him a voice in the administration. All this was delayed longer because Pedrarias fell gravely ill and was sick for many days, during which time he gave the bishop and officials power of attorney to govern in his place.

Before Pedrarias arrived in Darién, a gentleman merchant from Bilbao named Pedro de Arbolancha had passed through. Arbolancha was a man with legal connections and well known at court. Vasco Núñez gave him letters and testimonials of service detailing his discovery of gold deposits and his pacification of the major portion of that land to take back to King Ferdinand and Vasco Núñez soon expected a favorable response from court.[4]

While Vasco Núñez's residency lasted and even after, many newly arrived men fell sick and, since their rations had run out, many died of hunger. To make up for these deaths and fearing that Vasco Núñez would receive favorable dispatches from Spain, Pedrarias decided to occupy his men in the settling of the other coast. Thus began the destruction of that land (which they called conquest and pacification). Lieutenant Juan de Ayora was sent out as captain-general with Captains Hernando de Meneses, Francisco Dávila, Gamarra, and others, with four hundred men. Ayora's instructions were to proceed to the South Sea coast and settle the men in the site he found most suitable. He was to take special care to make the Indians understand the Requirement in order to satisfy the royal consciences of the monarchs and of Christians in general. The Spaniards were ordered never to be the aggressors nor allow any harm to the Indians without good cause and to give them an opportunity to respond to the Requirement made up by theologians and read to the savages in a language unknown to them. Indians were not to be attacked until they declared themselves for peace or war. But, in truth, the real purpose of the expedition was that even if the king found out that Vasco Núñez had discovered the other sea and sent him some appointment over the area, Pedrarias would have already settled there. That way, Pedrarias could deny Vasco Núñez the use of whatever reward he received by alleging that Pedrarias had settled an area that Vasco Núñez merely saw and where, in the process, Vasco Núñez had mistreated the Indians. To that end, Pedrarias had some documents prepared to use against Vasco Núñez.

CHAPTER IX—HOW JUAN DE AYORA AND OTHER
CAPTAINS WERE SENT WITH PEOPLE TO SETTLE THE
SOUTH SEA COAST; AND HOW THE KING REWARDED
VASCO NÚÑEZ WITH THE TITLE OF *ADELANTADO*[1]
OF THE SOUTH SEA AND THE GOVERNANCE OF THE
PROVINCES OF COIBA AND PANAMÁ; HOW PEDRARIAS
MANAGED TO THWART THIS APPOINTMENT; AND OF
THE ROLES OF THE GOVERNOR AND OFFICIALS IN THE
EXPEDITIONS, THE PRINCIPAL CAUSES OF THE DIMINU-
TION IF NOT LIQUIDATION OF THE INDIANS AND THE
DEVASTATION OF THE LAND, ETC.

As previously reported, upon his arrival, Pedrarias learned from Vasco Núñez's written report the state of affairs in Darién and which Indians were pacified and which were not. Even though Vasco Núñez's written report was truthful and contained good advice, Pedrarias did not give it credit, thinking that Vasco Núñez was trying to trick him. As I said, he decided to send Juan de Ayora with other captains and men to the other sea. The expedition followed the coastal route west to the harbor of Santa Cruz in the territory of the chief of Comogre. There Juan de Ayora established a settlement, leaving about eighty men, most of them sick. For their captain and magistrate Ayora appointed a youth named Hurtado, an almost unknown person of no experience who had recently arrived in the fleet. From there Juan de Ayora continued to the province of Tamao, where he left Captain Hernando Pérez de Meneses to construct a town. Another group went with Captain Francisco Dávila to the Panamá coast in the southern zone but he saw very little of the South Sea and dispersed all his men among the chiefs of that region.

On this expedition not only did Juan de Ayora fail to comply with the provisions of the Requirement about warning the Indians before attacking them, but he sprang on them at night. He tortured chiefs and principal Indians, demanding gold. Some he burned alive, some were fed to the dogs, some were hanged, and others were subjected to new forms of torture. Moreover, wherever he went he took their wives and daughters and enslaved the Indians, who were distributed among the Spaniards at his whim and that of the other captains.

These people occupied themselves for several months with this diabolical Indian hunt. Meanwhile, in Darién, disease and fevers spread among the Christians, especially among those newly arrived in Pedrarias's fleet. Each day, fifteen to twenty died, some days more. In a short time some five hundred died, most for lack of nourishment even though the royal stores had food to spare. Since the officials were zealous in safeguarding the royal supplies and they themselves did not lack food, they had little pity for others. The officials had built a large thatched structure called the Toldo on the coast near the beach to store many barrels of wine, flour, and other provisions unloaded from the ships. From there were transported little by little what they wished to the House of Trade headed by Factor Juan de Tavira.

God, seeing the little service He and the king received from those provisions and the poor men dying of hunger in the streets, permitted a fire to break out in that warehouse. And so everything that could have saved the lives of the many starving men was destroyed. If they had been given that flour and wine many would have lived and the king would have profited. I cannot help but suspect, as did many others, that the stewards who guarded the stores for the factor were the spark that caused the fire, thus covering the theft of one hundred barrels by burning ten and then writing off the entire amount as an accident. God will be the judge of it and I wish to God that other worse things had not happened in that land.

Because of so much sickness, death, and intolerable hunger, many who came in Pedrarias's fleet fled the land—some returned to Spain; others came to this our Island of Hispaniola, to Cuba, to Jamaica, or to San Juan. In the space of seven or eight months there were more deaths and departures than there were people remaining in that land. Among the living there was so much discontent that no one was there willingly. Even the governor, bishop, and officials would have abandoned the place if they could have done so without disgrace. Everyone wrote to the king and the council that the city was very unhealthy, deeming it the worst place in the world but, in truth, it was not so. The sickness was caused by accidental fevers and the loss of the food imported from Spain. Compounding this problem was the destruction of the local corn fields by a plague of locusts so thick they filled the air. Once those misfortunes passed the region was very healthy. There were abundant harvests, gold mines three or four leagues from the city, a river of good water abounding with fish, and plentiful supplies of deer, pigs, and other game. Those who persevered in Darién will have to admit that it is the best site on the mainland.[2] But, let us return to the history I was previously relating.

As I have said, the situation in Darién was so bad for everyone that even Governor Pedrarias tried to return to Spain. However, the citizens of Santa María del Antigua del Darién did not allow it and told him plainly that he could not leave without first being ordered to do so by the king and then undergoing a residency. Because of this he conceived such antipathy against the city that he did not rest until he depopulated it, as will be related later.

At that time the residency of Bartolomé Hurtado, Vasco Núñez's high constable and comrade, dragged on. To evade it and cover up his misdeeds, which well deserved punishment, Vasco Núñez's friend the bishop came up with a plan. He hinted to the governor that it would be good to send Bartolomé Hurtado to see what had happened to Lieutenant Juan de Ayora's expedition to the South Sea coast as no one had yet returned and there was no news of them. Because Bartolomé Hurtado was an able man and familiar with the area, it was done. He and twenty companions were sent to look for Juan de Ayora because Bartolomé Hurtado had accompanied Vasco Núñez when he discovered the other sea and he knew which chiefs were peaceful and which were not. In truth, in those days before Pedrarias, there were more than two million Indians in that territory. There were many peaceful or at least neutral chiefs who were disposed to serve and be friends of the Christians. The land was rich and the Indians possessed many gold ornaments. Vasco Núñez's Christians wanted for nothing and were primed to become rich in short order by the disposition of the land.

Bartolomé Hurtado found Juan de Ayora and gave him letters and instructions from the governor, bishop, and officials and then returned. Juan de Ayora reported that all were well and that he would return to Darién in a few days. As Bartolomé Hurtado's residency was only suspended, in order to have it over with and be free, he sought to curry favor with the governor, bishop, and officials by picking up Indians on his way back to distribute among all of these. Even though he carried the king's Requirement, it did not bother him that the majority of the Indians he abducted were peaceful. On his return with more than one hundred Indian slaves he stopped at Careta, whose chief was the first true friend the Christians had in that province. He told the chief that the Indian bearers he had were exhausted and he begged the loan of a few more to get to Darién, some twenty-four or twenty-five leagues away, with the promise of returning them. The chief welcomed Hurtado warmly. He fed him, his men, and Indians and ordered twelve or fifteen of his people to help carry the baggage. Moreover, the chief sent along one of his principal Indians to oversee his Indians and return them to Careta. When Hurtado arrived back in Darién, the governor, bishop, officials, and everyone were extremely pleased to learn that Juan de Ayora and his men were well and would soon return. In gratitude for this news they quickly concluded Bartolomé Hurtado's residency, forgetting about his misdeeds so readily that he regretted not having committed more. The whole affair was an example to others to commit crimes without fear of punishment.

Some time later, after the King's Fifth was levied on the abducted Indians,[3] Hurtado came to a meeting of the governor, bishop, officials, and chief justice with some thirty handsome Indian men and women and gave six each to the governor and bishop, four each to the treasurer, controller, factor, and chief justice, which they all took to their homes. These Indians were the first shares of the spoils the governor, bishop, officials, and chief justice obtained without having won them themselves, being given them for no good reason. From then began the custom of giving shares of Indians at least to the governor and officials.

Bartolomé Hurtado paid the King's Fifth to the treasurer with one of every five Indians he brought back. The Indians comprising the Royal Fifth were the peaceful and friendly Indians and their leader from Careta that the chief had lent Hurtado to carry the baggage. They were branded and auctioned, the majority being shipped to other parts. Naturally, this wicked fraud was reported directly to the governor but he did nothing about it and Hurtado was not punished. The chief of Careta, however, did not forget the injustice, as will be seen farther on when other Christians paid for Bartolomé Hurtado's crimes.

Because the governor, bishop, officials, and chief justice received a part of the Indians, Bartolomé Hurtado was not called upon to give the particulars of that expedition and how he complied with the procedures and Requirement the king ordered made to the poor Indians. It seems that they were attacked, captured, and tied up before they were told anything of the pope and Church or anything that the document required. After they were chained, someone read them the Requirement without benefit of an interpreter, although even if someone who understood their language had read it to them they had already lost the liberty to respond. Immediately they were dragged away, the slower ones beaten. Rape of the infidel women was but one of the outrages committed. There was no punishment or even reproof given for all this. Instead, there was a great dissimulation that was the beginning of so many evils that they could never all be recorded.

A few days later Juan de Ayora returned to report on his expedition and dealings with the Indians. His report was as bad or worse than Bartolomé Hurtado's, but, as Ayora gave even more Indians to the bishop, all went in his favor and everything was covered up. On the chief justice's recommendation the report was accepted and even praised, although Ayora inflicted needless extreme cruelties and death on the Indians. Even when they came to welcome him peacefully he tortured and robbed them. Ayora said that he would live out his days in his hometown of Adamuz in the province of Cordova and not in Tierra Firme and would not see these people again and swore to God that they would either give up their gold or their lives. And so he caused many deaths by novel cruelties and tortures and fed others alive to the dogs. Ayora left that land in a state of total rebellion and he so completely and diabolically discredited the name of Christian that the indignant Indians ever after were implacable enemies with just cause.

A guilty soul has no rest nor can a sinner live without fear of punishment. Juan de Ayora knew that he himself was the best witness to his heinous misdeeds. Thus, he could not be content with Licentiate Espinosa's favorable judgment, which came at a time of division among the governor, bishop, and royal officials—the bishop, chief justice, and Vasco Núñez on one side and the governor, treasurer, comptroller, and factor on the other. Because of the discord, Juan de Ayora had managed to escape punishment by the distribution of Indians. Nevertheless, it was clearly dangerous for him to await the arrival of those members of his expedition not yet returned to Darién, some of whom he suspected would report things that would cause his case to be reexamined. So he sought permission to leave as soon as possible. As his luck would have it, there was a caravel at anchor in the harbor of Darién, and feigning illness and the need to seek medical attention in Spain, he took the ship to this city of Santo Domingo on the Island of Hispaniola and from here left immediately for Castile.

A few days after Juan de Ayora left Darién, the other captains who had gone with him on the expedition returned to find him gone. Soon his misdeeds were made known, although to no avail. It was certain that he took with him a great quantity of stolen gold that had not been registered nor assessed the King's Fifth. The governor and officials sent notice at once to this city of Santo Domingo for his detention but he had already left for Spain.

The remaining captains gave their reports: some maltreated the Indians less than others but even the least cruel had little to commend them, as they committed many excesses. Nevertheless, since Hurtado and Ayora had been exonerated, it seemed inappropriate to condemn those who by comparison had scarcely sinned, even though they certainly did not lack culpability. Since they too gave shares of the booty and Indians to the governor and officials, they were absolved as well. The sharing of booty was by now so customary as to become almost a law among the captains. Because of the profit in Indians and gold to the governor, bishop, and officials and because the expeditions kept the men, Negroes, and dogs busy, they continued to send captains out to all parts of the country, giving them the Requirement that the king ordered made to the Indians with very specific instructions for its delivery. The captains were sent out to their assigned provinces for a specified time. When they returned loaded down with gold and enslaved Indians, they gave the governor two shares of everything and two shares of Indians to each official. On their return the official reports of the expeditions were made to Chief Justice Espinosa, and although the captains committed many errors and failings, exceeding their instructions and not administering the Requirement as they should have, they were pardoned and the Indians enslaved. Many of these pardons were given by Bachelor Diego de Corral, to whom the governor and officials entrusted the investigations in the chief justice's absence. No matter how unjustified, all the pardons were ratified by the governor and officials because otherwise they would have had to return the shares they were given. Bachelor Diego de Corral was one of the messengers sent on behalf of Darién to call Diego de Nicuesa to govern that land, whom they later refused to accept, as was explained in Book XXVIII, Chapter III.

Things being as they were in Tierra Firme, I determined to go to Spain to report to the king and to live in a land safer for my conscience and well being. The governor tried to stop me from leaving, saying that I would first have to undergo residency. He did this because in the name of Secretary Lope Conchillos, notary general of that land, I oversaw the notaries for the governor's and chief justice's courts as well as the notaries who went out with the expeditions. On their return, the latter gave me the sworn reports of the captains' activities and I knew what each commander had done. So, even though I had not taken any shares of the spoils, my residency was announced for a period of sixty days. During that time no one presented any claims against me and the governor never stopped promising that he would help me become rich in short order, saying that since I had suffered illnesses, want, and difficulties I should not leave just as it was about to pay off. He said this because he knew I had seen all those captains' expedition reports and would tell the truth of their activities to the king and gentlemen of his council. But I told the governor that the land was damaging my health and that I wanted to convalesce in Spain and rejoin my wife as I could no longer bear separation from her, among other good reasons that were entirely truthful.

The governor, showing much unhappiness at my departure, gave me permission when he saw that he could not deny it. He said that I was losing much by leaving because he liked me and wished I were departing richer instead of having wasted my opportunity and having spent more than others. He gave me letters and memorials stating how the greedy and untrustworthy bishop was a great obstacle to good governance and how dishonest and shameless were his clerics. When the bishop saw that I was determined to leave, he became very friendly and gave me the task of informing the king of Pedrarias's faults—his greed and inconstancy—and of the thefts and malfeasances of the officials and the chief justice. He begged me very affectionately to say what an able and good servant Vasco Núñez de Balboa was and gave me a long memorial concerning his thoughts on these and other matters. I accepted his dispatch and promised to tell the truth if I were asked, the same response I gave to Pedrarias when he gave me his memorial.

A few days before my departure the differences between the governor and bishop deepened and each, not trusting the other, loaded me down with memorials so that I would tell the king that he was not well served by the other. When I complied with their charges, the king would learn all this from their sworn statements and more from me and that there was good cause to remove them and drive them from that land. I went to Spain and kissed his Catholic majesty's hand in Plasencia as he was on his way to Seville. He permitted me to go to Madrid and visit my wife before attending him in Seville, where he said he would hear my report and provide all that was necessary for the good of that land. However, twelve or fifteen days later on his way to Seville, God took him to glory and so my mission was fruitless.

About eight or ten days before I left Darién, his Catholic majesty's provisions for Vasco Núñez arrived, forwarded by his friend Pedro de Arbolancha, whom I mentioned in the preceding chapter. One granted him the title of adelantado of the South Sea and the other that of governor and captain-general of the provinces of Coiba and Panamá. This dispatch fell into Pedrarias's hands, as he always took care to intercept the letters arriving from Spain. But, it was not such a secret that Vasco Núñez and the bishop failed to know it and make it public, complaining about the governor, saying that, since all were free men and the king's vassals, everyone had the right to communicate freely with Spain and receive their letters. Moreover, the bishop publicly preached that it was like being in captivity to contravene the will of and service to God and King and that he would notify the king of this confiscation of his letters, which took away the freedoms of both the king and his subjects. As a result, Pedrarias decided to consult with the officials and the chief justice and have them vote as to whether the provisions should be given to Vasco Núñez.

This course of action was suggested to Pedrarias by the chief justice, who had returned and had changed sides, breaking with the bishop. I myself recorded the votes of each. Treasurer Alonso de la Puente and Comptroller Diego Márquez said that the provisions should be withheld until the king was notified of the results of Vasco Núñez's residency. This residency, although started ten months before, was never finished because of Pedrarias's and the chief justice's delays (and even the bishop's, who had advised the delaying tactic when previously they wanted to send Vasco Núñez in chains to Spain). The factor was neither in favor nor opposed, stating that as he was not a legal expert and did not know what was best, he would concur with the majority. The chief justice said that it was reasonable for the king to know first the merits and the process of the residency as well as the opinions of the governor and the others.

After the bishop heard them he became very angry. He said that it was very bad for them to dispute what the king ordered and that even contemplation of such an act was a sort of disloyalty and disobedience, especially since the royal provisions cited Vasco Núñez's services in the discovery of the South Sea and rewarded him for them in discharge of the royal conscience. He said other things to this effect that I duly recorded and everyone signed the minutes of the meeting and the tallies. Since the governor was so fearful of the bishop, he said that the bishop's opinion seemed good (although, truly he wanted the opposite). Finally, it was agreed to give Vasco Núñez his titles the next day as the meeting lasted until almost midnight.

And so then Vasco Núñez styled himself adelantado of the South Sea, but no good came to him from this title.[4] The governor recognized that the land from Darién east along the coast to Cape Vela was in the hands of the fierce Carib Indians and that twenty-four to twenty-five leagues west was Careta. Beyond Careta began the territories granted to Vasco Núñez in Coiba and southern Panamá, and so there would be very little of Pedrarias's territory left between that and Veragua, which was the Admiral Diego Columbus's jurisdiction. With Vasco Núñez as adelantado of the South Sea and governor of Coiba and Panamá provinces, Pedrarias's jurisdiction would be much reduced and, as a result, the profit of those lands would be lost to him and the royal officials if Vasco Núñez were to assume his offices. Accordingly, when Pedrarias and the officials gave Vasco Núñez the provisions and titles, they made him promise that he would not exercise the governorship granted by the king without Pedrarias's permission. Moreover, they proposed not to give him men or to permit him to outfit for the enterprise. The bishop and Vasco Núñez felt that prying the title of adelantado from the claws of Pedrarias, the officials, and the chief justice was enough for the present and the rest would come in time. And so, the negotiation came to this end, but because it was based on falseness and hate, in time it led to much tumult and disturbance, as will be reported in due course.

CHAPTER X—IN WHICH ARE RELATED SOME
EXPEDITIONS BY DIVERSE CAPTAINS THAT GOVER-
NOR PEDRARIAS DÁVILA ORDERED MADE IN HIS
JURISDICTION.

It is not a little tedious for me to write about and others to read and there
would not be sufficient paper nor time to completely express what the
captains did to rob the Indians and devastate their lands. However, as I
said before, since in Castilla del Oro there had been at least two million
Indians,[1] it is necessary to address how so many people disappeared in so
little time. Moreover, having previously mentioned the misdeeds of some
captains, it would not be right to pass over those of other captains as or
more culpable. As previously stated, the governor and officials had grown
fat on their shares of the booty. Treasurer Alonso de la Puente put together the expedition instructions carried by each captain, one of the first
clauses of which was that the governor would receive two shares of the
gold and Indians and the comptroller, treasurer, and factor would each
have two shares of captured Indians but no gold. And so it was put into
effect. Thus, even though each official took only shares of Indians, each
strove to make friends with the captains, who would take the officials'
retainers with them to gain shares. As a result, many captains were appointed who on return were defended by the favor of their official friends
even though they had committed a thousand cruelties.

After Lieutenant Juan de Ayora was sent to the South Sea along with
others who went to the interior, many other captains were sent out so that
there was no province or part of the land that did not suffer. The following captains went out:

Captain Francisco Becerra led an expedition with the backing of the
treasurer, who was either his relative or from the same part of Spain.
Becerra was one of the first and oldest soldiers in that land and these
islands and, knowing well the Indians' ingenuousness, committed more
atrocities than any of the previous captains. He was neither reprehended
nor punished because he brought back six or seven thousand pesos worth
of gold and more than three hundred male and female Indians in chains,
all of which he shared liberally with the governor, bishop, and officials.
This was sufficient to excuse his crimes and even to be praised rather
than punished. Soon after his return he was sent out again even better
equipped and with more men to other parts, where he paid for his mis-

deeds along with many others who were lost with him. However, on his first inland expedition, he raided along the river of the chief called Suegro until it debouched in the Gulf of San Miguel on the Southern Sea.[2] Many other rivers flow into this river, such as those of Chiefs Tocagre, Quemado, and, farther on, Queracha (also called the River of the Canoa Nueva), then those of Tutibra and Toto (son of Chief Ocra). Inland from the river to the left in the mountains are the territories of Chiefs Tapicor, Penaca, and Porore. Their lands are high and forested with many rivers and ravines containing gold deposits.

It may strike the reader that the names of Chiefs Suegro and Quemado are Spanish, not Indian, and that is correct. Before proceeding I should explain. The one chief was called el Suegro because the first Christian captains who arrived took (or were given out of fear) three or four of his daughters and for this hospitality and the adultery of his "sons-in-law" (whom he probably did not want) they called him the "father-in-law" (*el suegro*), although his proper name was Mahe. The other chief they called "the scorched" (*el quemado*) because they tortured him with fire when he did not hand over all the gold they demanded. Let us return to the history.

Captain Becerra and others who went with him on the first expedition told me that they found short-haired, reddish lions with good-sized claws and fangs somewhat larger than those of greyhounds. I have seen some of these lions, which do not have the manes of African lions. The men also reported seeing what they called tigers, although I cannot affirm that since they are not as fleet as what is reported of tigers. The "tigers" in that land are fierce and beautiful animals, reddish with black spots.[3] There were many deer, pigs like those called *báquiras*, black foxes, and *dantas* (if that is what they are). The Christians call them dantas because of their thick skin; the Indians call these animals *beorí*.[4] All these and other animals are common in Tierra Firme. Because Book XII is concerned with these animals, I will return to what Captain Becerra saw on his expedition.

From the chief of Penaca's lands to the South Sea there are beautiful savannahs and rivers. After Captain Becerra's company reached the Gulf of San Miguel, they followed the coast up to the east to Chief Jumento's territory situated on the banks of a beautiful river entering that gulf. From there they went to the river of Chief Chiribuca, going then upstream to the area of Chief Topogre and continuing on to the sierra, the lands of

Chief Chucara. After that they went to Chief Canachine, in whose territory there is a promontory that juts out into the gulf, a very impressive sight. In the distance they saw higher ground where, according to Chief Jumento, there lived a certain group of people who were black (but this was not verified, nor did the captain visit Point Canachine). They also saw in the distance the Perlas Islands discovered by Adelantado Vasco Núñez de Balboa, as I reported earlier. At Canachine the captain turned back to Chief Toto's area, crossed to the other side of the Gulf of San Miguel, and went on to the river of Chief Chape. At Chape they proceeded up the gulf coast to the river of Chief Tunaca, then on to the coast of Thamao, where they saw the Panamá coast but did not go there. At Thamao they turned back to Darién with the aforementioned gold and Indians seized illegally on the expedition.

After this gold was melted down, the King's Fifth assessed, the shares distributed among the governor and officials, and the rest divided among Captain Becerra and his men, he was outfitted for an expedition to the Gulf of Urabá with two hundred or more of the best men available. But, as God keeps strict account and had not punished him for his previous crimes, neither Captain Becerra nor any of his men returned from this second journey. None of them was ever heard from again and so that was the end of them and their ill-gotten gains.

In the same season Captain Francisco de Vallejo was also sent to the Gulf of Urabá toward the area settled by Governor Alonso de Hojeda. Likewise Captain Gaspar de Morales went out to the South Sea under the governor's orders to pass over to the Perlas Islands discovered by Adelantado Vasco Núñez. Captains Juan de Escudero, Gonzalo de Badajoz, and Antonio Téllez de Guzmán were sent to explore diverse provinces and Adelantado Vasco Núñez de Balboa went to Dabaibe Province. Factor Juan de Tavira explored the Grande River, called the San Juan River, with some ships and men and before that Captain Luis Carrillo went to Abraime Province. Also, other captains were sent out to various parts and provinces.

Because it would be intricate, almost infinite, if not tiresome to detail so many cruelties inflicted on the Indians by the majority of these captains, I will abbreviate. If the reader is attentive to this history he will see how God is just and how the captains paid for their crimes, proving to mortal eyes how true is that dictum of the glorious doctor of the church, Saint Gregory: "He whose works show disdain for God's wrath presumes in vain to hope for His mercy."[5] So, pay attention to the stories of these captains.

I have related that when Lieutenant Juan de Ayora passed through the harbor of Santa Cruz in Comogre Province he left behind a settlement of eighty men under the command of a magistrate named Hurtado. Hurtado and his company mistreated the Indians, stealing all they had, including their wives and children, as well as committing other iniquities. The Indians suffered it all and did not rise up to avenge their wrongs because they feared that Juan de Ayora would return through Comogre on his way back to Darién. When they saw that Juan de Ayora's expedition had returned to Darién, they massacred every last person in the settlement of Santa Cruz with the aid of Chief Pocorosa. In response, the governor harshly punished the Indians of these chiefs by pronouncing them slaves even though they were not the aggressors nor had they killed any Christian who had not well deserved it.

Pedrarias entrusted another captain, Lope de Olano, who betrayed Governor Diego de Nicuesa, with the construction of a fort and town in Careta Province.[6] The site was chosen because it offered a good port on the northern coast for developing trade in the South Sea. Olano built the fort and town, which Pedrarias ordered named Acla. Now, let us briefly relate the deeds of the captains:

The governor sent out Luis Carrillo, the brother of Doña María Niños, Secretary Lope Conchillos's wife, but, because of his youth, Francisco Pizarro went along as cocaptain. Pizarro had been Governor Alonso de Hojeda's lieutenant in Urabá and was later marquis and governor of Peru. This expedition went out to Abraime and Teruy provinces. There, as you have heard, the Indians build their dwellings in trees in the middle of large lakes and lagoons secure from fire and from their enemies. From there they go by canoes to their maize fields on dry land. From this and other lands Luis Carrillo, Pizarro, and the others of the expedition brought back many Indian slaves and high-quality gold. They treated the Indians with the customary cruelty that Pizarro had learned so well during his many years in the Indies.

Captain Escudero did even worse on his expedition—he fed two chiefs to his dogs. As he brought back little gold, there was not enough to distribute to the governor and officials and he was arrested. However, he was absolved and set free because before Escudero left he had deposited a certain sum of gold with the chief justice, who was to prosecute him later. Because Escudero's misdeeds were so horrible and public, his lenient treatment led people to suspect that the chief justice wound up with the gold in his custody. So, even though Escudero well deserved punishment, he was absolved and not punished except for the loss of his money, which instead of going to the treasury went to someone who should not have had it.

Captain Francisco de Vallejo passed over to the other side of the Gulf of Urabá, where he stole three thousand pesos worth of fine gold, but the Indians gathered together and forced him to retreat. Had he been more skillful and courageous he could have avoided a shameful rout and saved all his men, but his fear was so great that he abandoned them. When the rivers flooded, he and a few Christians got on rafts and fled downstream, leaving behind seventy men, who all died because of his cowardice when he could easily have rescued them. Many of the abandoned men sought refuge in the trees along the river, but when Vallejo's rafts passed them he had no pity on them and went on, leaving them to die. With this "happy" end to his expedition he returned to Darién, where no captain to date had been punished for evil deeds. Because of the shares given to the governor and officials who assigned the captains their commands, the same officials protected them later. However, because what this Captain Francisco de Vallejo did was so widely known, losing so many Christians by his negligence and cowardice, his punishment was to be deprived of any command in the future. So, within a few days he left the territory with what he had stolen. Later when our lord emperor appointed Captain Rodrigo de Bastidas governor of Santa Marta, this Vallejo went with him and died in that territory.

Captain Antonio Téllez de Guzmán, favored by Comptroller Diego Márquez, led an expedition inland on the South Sea route, where he did as bad or worse than the others and was infamous for his widely known cruelties. Whatever one official wanted, the others approved because they were given the best of the enslaved Indians, and so Téllez de Guzmán escaped punishment. In truth, the governor acquiesced to everything he saw that the others clearly wanted and, as he himself enjoyed part of the spoils, he could scarcely point the finger of blame, being himself the principal tyrant.

Adelantado Vasco Núñez de Balboa went out to Dabaibe Province with a well-equipped and well-manned expedition. En route, the Indians attacked and he returned seriously wounded and with many of his men in bad shape. Captain Luis Carrillo, who was with him, died of a chest wound a few days after returning to Darién and so paid for his misdeeds in Teruy and Abraime provinces, as recounted earlier.

Captain Gonzalo de Badajoz went inland from the southern coast, where he and his men were the first Christians to see the Taboga Islands and other islands two to six leagues off the site of the city of Panamá. Badajoz went as far as Natá and Escoria. Before he arrived at the territory of the chief of Escoria, he had captured more than twenty thousand pesos worth of gold and many Indians. Although he was somewhat less cruel than the other captains, he was hardly blameless. The chief of Escoria voluntarily gave him nine thousand pesos worth of gold, which Badajoz repaid by taking from him one of his daughters and his wives. One of the wives was the sister of the chief of Paris, whose lands were farther on and who was one of the most powerful and richest in gold and subjects in all those provinces. When Chief Escoria saw that Captain Badajoz was taking away his wives and daughter, he followed him for more than a league begging their return. The captain refused and threatened to take him away as well or kill him unless he desisted. Hearing this, the chief raised his hands and eyes to heaven protesting to God then fell to the ground, biting it and raving. The captain and his company, laughing at these desperate convulsions, passed on, leaving the prostrate chief to lament his misfortune.

Chief Escoria complained to his brother-in-law Chief Paris and begged his help; however, the latter replied that the Christians had done him no wrong and he did not wish to harm them. Chief Paris had his wives send Captain Badajoz a present of six thousand pesos worth of gold with the message that he wished to be his friend as well as a friend of the Christians. Then he sent one of his principal Indians to see Captain Badajoz with three thousand pesos worth of gold. The envoy came with his wife, a cousin or sister of Chief Paris, a young girl of refined manner. That same night a "devout" cleric of the captain's expedition (the majority of the captains took along a priest) had the envoy sleep under his hammock and put the envoy's wife in the hammock to sleep with him, although she did not get any sleep nor was this adultery unperceived. Certainly this so-called cleric would better be called *onocentauro*, since *onos* in Greek means "ass," a symbol of lasciviousness as the Prophet Ezekiel notes: "The flesh of the women will be as the flesh of asses" (Ezekiel 23).[7] If this cleric had any knowledge of Saint Peter, he would have known that neither fornicators nor idolaters nor adulterers will enter the kingdom of God (I Corinthians 6).

The prudent Indian dissimulated his affront and the next morning with a smiling face under his cuckold's horns courteously took leave of the captain, taking with him his wife. He hastened to Chief Paris and, recounting his humiliation, told him that those Christians were evil, villainous people. Chief Paris was indignant, considering what had happened to his brother-in-law Chief Escoria. He quickly gathered his forces and other neighboring chiefs and set out to attack the Christians. They caught up with the Christians, who were staying in a town in the territory of Paris. The Indians attacked the few Christians there, who were guarding nine large baskets containing almost fifty thousand pesos of gold and many captured and chained Indians, all of whom had been gathered over the course of the expedition. The Indians set fire to many of the houses, killing and wounding some Christians, and certainly all would have died in the battle if timely help had not arrived. During the fighting, some courageous Christians managed to save seven of the nine baskets of gold from the burning town and took them to a small hill nearby, but the other two baskets were destroyed.

Captain Gonzalo de Badajoz and the majority of his men who had been looking for Chief Paris arrived during the battle and fell on the Indians, killing many and putting the rest to flight; however, the Indians managed to carry off the gold placed on the hill. The Indians regrouped to renew the attack with even more forces. In the meantime Captain Badajoz and his men were in a bad situation and decided to leave the territory of Chief Paris, losing their gold and Indian prisoners. Sadly, the enslaved Indians all perished; because of their chains they could not escape the fire nor could the attacking Indians save them.

The captain made for a river, where fortunately he found some canoes in which he and his men were able to escape. If they had not fled, none would have escaped alive, as Chiefs Paris and Escoria were in pursuit with many men and the whole territory was up in arms against the Christians.

After he fled the territory of Chief Paris, Captain Gonzalo de Badajoz headed for Darién, gathering as he went some twenty-two thousand pesos worth of gold. By sharing the gold and Indians with the governor and officials, his crimes were smoothed over and pardoned with no word of the many cruelties he had committed, although there was no lack of persons who spoke of them.

Captain Gaspar de Morales, Governor Pedrarias's cousin and retainer, went out to the South Sea and to Rica Island, where he gathered many pearls and much gold from the chiefs of the provinces through which he traveled. To diminish Vasco Núñez de Balboa's discoveries of that sea and its islands, he drew up duly witnessed and notarized documents of possession of the islands and other parts in the names of their highnesses and that of Governor Pedrarias Dávila. Morales changed the name of Rica Island to the Flores Island on the orders of the governor. Enriched by much gold, pearls, and slaves, he marched on to the province of the chief of Chochama, where he set up camp on the banks of a river. There he was faced with a large army of advancing Indians who came to recover their wives, children, and relatives stolen from them by the captain. In this difficult moment Captain Gaspar de Morales consulted with Andrés de Valderrábano and a young man called Captain Peñalosa, a relative of the governor's wife. Imitating Herod's cruelty, they agreed to cut the throats of all the enchained Indians, women and children, young and old, thinking that the Indian war party would stop at the sight of such a horrid spectacle. So, they killed ninety-five to one hundred persons. This cruel stratagem saved their lives because while the Indians stopped and wept over their dead, Captain Gaspar de Morales's party escaped as fast as they could.

Captain Morales returned to Darién, where, as Pedrarias's cousin and retainer, he escaped punishment and even reprehension for what he had done on his expedition. In his booty were many pearls; one in particular was pear-shaped, weighing thirty-one carats. A merchant named Pedro del Puerto bought it at auction for twelve hundred gold pesos. He kept it for one or two nights, all the while sighing and bitterly lamenting that he had paid too much for it. The governor coveted the pearl and found a way to buy it from him at the very same price, some saying that the whole affair had been arranged in advance. This pearl is the very one mentioned in Book XIX, Chapter VIII, which our lady empress, of glorious memory, later bought from Doña Isabel de Bobadilla, wife of Governor Pedrarias Dávila.[8]

Rich and sick, Gaspar de Morales returned to his home in Mojados in Spain. He died soon afterward and, God willing, repented of his sins.

Captain Peñalosa left for Cuba (also called Fernandina), where he was killed by Indians. As for Andrés de Valderrábano, I will recount his end later but, suffice it to say, it was befitting the death he ordered for the enchained Indians, except that when he was beheaded it was by royal decree as a traitor. In my opinion, he was innocent of the charge of treason but, as the Indians he had killed also did not deserve to die, it was God's will that Captain Valderrábano suffered and died for this and other crimes.[9]

Factor Juan de Tavira, now a rich man with more than fifteen thousand gold pesos, not being content with that nor remembering that three years before his only possessions were a cape and sword, observed how quickly the captains accumulated wealth. Because of a certain false report concerning the San Juan River (also called the Grande), which empties into the Gulf of Urabá, he believed that leading an expedition there would make him the richest man in his hometown of Ocaña. Obtaining the governor's license for this expedition, he built and outfitted three ships the size of small caravels, which cost him more than would three two-hundred-ton ships in Vizcaya. With these ships, some canoes, and almost two hundred men, he went to the Río Grande and sailed up it for seventy to eighty leagues, taking about as many days to do so because of its very strong current.

Along the river banks they found many settlements of *barbacoas,* or houses, constructed high off the ground on posts of black palm trees. These admirable houses are stronger than they appear and almost impregnable because of their locations and construction. More than two hundred Spaniards attacked one of these houses in Tatuma Province and could not capture it. After a two-day siege the Indians abandoned it at night, passing unseen through Christian lines and escaping to other barbacoas. From that it was deduced that there were very few defenders since they managed to escape undetected. When the Spaniards stormed the house the next day they met no resistance, finding only the bodies of three or four Indians killed by our musket or artillery fire. In that one barbacoa there was more than enough room to billet all the Christian soldiers even though there were more than two hundred of them.

The factor's expedition continued upriver but it seemed to them that the farther they went, the more powerful became the current and the greater the volume of water. When they went ashore to search for food the Indians killed them so that, even though they were starving on the ships, they only rarely dared to land.

One day while the factor was trying to go from one ship to another in a canoe, it capsized. The fleet's treasurer, a gentleman named Juan Navarro de Virués, tried to save the factor but both sank clutching each other and were never seen again. With that, the fleet returned to Darién, having lost many men and with the majority of the survivors ill. The factor spent most of his fortune on this expedition and what remained was forfeited to the crown to settle his official accounts. In this manner he paid the price for the flour and wine lost in the Toldo fire, which could have saved the lives of the poor Christians dropping dead in the streets, as was reported earlier.

A few days before I left that land by the governor's permission, Pedrarias Dávila the younger (the governor's nephew) arrived from Cenú Province on the coast of Cartagena, where Bachelor Enciso reported huge gold deposits. Pedrarias the younger had gone there with Captain Diego de Bustamante and two hundred other gentlemen and soldiers. They gave such a "good" account of themselves that Captain Bustamante and other Christians were killed and the rest returned broken and sick. They brought back so little gold that it only amounted to less than one gold peso per man. This same Pedrarias the younger was later killed after he returned to his native city of Avila, thus paying for the lives of all those who died in Cenú because of him.

I ask pardon if these brief accounts recording the captains' deeds offer them some offense. They should bear in mind that I write when witnesses are still alive to recall the events and that as inspector I was present when the expedition gold was melted down. Moreover, in the name of Secretary Lope Conchillos, I appointed all the notaries who accompanied their expeditions, whose reports of the captains' deeds and merits came to me. I read them as well as the documents of the residencies that were held. Rather than take offense, these captains should thank me for all that I have not included in these summaries. If they have any consideration and respect for my pen, they will see that I have treated them as friends and truly dispassionately. Certainly, I would rather have had praiseworthy things to report to make the reading more edifying and the writing a more pleasant occupation for me. Nevertheless, as I said previously, my aim was to account for the current state of this land, almost deserted and without Indians, and the principal cause is as I have stated. Farther on I will write a chapter summarizing these captains' fates as well as that of others who will be dealt with later, so that it cannot be said that I criticize the former and excuse the latter, but rather I give to each the name he deserves.[10]

CHAPTER XI—HOW INSPECTOR GONZALO FERNÁNDEZ DE OVIEDO WENT TO SPAIN SEEKING RELIEF FOR TIERRA FIRME; AND HOW A FEW DAYS AFTER HIS ARRIVAL IN CASTILE, GOD TOOK HIS CATHOLIC MAJESTY TO GLORY; AND HOW GONZALO FERNÁNDEZ DE OVIEDO CONTINUED ON TO FLANDERS TO MAKE HIS REPORT TO OUR LORD KING CHARLES; AND HOW LOPE DE SOSA, A KNIGHT OF CORDOVA, WAS APPOINTED GOVERNOR OF TIERRA FIRME AND OF HIS SUBSEQUENT DEATH.

After I received Pedrarias's license to leave Tierra Firme (as reported in Chapter IX), I embarked on a royal caravel whose master and pilot was Andrés Niño. On the same ship were the Franciscan provincial, Friar Diego de Torres, a revered person and very good cleric, with his companion, another Franciscan named Friar Andrés de Valdés, presently residing in the city of Santo Domingo where I am now. Also on board was Captain Rodrigo de Colmenares, who had been sent out as procurator of Darién when Pedrarias was appointed governor of Castilla del Oro. As it often happens on long voyages, one's shipmates reveal themselves and their missions and I found out that Friar Diego de Torres, among other items of business relating to his order, was sent by the bishop to counter my mission. Under the guise of their habits these priests often have a hand in many other affairs besides those of their orders. Moreover, Captain Rodrigo de Colmenares was sent by Pedrarias, who feared that I would tell the truth about everyone and everything and both were correct to think so. Although I was aware of their secret missions, I continued to be friendly and we were messmates until we came to this city of Santo Domingo in the Island of Hispaniola.

From Santo Domingo, Colmenares departed first in a fleet ready to sail and arrived in Seville much before I did. The more sagacious priest, to keep an eye on me, did not leave the Franciscan convent here until I departed more than two months after Colmenares.

Pedrarias, ever astute and careful, always chose Darién's aldermen from his clients and friends favorable to his interests and not the republic's. In the city council, nothing was debated or done and nothing was written without his knowledge. Thus, the king and his royal council never learned anything about that city other than what the governor wanted them to know. However, by other ways and by letters from important private persons and even from some officials themselves (although they were not happy with me for saying that they illegally shared expedition loot), everyone wrote of the governor's and bishop's scandalous behaviors and thus supported my denunciations. All these letters proved even more than what I could say.

The friar sailed from Santo Domingo in a ship I captained. I carried several thousand gold pesos consigned to their majesties put in my care by Treasurer Miguel de Pasamonte and other officials. The treasurer was King Ferdinand's old trusted servant and fellow Aragonese. Moreover, the treasurer was a friend of Juan Cabrero, the royal steward, and of Secretary Lope Conchillos (all Aragonese as well). Pasamonte gave me letters of introduction attesting to my credit to both of them. The treasurer also sent with me six handsome female and six male Caribs, many parrots, six loaves of sugar, and fifteen to twenty cassia pods. That was the first sugar and cassia that the king received from these parts and the first sent to Spain.[1]

On our voyage to Spain from Santo Domingo we stopped at Funchal on the Island of Madeira belonging to the king of Portugal. Because of bad weather and rough seas, the voyage had taken seventy-five days. Thinking that our ship would remain there for a while, Friar Diego de Torres, his companions, and some of the crew and two or three passengers went ashore for provisions and especially for two or three barrels of water, as we were down to one barrel for ninety persons. As it happened, that night after the first watch such a strong southerly wind sprang up perpendicular to the coast that our ship as well as many other ships and caravels could not remain at anchor. All fled the port to avoid being blown aground on that rocky coast and so we set sail the evening of the very day of our arrival. The other ships took shelter at Puerto Santo Island, but we continued on to Spain, making do with the little water we had. The friars were left behind but in a few days took passage on another ship. Unfortunately, Friar Diego de Torres fell sick and died in the Bay of Cádiz before he could disembark. In my estimation, he was such a good person that he would not have failed to report truthfully had he come to court.

After arriving in Seville I went in search of the king and found him in December of 1515 gravely ill in Plasencia on his way to Seville. I kissed his hand and delivered the letters and reports of all those who wrote him from Tierra Firme and those of Treasurer Miguel de Pasamonte. The king was delighted with the presents and the Indians, as his highness had written the treasurer that he wished to see what sort of people were these Caribs who eat human flesh. The Caribs were from the islands of Dominica, Matinino, and Cibuqueira (called Santa Cruz by the Christians) and from other nearby islands. The king listened to me and questioned me about general things and of the voyage from that land but, as to the governance and how he was served there, he desired to consider everything carefully and told me that he would hear me and decide when he got to Seville. I requested leave to go to Madrid to visit my home and wife, whom I had not seen for three years.[2] His highness graciously consented, saying that since he was told that what I had to say was important to his service he would attend to it in Seville. In the meantime, until I returned to court, I was to provide Secretary Conchillos a memorial stating all that should be done. I did that and left for my home in Madrid.

A few days after I arrived in Madrid, the following month, January of 1516, on his way to Seville, his Catholic majesty died in Madrigalejo, a village near Trujillo. As soon as I learned that God had taken King Ferdinand to His glory, I left for Flanders to report on conditions in Tierra Firme to the new king, Our Lord Charles. I departed not having rested from the long voyage from Tierra Firme and disregarding personal expense and hardships.

On the voyage to Flanders we sailed from Portugalete but almost to the coast of Brittany we ran into a storm that forced us back to Laredo.[3] Setting out again and about halfway to our destination, we ran into such a strong nor'easter near the Island of Ushant that we were forced to jettison the cargo and everyone feared for their lives.[4] Again the winds pushed us back to Spain to La Coruña. At La Coruña several of us made a pilgrimage of thanksgiving to the shrine of the Glorious Apostle Saint James.[5] Three days later we returned to La Coruña and set out once again for Flanders. In the English Channel another storm hit and only by the greatest effort and fortune did we reach one of the Scilly Islands,[6] where we were stranded for eight days under worse conditions than in the Indies. The only shelter was a ruined fortress of the king of England and four or five thatched huts that could not compare to the native dwellings in Tierra Firme. Nevertheless, we had some wine (more expensive by far than the wine we drink here in Santo Domingo) and a little flour with which we made cakes cooked in the ashes. That was all we had to eat except for the rabbits some crossbowmen managed to kill. We fasted there some eight to ten days in sight of the British Isles and six or seven other islands waiting for the weather to clear. If we had not been able to take shelter on those small islands, the winds would have blown us around Ireland and perhaps a year would have passed before we could have returned to Flanders.

Finally God was pleased to send us the weather we needed and we returned to the Channel and soon disembarked at the Dunes, two or three leagues south of Dover. From the Dunes we passengers went to the Port of Dover and the ship sailed on to London. We crossed the Channel to Calais and then traveled by land to Brussels, where the king was in residence. This entire journey took almost four months, costing me more effort and money than twice the voyage from Seville to this city of Santo Domingo. By way of contrast, the return trip from Zeeland to Portugalete took three and a half days.

After I kissed our lord king's hands he ordered his grand chancellor of Burgundy to hear me and it was done.[7] But because the majority of the royal council were foreigners and the few Spaniards among them had little experience in such matters, I was referred by his highness to his regents in Spain—the Cardinal-Archbishop of Toledo, Friar Francisco Jiménez de Cisneros, and the Cardinal of Tortosa (later Pope Adrian). The king ordered them together with other persons in charge of affairs of the Indies to consider the memorial I had given his majesty and which had been countersigned by his secretary, Ugo de Urríes, Lord of Ayerbe,[8] and then decide what was best for the royal service and the good of Tierra Firme. Also, in gratitude for my efforts on his behalf, I was to be reimbursed for my expenses and services as a servant of the royal household.

I returned to Spain with this order of referral but, as I was about to leave Brussels, I chanced upon Rodrigo de Colmenares, destitute and sick, who begged me for the love of God to take him with me to Castile, which I did, even lending him money that was never repaid. He told me that what he had said and negotiated was for the benefit of Tierra Firme and that he also was referred to the cardinal-regents.

After we returned to Madrid, where the regents were, Captain Colmenares left for Naples as his mission was not successful. Later, he returned to Tierra Firme a year after I did, which was four years after we came back to Spain from Flanders.

I presented the order of referral and my memorial to those very reverend cardinals with a request for a hearing as our lord king had ordered. However, they never responded or attended to anything relating to Tierra Firme, nor did I receive the disbursement ordered by his majesty. And so, that land was not relieved of its troubles, which grew daily, nor I of mine, being two thousand castellanos the poorer for what I spent in those journeys. Praise God for everything.

The reason I was not heard and the royal referral was not successful was that the Spanish Cardinal was occupied in sending, and did send, three Hieronymite friars to govern this city of Santo Domingo and the Indies. They were Friar Luis de Figueroa, prior of La Mejorada; Friar Alonso de Santo Domingo, prior of San Juan de Ortega; and Friar Bernaldino de Manzanedo, prior of Montamarta, all venerable personages selected to remedy New World affairs. With great and far-reaching mandates they came to reside in this city of Santo Domingo. In truth, their arrival was beneficial to this island, not only by their example and teaching but also in fomenting plantations of cassia trees and sugar mills as well as other things I will not stop to detail as I touched on them in the first part, Book IV, Chapter II. However, with regard to the reforms in Tierra Firme they did little or nothing, nor did they visit it.

To continue with my journeys and troubles, which did not cease: at that time, Admiral Don Diego Columbus was in Madrid engaged in lawsuits concerning his privileges with the royal attorney-general. After our lord king came to Spain to begin his reign, he ordered the admiral to return home to this city and the Hieronymite clerics back to Castile. That was in 1517. That same year Cardinal Friar Francisco Jiménez died and I returned to my negotiations, which lasted until 1519 when the king went to Barcelona, where he received news of his election as King of the Romans and future emperor. In Barcelona I had another audience with the king. I had spent five difficult years and much money pursuing my mission without obtaining the needed remedies for Tierra Firme, where constant misdeeds and robberies became so customary that there was no hope for cure.

In Barcelona, his majesty provided as governor of Castilla del Oro a Cordovan knight named Lope de Sosa, who was living in Grand Canary Island, where he had been governor. He was an ideal person for the well-being of Tierra Firme. I was ordered to return there with him and just as I was ready to leave Barcelona, I learned that Bishop Friar Don Juan de Quevedo had arrived in Spain. He wrote me to wait for him at court, which I did, as I would have been very pleased to declare in his presence what I reported in Flanders and in the council. However, a few days later, on his way to court, he died near Barcelona. At the same time, news arrived that Governor Pedrarias had executed Adelantado Vasco Núñez de Balboa and others as traitors and confiscated their assets for the crown. Then our lord emperor by royal warrant ordered me to collect those assets, which rumor estimated at more than one hundred thousand gold pesos. With this and other dispatches I left Barcelona for Madrid, where I gathered up my wife and children and went to Seville to sail for the Indies.[9]

And so, at the beginning of the following year, 1520, I left Spain and went to Grand Canary Island, where I found that Governor Lope de Sosa had gone on ahead. From Grand Canary I came to this island, where my wife, two children, and I spent eight days in Santo Domingo before crossing to Tierra Firme. We dropped anchor in the harbor of Darién at night and I found out from another ship there that Governor Lope de Sosa had arrived but that he died before he could disembark. That was the cause of the almost total perdition of that land, as he was a man of good conscience and long experience in governing, a very just man who would have remedied the ills of those parts. As for me, I was in a state of confusion, repenting of all I had tried to do. Naturally I suspected that things would go badly for me because Governor Pedrarias believed that I was his enemy and had solicited his replacement by Lope de Sosa. However, he welcomed me and seemed pleased at my arrival and later favored me and my household. As I had brought my wife and young children, I could not fail to attend to my mission there, as I will relate farther on.

First, however, it would be well to recount the cause of the deaths of Adelantado Vasco Núñez de Balboa and the other sinners accused of treason who perished with him. As to whether or not they were traitors I cannot say, even though I collected their assets in his majesty's name for his treasury.

CHAPTER XII—CONCERNING THE DEATHS OF
ADELANTADO VASCO NÚÑEZ DE BALBOA, ANDRÉS
DE VALDERRÁBANO, HERNANDO DE ARGÜELLO, LUIS
BOTELLO, AND HERNANDO MUÑOZ, ALL EXECUTED
IN THE SPACE OF AN HOUR IN THE TOWN OF ACLA IN
TIERRA FIRME.

The Catholic Monarch King Ferdinand, fifth of that name, rewarded Vasco Núñez de Balboa's services by naming him adelantado of the South Sea and governor of the provinces of Coiba and Panamá, as I detailed earlier. Likewise, I reported how Pedrarias tried to delay implementation of his appointments while Bishop Friar Juan de Quevedo worked to have them effected. All this resulted in the undying enmity of the governor, officials, and Chief Justice Licentiate Espinosa toward Vasco Núñez.

The astute bishop, well knowing the disposition of their minds and their malicious schemes, came up with even better ones to achieve his goal, which was to see Vasco Núñez in full possession of his appointments. Seeing that the governor was old, ill, greedy, and burdened with unmarried daughters, the prelate proposed to him the marriage of one of his daughters to Adelantado Vasco Núñez, a young and energetic man. There would be several advantages for Pedrarias: Vasco Núñez would serve him as a son, he was a good match for Pedrarias's daughter as a gentleman and an adelantado, as his lieutenant he would relieve Pedrarias of military matters and the king would be well served, Vasco Núñez would increase the family honor and wealth, and, most important, the feuding with the officials would cease, allowing the governor to live in peace. The bishop made these and other arguments in the same vein to Pedrarias and to Doña Isabel de Bobadilla, his wife, who liked Vasco Núñez, as he had spent much time cultivating her friendship. The governor and his wife agreed on the provisions of the marriage contract and Pedrarias took Vasco Núñez as son and son-in-law. The daughter Pedrarias offered was in Spain and they agreed that within a certain amount of time they would bring her to Darién.[1] Thus Pedrarias began to call the adelantado son, to honor and favor him, and married his daughter to him by proxy with all due documents and pledges. Pedrarias communicated the news of the marriage to the king and the gentlemen of the Royal Council of the Indies as in the best interest and service to God and their majesties.

In my opinion, it is very plain that if the bishop had remained in that land, the adelantado would not have died. Nevertheless, the bishop thought the marriage made Vasco Núñez secure from the governor's cunning and that of Treasurer Alonso de la Puente, the person who most hated Vasco Núñez, as he well demonstrated later. Thus, soon after arranging the marriage, the bishop left for Spain thinking that the governor would favor Vasco Núñez. As I related in the preceding chapter, the bishop died on his way to court in Barcelona on Christmas Eve, 1519.[2] Friar Vicente Peraza of the Dominican order was elected to replace him as the second bishop of Castilla del Oro.

To return to the history: Adelantado Vasco Núñez, being in his father-in-law's good graces, sought his license to go to the South Sea and construct some ships to explore those waters and their riches. The governor was very pleased with the plan and even arranged a loan from the royal treasury for the fleet's construction. To that money Vasco Núñez added his own and the entire capital of his friend Hernando de Argüello. (As I reported in Book XXVIII, Chapter XXVIII, Argüello, from Torre de Lobatón, was the notary who formally wrote the oath in Darién by which Vasco Núñez and others conspired to reject Diego de Nicuesa as governor.)[3] With these funds, the adelantado began to work on his expedition to the South Sea coast.

At that time work on the fort and town of Acla was completed and Captain Lope de Olano was named its warden.[4] Olano's Christians badly mistreated the Indians and Chief Careta, in whose territory Acla was built. The chief had not forgotten how Captain Bartolomé Hurtado, on his return from the search for Lieutenant Juan de Ayora, had given the peaceful Indian bearers and their leader that the chief had lent him as slaves for the King's Fifth. Likewise God had not forgotten Lope de Olano's part in Nicuesa's death and his other evil deeds. The chief, no longer able to suffer the adulteries, robberies, and other affronts, killed Olano together with twelve or fifteen Christians who were with him. Instead of considering the chief's just cause in avenging himself, the Christians committed many more cruel deeds and declared slaves all Careta Indians. In spite of everything, that outpost on the northern coast endured as a small settlement now known as the city of Acla in the territory of Castilla del Oro.

Adelantado Vasco Núñez sailed to Acla and then crossed to the other coast, where the ships were constructed with great effort and expense.

Vasco Núñez and his men carried wood on their own backs from the forest to the shipyard for this project. Five hundred Indians died transporting hawsers, anchors, rigging, and other materials from one sea to the other on extremely rough trails through mountains and forests and across many rivers. While the materials were being assembled, Vasco Núñez sent out captains to round up all the neighboring Indians they could find, reading them the Requirement as they were bound, but then not abiding by any of its provisions. Part of these captives were occupied in ship construction and the rest were sent to be sold in Darién by Hernando de Argüello without being officially declared slaves or not. Everything was hushed up because of the marriage of Pedrarias's daughter with the adelantado. All this was done in disservice to God and King and resulted in the total desolation of that land and its Indians because the ship construction lasted a long time.

When the governor's license for the projected South Sea voyage expired, Pedrarias was given to understand by Vasco Núñez's enemies that since the adelantado had not written or come to explain the delay, he must have rebelled, planning to take his ships and settle South Sea areas where he would rule independently of king and governor. The officials and Bachelor Corral, the adelantado's enemies, took advantage of every opportunity to inflame the governor's suspicions by speaking against Vasco Núñez. All this the governor believed. Finally, the adelantado's letters arrived, offering excuses for the delay in constructing and launching the ships and requesting an extension to effect the expedition. His petition was denied because the officials and Bachelor Corral told the governor that by no means should it be granted. And so, the governor delayed, not saying yes or no but sending evasive responses to draw out the negotiations.

In a letter that was to cost Hernando de Argüello his head, Argüello informed Vasco Núñez of what was going on. He wrote that they did not want to grant the extension but that Vasco Núñez should not worry about it nor desist in his projected voyage since the Hieronymite fathers (governing from this city of Santo Domingo as the superior authority) had written Vasco Núñez to carry out his project so vital to the interests of God and King. Hernando de Argüello told Vasco Núñez to do that and disregard the governor and officials since all of Vasco Núñez's capital and that of his friends as well as much time and labor had been expended in the enterprise. This letter fell into Pedrarias's hands.

About the same time there were rumors that, through my petitions and the reports our lord emperor had about Tierra Firme, a new governor had been appointed to replace Pedrarias. Because of these rumors, Vasco Núñez agreed with Andrés de Valderrábano, Captain Andrés Garabito, Luis Botello, and Hernando Muñoz to send to Acla to find out what news there was of the new governor's arrival. If a new governor had arrived, a messenger was to return proclaiming publicly: "Good news, good news, Adelantado Vasco Núñez is governor of Tierra Firme!" They gave him certain letters to display that purported to contain this news. This plan was devised because if Vasco Núñez's people found out there was a new governor in the territory, they would abandon him and return to Darién. Moreover, Vasco Núñez suspected that a new governor would give the enterprise to some relative or friend or at least would temporize, and all Vasco Núñez's time, work, and investment would be lost. Alternatively, if the agent sent to Acla found no news of the new governor's arrival, he was to proclaim that and that Pedrarias was content to hear from Adelantado Vasco Núñez and was sending the requested extension.

These letters and spies were detained by one Francisco Benítez, a notary in Acla, who at once informed Pedrarias. The governor then sent the adelantado a very affectionate, paternal letter calling him to Acla, where Pedrarias had gone. Vasco Núñez, as the obedient son, obeyed, thinking, as was natural, that he was in Pedrarias's good graces. But as soon as he arrived he was arrested along with Captain Andrés Garabito, Luis Botello, Hernando Muñoz, Andrés de Valderrábano, and Hernando de Argüello, the author of the aforementioned letter. The imprisoned Garabito was advised to tell what he knew of the affair and beg the governor for his life. This he did, telling the governor under oath the details described above. By his confession, his participation in the plot by the adelantado and his cohorts was pardoned.[5] The governor ordered Chief Justice Espinosa to proceed very diligently in Vasco Núñez's residency, which was publicly proclaimed. The governor added material from the first incomplete residency of five years before and all the crimes and excesses imputed to the adelantado in the matter of Captain Diego de Nicuesa's death. In addition, the governor added crimes from the time Vasco Núñez governed before Pedrarias, among them that of taking Inspector Silvestre Pérez's royal gold-marking stamp and then murdering him by starvation.

Seeing Adelantado Vasco Núñez's tribulations, Treasurer Alonso de la

Puente, Comptroller Diego Márquez, and Bachelor Diego de Corral happily joined together to produce a long criminal indictment signed by all three and presented by Vasco Núñez's old enemy Bachelor Corral. The chief justice displayed no less delight in the prosecution and finally sentenced all to forfeit their heads for treason and their assets were confiscated to their majesties' treasury.

Before sentence was passed, the chief justice arranged with certain representatives of the expedition company that had constructed the ships to petition the governor to make short work of Vasco Núñez's residency and to send Chief Justice Licentiate Espinosa to be their lieutenant general and captain, declaring that they wanted him and no other since no one else was so qualified for the task. They stated that if this were not done, the many men involved in the expedition company would be ruined. This petition with many phrases in the chief justice's favor was composed by the chief justice himself, who made the company's representatives sign it.

After the sentence was handed down, Adelantado Vasco Núñez appealed to our lord emperor and his Royal Council of the Indies. The chief justice sent one Cristóbal Núñez, the notary in charge of the case, to notify the governor of the appeal and ask him if he would permit it in consideration of Vasco Núñez's title as adelantado or if he would reject it. The governor responded in writing that the appeal was denied and not to be sent forward and sentence was to be carried out. Both the document notifying Pedrarias of the appeal and the governor's response were drafted by Licentiate Espinosa and written up by his servant Antonio Cuadrado and Pedrarias signed them. The sentence was publicly proclaimed and the adelantado, Hernando de Argüello, Luis Botello, Hernando Muñoz, and Andrés de Valderrábano were beheaded in the plaza at Acla. Captain Andrés Garabito was absolved for revealing the treason. Pedrarias watched the executions, peeping through the canes in the wall of a native hut situated ten or twelve paces from the site to which they were led like sheep, one after another. The adelantado's head was displayed on a stake for many days afterward.

Thus ended the governorship of Vasco Núñez, discoverer of the South Sea, and thus he paid for the death of Captain Diego de Nicuesa. For this and other crimes God permitted Vasco Núñez's death, but not for what the sentence said, for no one thought he was guilty of treason.

Likewise, Hernando de Argüello paid for the testimony and oath of

Darién against Nicuesa, and Andrés de Valderrábano paid for the advice he gave to Captain Gaspar de Morales to murder so many helpless Indians, their wives, and children on the way back from the Perlas Islands. (Captain Peñalosa, also a participant in the Herodian massacre, was later killed by Indians on the Island of Cuba.)

Luis Botello and Hernando Muñoz were among the first conquistadores in that land and old friends of the adelantado, with whom they had participated in many of the expeditions I have detailed. Their hands were not so clean of human blood that they lacked merit for their fate.

Several years later in León, Nicaragua, Captain Andrés Garabito and others took part in a joust wearing Moorish costumes.[6] He and another horseman rode up to some Spanish women spectators saying, "Ladies, convert to Islam" and other foolish things. In the very act of praising Mohammed's sect he suddenly fell dead without saying another word.

Francisco Benítez, the notary of Acla, who had discovered the adelantado's spies and informed the governor, died suddenly three years later in Panamá. He was found dead in his hammock, having retired the night before in good health.

Such were the ends of these sinners. I pray God have mercy on their souls, since their bodies did not escape His punishment.

CHAPTER XIII—HOW LICENTIATE GASPAR DE
ESPINOSA, PEDRARIAS'S CHIEF JUSTICE, WENT AS HIS
LIEUTENANT-GENERAL TO EXPLORE THE SOUTH SEA
IN THE SHIPS CONSTRUCTED BY ADELANTADO VASCO
NÚÑEZ DE BALBOA; WHAT HE DID ON THIS VOYAGE;
AND OF OTHER THINGS IN WHICH LICENTIATE
ESPINOSA WAS INVOLVED PRIOR TO THE EXPEDITION.

Even before Adelantado Vasco Núñez de Balboa's death, Chief Justice
Licentiate Espinosa was well instructed and expert in the cruelties the
other captains customarily practiced upon the Indians. He had even sur-
passed them when, as the captain-general's lieutenant, he had gone to
the South Sea coast. En route he had caused many Indian deaths in
Comogre, Pocorosa, and Chimán provinces under the pretext of punishing those who had killed the Christians of the city and port of Santa
Cruz. Then he went on to Natá and to Paris provinces in search of Captain Gonzalo de Badajoz's lost gold. After spending some days on the
plains deep in the territory of Chief Paris with two hundred select men
and not finding a trace of that chief, he sent ahead Captain Diego de
Albítez with one hundred men while he remained with the rear guard
and their fifteen or sixteen mares and horses.

I cannot help but laugh when I recall the Indians' description of this
captain when they returned to their people and were questioned about
him. To communicate what they had seen and where he was headed they
imitated the braying of asses because Licentiate Espinosa had one in his
expedition and the Indians had never before seen such an animal. Seeing
that the Indians were frightened by the braying, the Christians gave them
to understand that the animal was asking for gold for the king and his
captains and some Indians did give it to placate the ass.

Returning to the history: Diego de Albítez, proceeding on, came upon
the chief at the bank of a river, and in the ensuing battle fifty or sixty
Indians were killed and some Christians were wounded. The chief justice
arrived with reinforcements and put to flight the chief and his men, who
fell back to regroup with more men. At that time Captain Hierónimo de
Valenzuela arrived with one hundred more soldiers sent by Pedrarias to
help the chief justice. Now that the Christians numbered three hundred,
the chief, seeing that he could not expel them without devastating his
land and people, came up with a plan. He arranged for the Christians to

capture two of his Indians, whom he told to reveal the whereabouts of the gold the chief had taken from Captain Gonzalo de Badajoz. When they were captured near the Spanish encampment, Diego de Albítez asked them where Chief Paris was and, not wishing to reveal his location, they said that he was in another province. Interrogated about the gold, one of them said he would show the Christians where it was and that the chief wanted them to take it and leave his lands as soon as possible. Since gold was our peoples' principal intent, rather than establishing friendly relations with the chief or converting the Indians, Diego Albítez went to where the Indians said the gold was hidden. In an Indian dwelling in a ravine they found ten baskets containing thirty thousand pesos worth of gold. Of the gold Badajoz gathered there was missing only the six thousand pesos that Chief Paris's wives had sent to Badajoz and three thousand pesos that Paris had given to that principal Indian cuckolded by the "kindness" of that "devout" cleric. The chief took these nine thousand pesos, leaving the rest as Badajoz had collected it.

With this gold and more taken on that expedition, the chief justice returned very prosperous and proud to Darién. From then on he was reputed a person well versed in the martial arts and in wrongs practiced upon the Indians. He even invented an atrocity unknown in those parts. He had tied to a tree one of the Chimán Indians sentenced to death for the murder of the Santa Cruz Christians. Then at a distance of ten or twelve paces he ordered set up a small cannon and had him shot in the chest. The entry wound was the size of a nut, but the exit wound in his back was the size of a ten-gallon jug. This execution greatly frightened the Indians and was even considered very cruel by the Christians who witnessed it.

Licentiate Espinosa returned to Darién with more than thirty thousand pesos worth of gold and many Indians in chains. There the representatives of Vasco Núñez's company found him as arranged and requested that he command the adelantado's ships. The governor granted their request and authorized him wide powers to proceed with the ships and men on the voyage the unfortunate Adelantado Vasco Núñez was to have made.

Licentiate Espinosa, with the title of lieutenant to the captain-general, went to the South Sea and explored the sea and coastal area toward the west. From this second expedition he took forty thousand pesos of fine gold from Chief Paris, twenty thousand pesos of which he buried in Panamá within the city near the coast, and he left Captain Gonzalo de

Badajoz there as his lieutenant. The other twenty thousand he had taken to Darién, the residence of the governor and officials. Part of this sum was used to pay the Royal Fifth assessed on the forty thousand and the remainder was melted down to buy needed supplies for the expedition members. From Panamá, Licentiate Espinosa continued his expedition, sailing along the coast twenty-five leagues in a westerly direction to Point Chame, where he had been before.

Point Chame is seven and one-half degrees north of the equator.[1] From there he went to reconnoiter Point Güera, twenty leagues west at six and one-half degrees north. Between these two points lies the small Gulf of Paris, so called because Chief Paris is the lord of that territory. From Point Güera he proceeded west another twenty leagues to Point Buena Vista at six and one-third degrees north latitude.

Between Point Buena Vista and Point Santa María, a distance of another twenty leagues west, there is a bay oriented north-south that is twenty leagues long and contains many islands. Among them are the Cebaco Islands, where the Venetian cosmographer Codro is buried (and not in Zorobaro, as the first edition of this history erroneously reported in Part I, Book X, Chapter III).[2] Also in this inlet is another large island, the Island of Santa María, with the Ponuba harbor at its northern point.

Point Burica, six and one-half degrees north latitude, is some twenty leagues southwest of Point Santa María. This very fertile region produces abundant harvests of maize, yuca, and other crops for the Indians. Deer and wild pigs abound for hunting and there are plentiful supplies of fish and fresh water. There are beautiful large mamey trees and coconut palms. All in all, it is one of the best provinces on that coast with the best people. The Benamatia Islands lie between Points Santa María (six and one-third degrees north) and Burica in a small bay or inlet about ten to twelve leagues wide called the Gulf of Osa.

Sailing on west from Point Santa María another twenty leagues, close to the coast, is Caño Island, at a little more than six and one-half degrees north. The island received its name because a jet (*caño*) of very good spring water about the size of one's wrist spouts from a cliff there and falls into the sea. Caravels can sail underneath and collect fresh water without any danger.

From Caño Island there are ten to twelve leagues to some islands near Point San Lázaro, which is at seven and one-half degrees north. Licentiate Espinosa sailed west fifteen to twenty leagues from these islands in what he named the Gulf of Sanlúcar (called San Lucas by others), but he did not see nor enter the large bay there between Cape Blanco and the point at Herradura harbor. On this voyage he explored a total of about one hundred eighty leagues of this coast. As will be detailed later, Gil González de Avila and the pilot Andrés Niño continued the exploration of the Gulf of San Lucas to Posesión harbor and then on to the Bay of Fonseca. All these places are on the western Panamanian coast of the South Sea.

While Licentiate Espinosa's fleet of three or four ships was off exploring, in May 1520, Governor Lope de Sosa arrived at Darién. As previously related, he had come on the emperor's orders to govern Castilla del Oro and to carry out the residency of Pedrarias and his officials. After his ship anchored, he began to dress for his formal arrival. He had just finished giving orders for the landing when he suddenly expired on board ship. Governor Pedrarias, who had prepared his reception, had his body taken ashore with all honors and interred in the cathedral in the preeminent location at the foot of the steps before the high altar. All this he did with a great show of grief, but in his heart of hearts there was great joy as certainly it seemed to him a miracle and a sign that God wished him and no other to govern that land. Nevertheless, as I have determined to speak the truth in my history, one cannot deny Pedrarias's good breeding and deportment, which, as an old courtier, he displayed when he wished. And so, Pedrarias treated well Lope de Sosa's son, Juan Alonso de Sosa, and all the members of the governor's household, aiding and favoring them all. Most favored among them was Juan Rodríguez de Alarconcillo (who was to be Lope de Sosa's chief justice). It was suspected that Pedrarias did so for reasons that will be explained farther on.

Returning to Licentiate Espinosa's voyage in the South Sea: he discovered Culebras Gulf, named for the innumerable snakes (*culebras*) found on the surface of its waters. These snakes are three hand spans or more long and are black with yellow bellies. They have downward-pointing scales on their sides and upward-pointing scales on their bellies with which they intertwine as you would the fingers of both hands, joining the two colors. The thickest ones are a little larger than the big toe or the fingers on one hand together.

The chief pilot on this voyage was Juan de Castañeda, a good man and skillful mariner. Such were the voyages these Christians made in the South Sea up to the year 1519.

CHAPTER XIV—HOW, BY ORDER OF THE EMPEROR,
CAPTAIN GIL GONZÁLEZ DE AVILA AND THE PILOT
ANDRÉS NIÑO CAME TO TIERRA FIRME TO EXPLORE
THE SOUTH SEA FROM PANAMÁ; HOW THE AUTHOR OF
THESE HISTORIES RETURNED TO CASTILLA DEL ORO;
AND HOW PEDRARIAS MANAGED TO DEPOPULATE
DARIÉN.

A pilot named Andrés Niño had been in Tierra Firme for some time.[1]
When he learned of Adelantado Vasco Núñez's arrest he suspected that
the adelantado would not leave prison alive and that by gaining possession of the ships Vasco Núñez had constructed the pilot could make great
discoveries and find great riches in the South Sea. Treasurer Alonso de la
Puente backed the plan and sent one of his men, Andrés de Cereceda,
with the pilot to Spain. Once at court, Andrés Niño attempted the negotiations but, although he was a skilled pilot and expert seaman, he did
not have enough influence to be granted the appointment. So, Niño
and Cereceda joined with Gil González de Avila (the emperor's comptroller in this city of Santo Domingo in the Island of Hispaniola), who
at that time (1518) was at court. González de Avila formerly had been
in the household of the bishop of Palencia, Don Juan Rodríguez de Fonseca, president of the Council of the Indies. They informed the bishop
of Vasco Núñez's imprisonment and came to an agreement. With the
bishop's backing, they requested and received the license for Gil González, Andrés Niño, and others to outfit the expedition at their own expense, their majesties taking whatever share it pleased them to do so.

With the provisions completed, a royal warrant was issued stating that
the king, being informed that, one, Vasco Núñez de Balboa without his
majesty's express license had gone to the South Sea to make certain explorations with certain ships and men and, two, he took and held some
things and since Vasco Núñez was presently imprisoned, his highness was
sending Gil González de Avila and Andrés Niño with a certain fleet for
the exploration of the South Sea. The king ordered his deputy general
and governor of Castilla del Oro that on receipt of his warrant he should
hand over to Gil González all ships and skiffs that remained of Vasco
Núñez's fleet so that together with other ships arriving from Spain the
said voyage and exploration could be undertaken; that an inspector to be
named by the governor of Castilla del Oro should inventory everything;

and that the governor should handle everything with dispatch as it was a matter of much importance to the royal service.

I saw this warrant, which was issued in Barcelona, June 18, 1519. The governor's name was not specified because at that time they were trying to send another to Castilla del Oro and remove Pedrarias Dávila from office. To that end, a few days later in Barcelona, Lope de Sosa was given the governorship. However, when Gil González arrived in Tierra Firme all that I reported in the preceding chapter about Licentiate Espinosa's expedition had already taken place.

In 1520, a few days before Lope de Sosa's death, Captain Gil González de Avila and Pilot Andrés Niño arrived in Darién to begin work on their expedition. His majesty contributed a certain portion to the royal company and appointed as captains Andrés de Haro from Burgos, Gil González, Pilot Andrés Niño, and the aforesaid Andrés de Cereceda, who was appointed treasurer. Other individuals also contributed their parts to the expedition. Gil González set about preparations in Acla with the construction of certain ships in the Balsa River, which debouches into the South Sea at the Gulf of San Miguel. Even though he presented the previously mentioned warrant to Pedrarias, it did him little good because many opposed the transfer of Vasco Núñez's ships, saying that they belonged to his company. Pedrarias was happy to draw out the matter to hinder Gil González. Seeing that the ships would rot away if the conflict were not resolved, it seemed better to outfit them than build new ones.

Treasurer Alonso de la Puente and Comptroller Diego Márquez (both officials of Castilla del Oro) entered the enterprise to save the day for Gil González and his associates. If they had not, it would have been impossible because the governor was upset. He felt that, in addition to its being an insult for another person to come to his territory to outfit an expedition with the king's license, it was a personal affront that lessened his authority. He did not want anyone else to discover or do anything concerning the South Sea. And so, in every way possible with all his cunning he hindered the expedition and its preparation.

Gil González sensed this and understood somewhat the governor's greed. On the advice of Treasurer Alonso de la Puente and Comptroller Diego Márquez, who knew the governor longer and better, Gil González decided to involve him in the armada company as the easiest way to move the matter forward. And so, Gil González came up with a clever plan, which was that Pedrarias would sell him a flighty young Black slave for three hundred pesos, but instead of cash he would receive armada shares, which would entitle him to enjoy a proportionate amount of expedition profits. Pedrarias sold the slave, the amount being credited to him on the company's books as participant and backer of the company, as if a good-for-nothing Negro not fit to be cabin boy were the thing they most needed. Then the governor began to favor Gil González and allowed the project to proceed although, truthfully, in spite of the fact he dissimulated it, this expedition (detailed in the next chapter) still displeased him.

A few days after Lope de Sosa died and some months before Gil González set out on his exploration, I landed at Darién with my wife and two children thinking to find Lope de Sosa governing the land. Arriving at the harbor of San Juan on the evening of June 24, 1520, I found out from another ship at anchor the shocking news of Sosa's death. At that moment I felt more trapped than if I had found myself in the land of the Moors because, in truth, I had put my heart and soul into procuring Pedrarias's removal. I truly (and correctly) thought I was lost and would not have disembarked if it had not been for my wife and children but, since there was nothing else to do, I commended myself to God hoping for His help, not expecting any on earth.

The next morning I sent a man ashore to notify the governor of my arrival. He replied that he was pleased and that I was welcome to come ashore, for he regarded me as his majesty's friend and good servant, whom he intended to aid and honor as much as possible as if I were his son or brother. Finally, although I did not believe all this, I disembarked with my household and there on the coast Bachelor Diego de Corral and Diego Maldonado came to greet and accompany me, giving me the governor's message as reported above as well as other loving words. In Darién, I went to pay my respects and the governor showed himself to be very pleased by my arrival to all appearances. Later the governor came to the inn to visit my wife and spoke to her very graciously.

En route to Tierra Firme I had stopped in this city of Santo Domingo and learned that Pedrarias's wife, Doña Isabel de Bobadilla, on her way to Castile had put in at the harbor of Yaguana on the western end of this island.[2] According to reports, the governor was sending her to Spain with a large quantity of gold and pearls. He did this to free his time for his residency that he assumed Lope de Sosa would conduct and to safeguard his assets. The governors and judges of these parts whose terms expire frequently flee with their money before the final accounting or else send the money home before undergoing residency.

Two months after I arrived in Darién, God took from me one of my sons, who was only eight years old. Because of this grief, together with the grief I felt at the death of governor Lope de Sosa, many times I was determined to return to Spain on the same ship that brought me, but necessity and shame restrained me because of my heavy obligations to my wife and household. What most obliged me to await whatever would come was that by imperial order I was charged to collect the one hundred thousand gold pesos that his majesty was given to understand constituted the confiscated assets of Adelantado Vasco Núñez de Balboa and his confederates. Once I was in that land, to return without carrying out the emperor's orders would have been a grave error and besides that I had spent most of my funds.

All these reasons made me stay in spite of my certainty that the governor would try to destroy me because he had been informed that in Spain I had not spoken well of him and had procured Lope de Sosa's appointment. Also, it was true that I had requested and received the governorship of Santa Marta. However, I gave up that post because I was not also granted the one hundred knighthoods of Santiago for the gentlemen to accomplish the enterprise as I detailed in Book XXVI, Chapters I and III.[3] (Santa Marta was later removed from Pedrarias's jurisdiction.) Principally, I feared that he would do me harm for the above reasons and because of what he had done to me in the past. Many persons told me that he regarded me as his enemy. Moreover, he was resentful that I came as his majesty's collector of the assets of the adelantado and his confederates and of all fines accruing to the royal exchequer. Not only that, I held the chief notaryship for Secretary Lope Conchillos and the office of assayer, as well as the inspectorship of mines, and as such would have a hand in everything. What made me most dangerous in Pedrarias's opinion were my distrust and the appointments that I had negotiated as perpetual aldermen of the city of Darién for myself, for other officials, and for Bachelor Diego de Corral. I received neither thanks nor reimbursement for the fees to dispatch their appointments. All these appointments I procured as much to honor these people as to serve God and King by stopping Pedrarias from annually naming his retainers and servants as aldermen of that city. Naturally, Pedrarias resented all this.

In addition to the above, I brought a warrant allowing the governor to rule alone without consulting the officials and, although this was beneficial for Pedrarias, I gained nothing by it, as I thought that the governor would be Lope de Sosa. I brought another warrant prohibiting officials from trading with the Indians and another requiring the governor and his guarantors to certify gold purity and make up the difference if in Spain it were found less pure than marked. I brought the ordinances and rights of the smelting office. I brought a remission for four years of fees from the inland import-export duties. I brought a warrant that reduced the king's share of the gold mines to a tenth and then would raise it a point year by year to a fifth. I brought other grants and franchises for the territory and settlers that were useful and beneficial to all except me. No one thanked me or reimbursed me a penny for all my work and expenses even though, as I said before, I spent the majority of my capital going to Flanders with the sole purpose of seeking remedy for that land and community. On the contrary, the governor and officials were displeased by several of these warrants. In truth, the only fruits of my labors for me were many problems and much time and money lost, as I will tell farther on. Nevertheless, the governor and everyone feigned great content at my return with such notable grants for the city and entire province.

When I presented all these warrants and provisions Pedrarias praised me to the skies for what I had done for that land. He excused himself to the officials, saying that he did not wish to rule alone but that I had brought the warrant to that effect as well as the one prohibiting them from engaging in trade. One and all were very unhappy because it was a great hindrance to their greed, taking away their control and business interests. They dissimulated their resentment against me but did whatever they could to get even.

A few days later the governor decided to go to Panamá to await Licentiate Espinosa, the chief justice, who had been exploring the southern coast for two years in Vasco Núñez's ships, grabbing everything he could like a man planning to return to Spain and not remain in that land.

When I saw that the governor was going to the other sea, I sent him a formal protest, pointing out that his departure at that time would depopulate Darién because the officials were going with him and all were determined to establish residence in Panamá on the southern coast and some at Nombre de Dios on the other coast.[4] I detailed many reasons he ought not to go, but he paid no attention and took with him Treasurer

Alonso de la Puente, Comptroller Diego Márquez, and Factor Miguel Juan de Rivas. Because the treasurer and comptroller were aldermen in Darién and so that they would not return to that city, the governor gave them grants of Indians to serve them in Panamá, which is eighty leagues away. Clearly the governor wanted to depopulate Darién because his son-in-law Vasco Núñez, whom he executed, had won and settled the land and because once when Pedrarias wanted to return to Spain without undergoing a residency, the city council stopped him. Also, he wanted to go to Panamá to be present to collect the booty he expected the chief justice was bringing back from the south coast expedition and because that part of his jurisdiction was free of warlike Indians (apparently where there were such Indians was not to his liking). Moreover, it was said that the chief justice and Captain Badajoz had already returned there with much gold. For all these reasons, neither my words nor those of many others had any effect on him.

Determined to go, Pedrarias came up with a clever stratagem to satisfy requirements in a way favorable to himself. Pedrarias made Licentiate Alarconcillo, who came with Governor Lope de Sosa, his chief justice and lieutenant and had proclaimed in Darién a thirty-day residency for himself. The residency was entirely favorable as Pedrarias remained in office and made his lieutenant a judge. All this pointed to a guilty conscience and was the subject of much laughter but, of course, anyone who had a complaint about him did not dare come forward. This fraudulent residency was sent to court at just the right moment, when our lord king was not in Spain and his regents were totally occupied in putting down the Comunero Revolt.[5] Doña Isabel de Bobadilla, Pedrarias's wife, and Francisco de Lizaur, his attorney, importuned the regents—the most Reverend Cardinal of Tortosa (later Pope Adrian VI), the Constable of Castile Don Iñigo de Velasco, and the Admiral of Castile Don Fadrique Enríquez—who sent a commission to Licentiate Alarconcillo to take residency of his master, Licentiate Espinosa, and those judges appointed by Pedrarias. When these provisions arrived from Spain, the governor, treasurer, and factor were in Panamá. Comptroller Diego Márquez and I, the inspector, were in Darién with our wives. Pedrarias's lieutenant in Darién was Martín Estete, a man inexperienced in either arms or letters, who was married to one of the ladies of Pedrarias's wife.

Shortly before the governor left Darién he sent out Bachelor Diego de

Corral as captain with some men to explore and pacify the region toward Abraime, Zaranura, and other provinces. His deeds will be addressed farther on.

So, with this state of affairs, Licentiate Espinosa returned to Panamá with more than thirty-three thousand pesos worth of gold plundered from the Indians along the western coast. This amount was in addition to the twenty thousand he had buried there, as reported earlier. The governor then sent to Darién for Comptroller Diego Márquez and me or our deputies to come to Panamá. We were to melt down and receive the Royal Fifth and fees of the fifty thousand pesos plus the gold from trading and from the mines and distribute the rest to whomever it belonged. My presence was especially enjoined by Pedrarias's procurator because the smelting of bullion was my responsibility and I had the royal mint stamps as well as the charge to collect the assets of Adelantado Vasco Núñez de Balboa and his confederates. That being the case, Comptroller Diego Márquez and I decided to go to Panamá. Diego Márquez pulled up stakes and took along his wife, determined not to return to Darién. I left mine behind, even though every day residents were leaving, lured away by the governor's promises of grants of Indians and other rewards for those who left that city. While others were abandoning it, I began to build, giving to my wife money and the design to construct my house. She completed it so well that there was no house to compare at that time in all Tierra Firme. With the construction of this house, the city had some hope because I had not abandoned it like the other royal officials, and the city granted me powers of attorney to negotiate on its behalf with the governor.

After I arrived in Panamá, the twenty thousand pesos worth of gold from Paris were disinterred in my presence. The chief justice brought this back from his first expedition, leaving Captain Gonzalo de Badajoz and a few men to guard it. They had buried it to keep it safe from the Indians. This gold brought by the licentiate together with that mined in Panamá, Capir, and Juanaga by the settlers of Panamá and Nombre de Dios amounted to seventy thousand pesos.

About this time, Diego de Corral and his men limped back to Darién. Having found the land through which he traveled at peace, he left it up in arms by virtue of his "intelligence" and ineptitude. To compound this disaster, Lieutenant Martín Estete entered the area by canoe and was even worse than Corral. Each of them bore heavy responsibility for starting the Indian rebellion and the destruction of Santa María, which at that time was the largest and best Christian settlement in Tierra Firme.

While Bachelor Corral and the lieutenant were giving such a bad account of themselves in Darién, the gold was melted down in Panamá and Captain Gil González de Avila (who by the purchase of the flighty little Negro involved the governor in the expedition) finished outfitting and began his voyage. He had been delayed until now because the first ships he built in the Balsa River rotted away in the sun and rain while the governor temporized. If he had not taken that Black boy, he would never have left.

Finally, in 1522 he set out on the western route and his discoveries will be reported farther on. Before that, in 1521, I left Panamá for Nombre de Dios and from there went to Darién in a caravel that I owned. At the time of my departure, in the name of the city of Darién, I made a formal written complaint to the governor setting forth the reasons he was the cause of its destruction. As he was upset that these things were written down, he resolved to beg me to take charge in Darién by accepting the staff of office of lieutenant, saying that I would give such a good account of myself that the city and territory would be sustained. His explanation for this charge was that at that time he could not leave the South Sea. I did not want to accept, for being a royal official was more honorable than being his lieutenant and for not wanting the problems of that office. I excused myself, saying that as the king's officer I could not also serve the governor without conflict of interest. Finally, at his and others' insistence, reminding me that the city would be abandoned with the loss of my investments there if there were no one to care for it, I accepted the charge. In spite of my other offices as bullion inspector, alderman of Darién, and general collector for their majesties' exchequer, the governor ordered me to take up the staff, saying that it was vital to their majesties' service. And so he signed the order and I accepted it, as my household and wife were in Darién, the care of which I had inherited to my sorrow and because it was God's will.

When he gave me the provisions by which I was to govern that city and to be captain of that province, Pedrarias told some people that taking up that charge would be my ruination. And so it was, because my nature could not tolerate shameful or ugly things and to try to impose justice upon people accustomed to its absence and to evil living would not be without considerable risk to my person. All the more so considering how ill disposed the governor was toward me. Although I was not ignorant of all this, so as not to see the city, my household, and revenues lost, I bowed my head, trusting in God Almighty, and returned to Darién. I had left in August and returned Saturday, November 9, 1521. The very next day, Sunday, I buried my wife, who had been ill for ten days. The intense pain of the loss of the woman I loved more than myself almost made me lose my mind for, in addition to her sweet companionship and my desire to live in a state of Christian matrimony, I was not accustomed to taking concubines as had many of my neighbors, some even taking two.

My new position in Darién gratified my enemies for, as soon as I assumed the staff of office, I set about punishing public sinning, which many residents had grown old practicing. Very soon I was hated because I did not allow the sale or consumption of meat on Saturdays as had been done until then. Second, I issued a proclamation against public concubinage and, as they knew I would punish them, those who lived openly in concubinage separated. Third, I stopped the gambling and had all the playing cards in the city publicly burned in the plaza. Fourth, I punished blasphemers. Fifth, I sentenced a notary who was robbing the city to a fine and suspended him from office for one year. I was rigorous in punishing transgressors of everything I prohibited. I prevented the Indian women from being used as beasts of burden, as the Christians were using them like asses. Likewise, I did other things I believed to be in the service of God and King and to the benefit of the public good. All my travails were like sparks, igniting the animosity of those who were to place me in the great danger I was to face.

CHAPTER XV—HOW THE CHRONICLER REMAINED IN
DARIÉN AS CAPTAIN AND THE GOVERNOR'S LIEUTEN-
ANT; HOW CHIEF BEA'S INDIANS KILLED CAPTAIN
MARTÍN DE MURGA AND OTHER CHRISTIANS; HOW BY
THE PRUDENCE AND INDUSTRY OF THE SAID CAPTAIN
AUTHOR OF THESE HISTORIES WERE PACIFIED MANY
CHIEFS AND WARLIKE CARIB INDIANS OF THE COAST
AND MANY GOLD PESOS FROM TRADE WERE DEPOSITED
IN DARIÉN.

When I presented Pedrarias's provisions to the city council of Santa María del Antigua del Darién, all received me as his lieutenant with pleasure, recognizing the governor's enmity toward the city and the fact that the other royal officials had moved away. Both Treasurer Alonso de la Puente and Comptroller Diego Márquez had gone to Panamá and Factor Miguel Juan de Rivas to Nombre de Dios. Unlike them, I wished to persevere in that city and had bought for cash the houses of the comptroller and others and sold them on credit to others.

I bought cattle and swine to provide meat for the town, which until then had never had its own supplies. I formed an excellent gang of slaves and Blacks to work the gold mines throughout the entire jurisdiction. I settled all the differences between residents over debts that I could, in some cases using my own assets to reconcile the parties. I made many ordinances and statutes for the republic's benefit. However, as I said before, only a few of these things were well received because of the dissoluteness of the residents.

One thing I did that was especially beneficial for the city, for me, and for everyone in general was the following. I outfitted a caravel of mine with a crew, provisions, and arms for peace or battle and sent it east to the Cartagena Caribs, Codego Island, and other parts. Without any help from the king or others but at my own expense, I began trade with the wild Indians and started their pacification. I was not the first to try trading with them; as I reported before, Captain Cristóbal Guerra, Juan de la Cosa, Bastidas, Juan de Ledesma, Hojeda, and many others had traveled all that coast, the majority robbing and disturbing under the pretext of trading. However, what I did was to trade and calm what had been disturbed. In a few months' time, I amassed seven thousand pesos worth of gold.[1] By my example the Darién residents bought or constructed ships for trade and, in a short time, fifty thousand pesos worth of gold were deposited in that city without risk and without killing or angering the Indians. (This is detailed in Chapters III and IV of Book XXVI.) This sum greatly improved the city, and all because of my enterprise.

In spite of all this, I was a feared judge for not overlooking public sinning nor failing to apply just punishment, however mild. Everyone knew that they could not expect me to let them off without at least a moderate correction if guilty and, as a result, many were indignant. If the persons I punished appealed to the governor, they were absolved and even given money. The treasurer and comptroller at the governor's side had not forgotten those warrants I brought that denied them a vote in government affairs and the right to trade as they once had, and these two officials favored the appellants even though I had justly sentenced them. In short order I was hated by the appellants and their supporters but esteemed by the good citizens and those who were impartial. However, the latter were not influential enough to help me when they saw me in need. Very few persons dared to show themselves my friends, as they clearly saw that the governor was against me and spoke ill of me. Many times he had said these words:

> I know that another would do better in the good administration of these parts. Our lord emperor, being informed of this and at the petition of Inspector Gonzalo Fernández de Oviedo, provided Lope de Sosa, may he rest in peace, a good gentleman who would have governed very well. I would be delighted to be free and withdraw now if it were not God's will that I keep on with the trials and toils of sustaining these regions in the face of constant personal expense, little income, continual illnesses and having buried in this soil one of my sons.

Singing this refrain and others about how many other burdens his person owed to God and King, all who heard him said that without doubt God wanted him and no other to govern, and with such obsequious flatteries they passed the time, although the record was clearly the opposite. The governor, his ministers, and captains laid waste the land with robbery and cruelty, all with impunity as the history partially relates. What they called pacification was desolation, murder, destruction, robbery, and the elimination of the natives.[2] Because I said so several times, those who wanted me to conform like previous judges had a bad opinion of me.

To make matters worse for me, it happened that a Darién resident, a Basque named Martín de Murga, was Pedrarias's Indian agent for the Darién province and *repartimiento*.[3] He requested my permission to visit Chief Bea, who was one of his Indians and who resided in the lagoons near the Grande River. I refused him, telling him not to go there because I was informed that all the Indians of that area were in rebellion since the time that Bachelor Corral and Martín Estete passed through on their so-called visit. I said that I would certainly not give permission, fearing for his life and that of his men. He complained about my decision to many and, of course, someone told me. I had him come to see me and said to him:

> Martín de Murga, it has been reported that you are complaining about me. This is unwarranted because if I have not given permission it is so that your chief will not kill you. When you do go I would like you to be able to return safely and not be murdered. For your own sake, stop saying that I am ruining you and that I do not want you to profit from the one thousand pesos you say your chief promised you. I am only doing my duty to you and if you think otherwise bring a notary and make a formal demand of me for what you want. I will respond formally and henceforth discharge my conscience before God and everyone.

Martín de Murga thanked me courteously for permission to file the demand, asking me kindly not to take offense. I responded that it would please me rather than give offense. And so, he filed a claim of five hundred pesos against me if he did not receive permission to go to his Chief Bea, stating that the chief had asked him to come receive the one thousand or more pesos for trade and that the chief was not in rebellion but living in peace. I responded that it was publicly suspected that the chief was in fact in rebellion and that I advised him not to go there even though he did not need my permission, since, as Indian agent for Darién, he could go wherever he wished. Nevertheless, if he still wished my license, I would give it provided he took reasonable precautions so that he and his men would not be in danger.

After that, without any other contact between us, Captain Murga left.

He took with him in two canoes Ruy López de Talavera, Juan López de Llerena, Juan de Medellín, and ten or twelve friendly Indian oarsmen. He took along shirts, hatchets, and other items to give to the chief, his wives, and Indians. Those people of Bea live close to Darién on some lagoons near the Grande River (also called San Juan), which enters the Gulf of Urabá. In certain times of the year, especially during the rainy season, it is very dangerous to go there.

Captain Murga and his party were well received on their arrival, the chief embracing them all. The captain gave fine shirts to the chief, to his wives, and to some of the principal men, as well as Basque hatchets and other items.[4] To show the Indians how well the hatchets cut, they fitted them with handles. Then the chief prepared for the Christians and their Indian servants a bountiful meal of excellent fish and other local items. While they were enjoying their food, and their guard was down, the Indians split open the four Christians' heads from behind with the hatchets. They had no opportunity to defend themselves because after the first wounds they were quickly killed by a rain of blows from many Indians. Most of the Indian oarsmen who brought them were bound up to be branded as slaves, but a few of them escaped during the massacre and returned to Darién.

To solemnize his treachery, Chief Bea donned a gold belt and collar and with his Indians dragged Captain Martín de Murga's corpse by the feet a quarter mile away, where it was left to be eaten by the birds. Many Indian men, women, and children accompanied the body, laughing and singing their *areitos*.[5] From time to time the chief struck the corpse's mouth with his gold-studded war club saying: "*Chica oro, chica oro, chica oro,*" which means: "Eat gold, eat gold, eat gold."

After this "funeral service" of the imprudent captain, they dragged the bodies of the other three Spaniards to the fields as well. Some of the Indians who had accompanied these poor wretches returned to Darién three or four days later and within a week the majority came back to tell what had happened. As soon as I had the news, I determined to go or send someone to punish Bea and I prepared an expedition.

As none of the soldiers of these parts who met bad ends in one way or another lacked guilt for their punishment, you should know that this Murga had been constable and minister of the atrocities committed by Chief Justice Espinosa in his overland journeys through this province of Cueva.

Darién's population diminished daily as those who went to see the governor on business were given gifts and Indian grants there and few returned. Because of what happened to Murga, there was fear in the city, especially because it was suspected that another chief, Guaturo, had joined Bea as well as Corobari, who had rebelled some days previously and was a very notorious and formidable enemy of the Christians. Corobari's mother, wife, and children were in Darién in the household of Bachelor Corral as part of his Indian allotment. Moreover, Corobari's close relative was the bachelor's Indian concubine by whom Corral had children. We were greatly worried about this Corobari who, like a thief in the household, could be advised daily by his Indians in Darién of how few we were. With these well-founded suspicions, I had armed and readied three canoes, a small boat, and food, most of which came from my household or was purchased with my money. I ordered Captain Juan de Ezcaray to go with a force of forty men (ten of them crossbowmen) and two or three of the Indians who went with Captain Murga to capture Chief Bea and as many other guilty Indians as he could. I would remain behind to guard the city.

With these arrangements made, Ezcaray and his party were to leave after first hearing the Mass of the Holy Spirit. Bachelor Diego de Corral was greatly disturbed by this expedition, no doubt because he feared revelation of the full extent of his guilt in the rebellion of the areas through which he had traveled under the pretext of simply visiting. As Chief Bea was a relative of his Indian concubine Elvira and of his children by her, Corral began to work against the men's departure.[6] He spoke out publicly about the danger they faced, using many scandalous words, frightening those slated for the journey. In his capacity as alderman, he said many things to me to make me reconsider my plans, stating that I well knew that sending so many men would leave the city defenseless. If they became lost or something bad happened to them, it would be my fault, besides which I was reducing the city's forces, which were already quite small. Moreover, Corral stated that with the departure of these men, other regional chiefs would be emboldened to attack and burn the city. All the potential harm to those leaving and those staying would be my fault, if I did not change my mind and listen to his advice. He said many other things that seemed quite reasonable to common folk of limited intelligence, giving them to understand that I placed the city in danger and those I ordered to go were excused from such an obviously dangerous expedition and that my plan was ill-advised, rash, and unreasonable.

The majority of the citizens were listening attentively and favorably to his speech. As I was determined to send the expedition to punish the delinquents so as to avoid any other provocations, I replied to him in this fashion:

> Sir bachelor, it grieves me to have to respond to your words in a public forum but you have given these citizens and friends to understand something very far from the truth and very prejudicial to all. Your fictitious concerns are all directed toward your own interests; beneath them, in truth, is something else, the opposite of what you want us to believe. Clearly, if Bea's daring and treacherous murder of Captain Martín de Murga and the other sinners is overlooked worse dangers will ensue. Moreover, Bea himself and his confederates would have greater cause to burn our homes and kill us because the embers are in your own house, where he has his spies and relatives in your son Perico and your Elvira from whom you had him and who is Bea's cousin. You least of all should have anything to say in this matter. If anyone deserves Bea's punishment it is you, unless you think Bea will protect you because of your mutual relations. All your objections are groundless. These gentlemen I am sending with Captain Juan de Ezcaray are so worthy, loyal, and experienced that they are more than up to the task I have assigned. Each has so much at stake in this that, though few in number, their valor assures their success and that God and their majesties will be served and this city secured. I will remain here to guard the city from Bea's spies and relatives and those of your Corobari, who you and everyone knows is a dirty dog. Twice his disloyalties were pardoned and after being baptized and calling himself Christian he roams the countryside a third time causing trouble. He is this city's worst enemy because of you since in your house are his mother, wife, sons, and other Indian friends and he is a relative of your Elvira and your son.

My actions will show that my principal aim is the common good of all. I have no other interest except to serve God and their

majesties and to conserve this city in which I have as much to
lose as anyone. I could easily have left it like others of his majesty's officials and gained much advantage by Indian grants and
other things the governor offered me if I would leave it. Thus, by
this you will see that my desire is to sustain this city; to live and
die in it. Each day some of our Indian house servants disappear
and are not seen again dead or alive. Obviously, they could not
have been taken by tigers without our knowing it. Everyone in
this city suspects, I as well, that these traitor chiefs, Corobari and
Bea, your son's relatives, are enticing them away from us. Because
the thief and spy is among us, we sense the danger and do not see
the remedy, but no one is so completely blind or so ignorant that
he fails to understand that the remedy is to cut down and pull
up the roots of those evil weeds Chiefs Bea and Corobari. Be
assured that as long as my charge is the common good of all and
even at the cost of everything including my own life, I will clear
up all these suspicions and doubts for everyone. The punishment
appropriate to the Murga affair will be carried out and no one is
to say otherwise. And, by the way, Sir, it would be good if you
told us where you left the two or three Christians of the company
you led inland who, being sick and exhausted, were abandoned
even though you could have brought them out. For if they are
still alive the expedition may be able to collect them.

On hearing this the bachelor turned pale as a corpse.

Previously, I had been informed how these men on their knees before
the bachelor tearfully begged his aid and mercy and pleaded not to be left
to be killed by the Indians. He responded that they should get up and
walk since no such rogues would be carried. One of them said to him and
the others: "Sirs, since you are determined to go, pray to God for my
soul." The bachelor ordered the others on and left these men. He went
back to a native hut with two or three companions where there was a
Biscayan (the last of those who could not keep up) and he said to him:
"You, why are you not on your feet?" The poor man, who was lying in a
hammock with very swollen feet, responded with tears flowing from his
eyes: "Captain, Sir, you can well see that I cannot follow you; please remember that I am a Christian." However, the bachelor had no more pity
on him than on the other two he left farther back and he went away.

Nevertheless, the bachelor had his Indian women carried in hammocks when they became tired.

When the bachelor heard me speak of his guilt concerning those he left to die on that expedition he was very shaken and said to me: "Sir, so that you can see that it is not good for these men to go where you are sending them, I will supply you the signatures of one hundred principal men of this city who will attest to the same." I ordered a notary to set down his words and he did. Then I ordered the bachelor to sign the statement and he did. Next, I had a document drawn up ordering him to produce the signatures before me by vespers of the following day under pain of a fine of one hundred thousand maravedís to his majesty's exchequer. If what he said were true, I would bow to the general opinion of what should be done.

The bachelor set about gathering those signatures among clerics, friars, and others who had no business in voting on military affairs as well as from others who scarcely knew what they were signing. In total, he got about ten signatures, mostly from his adherents and from men of little repute. That very night the majority of the soldiers slated to go to Bea rebelled and refused to go. The next morning, Captain Juan de Ezcaray came to me and reported: "Sir, I am astonished at how much inconstancy and little shame there is in this city. Yesterday, everything was settled and last night they changed their minds. They seem as though men being led to the gallows and no man is disposed to go with me." Immediately I sensed the bachelor's evil hand in this and began to gather a good deal of evidence against him as to his part in the mutiny. This could not be done secretly so that he would not know and the bachelor took fright at his guilty involvement in the matter. Seeing that he was found out, he conspired against me with his longtime friend Dean Juan Pérez Zalduendo (a man without education).

Some months previously I had reviewed the files of the clerk Cristóbal Muñoz, who had processed the documents of the trial and execution of Adelantado Vasco Núñez de Balboa and his confederates. I requested the transcripts, because I wanted to determine the fees due to Secretary Lope Conchillos in his capacity as notary-general and also to see whether the adelantado and his confederates had more assets than what I knew, so that as receiver I could seize them for the royal exchequer. I had the documents in hand for a few days, during which time I read them all, numbering and initialing each page so that none could be abstracted without its absence being apparent. This clerk Muñoz later took this file to Panamá, where the governor and the chief justice observed my precautions and imagined that I had noted items and errors prejudicial to them. Because of this, I suspected that they had arranged for my tribulations and my death.

CHAPTER XVI—HOW THE AUTHOR BROUGHT TO
JUSTICE CHIEFS COROBARI AND GUATURO, WHO HAD
REBELLED AGAINST THEIR MAJESTIES' SERVICE; AND
HOW HE ARRESTED AND SENT TO SPAIN DIEGO DE
CORRAL; AND OF OTHER ITEMS PERTINENT TO THE
HISTORY.

No ships came to Darién for many months because of the disturbances
of the Comunero Revolt in Spain. Then it pleased God that a caravel
arrived at the port on Tuesday, July 1, 1522, the eve of the Visitation of the
Mother of God to Saint Elizabeth. On board was ecclesiastical and secular justice in two persons: the one was Licentiate Sancho de Salaya, coming as chief justice of the coast and South Sea in the names of their
Caesarean Catholic majesties;[1] the other was Archdeacon Rodrigo Pérez,
whom the dean, persuaded by Pedrarias Dávila and Licentiate Gaspar de
Espinosa, his chief justice, had sent in chains to Spain as participant in
the treason of Vasco Núñez and those who were executed with him. The
archdeacon returned absolved and with an order from their majesties and
from his prelate for the restitution of his assets. Note, reader, what must
have been the extent of guilt and treason of the unfortunate adelantado,
for this archdeacon was one of his strongest supporters and he returned
absolved to the territory!

Licentiate Salaya brought authorization from the new bishop, Friar
Vicente Peraza, to take possession of the cathedral church, remove its
officers, and replace them with whomever he wished. His first act was to
take possession for the bishop and then he removed the dean as diocesan
magistrate and selected Archdeacon Rodrigo Pérez in his place. Pérez
and Salaya then secretly investigated certain citizens. Since people could
then speak freely in discharge of their consciences they informed them
truthfully of how prejudicial Bachelor Corral was to the city. With the
arrival of justice in the territory, the bachelor and the dean, knowing that
I was against them and would make them answer for their misdeeds and
the soldiers' mutiny, asked Licentiate Salaya and certain Franciscans to
reconcile us. At their insistence, from then on I spoke courteously to
them when we crossed paths. However, I did not promise to forget my
duty; rather I said that regardless of whether we spoke I would not fail to
pursue justice when I could, since, because of them, Chief Bea was not
punished. The go-betweens were content with this proviso. But, as the

guilty sooner or later fear their punishment and are ever suspicious, even though we courteously doffed our caps to each other, our communications were not as sociable as before nor could I overlook their conduct because of my offices. And so their hatred of me was engraved on their hearts with diamantine letters.

When Licentiate Salaya was better informed of Bachelor Corral's conduct, life, and biases, he advised me to send him back to Castile to the wife he had left eleven or twelve years ago. At that time he lived in public concubinage in Tierra Firme. Salaya said that for Corral's excesses he should be expelled as prejudicial to the republic. I responded that Licentiate Salaya should make the appropriate interrogatory and investigation and if he thought there was sufficient compelling evidence I would do what he advised and say it was justice. The licentiate took pen and ink and wrote up an interrogatory with his own hand. Witnesses who were called responded with many other accusations and said abominations of the bachelor. This done, according to the licentiate's advice, I had him put in chains and placed on board a ship ready to sail for Spain. With him I sent a certain Luis de Córdoba, a Sevillian spice dealer imprisoned as prejudicial to the republic and living in Darién without his wife in public concubinage with two women. The officials of the House of Trade in Seville, on the basis of his majesty's warrant, sent me an order to remand the prisoner to Spain and make him live with his wife. I ordered both of them on that ship, which set sail to this city of Santo Domingo and from here to Spain. This departure greatly upset Pedrarias because he thought that in Spain Corral would turn against him and would say bad things about him.

Things being in this state, news arrived in Darién from an Indian who had belonged to Christians and now was with Chief Corobari, the enemy of our city. This Indian was arrested and brought before me for questioning. He reported the chief's location as in a mountain range seven or eight leagues from Darién and said he had come because two days before the chief had killed his wife, a Christian named Catalina, because she had said that Christians were good people. Moreover, Corobari had killed many other peaceful Christian Indians. This Indian offered to lead us to the chief. Since Corobari was the one who most worried us and we did not know where he was, after carefully interrogating this Indian I put together a force of thirty-five Christians under a good captain and ordered him to set out with the Indian as guide. They came upon the chief one night and captured him and some of his people. When he was brought to Darién he freely confessed that he had killed Catalina and many other Christian Indians and that he was an enemy of Christians; that he had rebelled twice, was pardoned twice, and then rebelled a third time against their majesties' service; and that he had done many other evil things. Among these things he confessed that Bachelor Corral had told him of Captain Martín de Murga's murder at a house the bachelor had half a league from the city, where the two had met and dined several times. These meetings occurred when the city feared attack by Corobari and Chief Bea after Captain Martín de Murga's murder. Because of this information, Licentiate Salaya said publicly that if Bachelor Corral had not departed, he would have well deserved being burned as traitor and enemy of the Christians alongside his Chief Corobari. He advised me to order Corobari burned at the stake and wrote the order and sentence with his own hand. I signed it and Corobari was burned. I ordered him strangled first because he was baptized and he wanted to die a Christian. He was executed at the stake because, while Indians have no fear of other forms of execution, they greatly fear burning.

After that, Licentiate Salaya went off to Panamá, where the governor was. About that time Doña Isabel de Bobadilla, Pedrarias's wife, sent him from Castile that advantageous residency he was ordered to undergo by the regents and Pope Adrian (then cardinal of Tortosa), who shared the governance of the kingdoms of Spain. They ordered the residency taken by the very same Licentiate Alarconcillo who had directed the other one that Pedrarias had him do. Likewise, the licentiate was to take residency of Licentiate Espinosa and all those who had exercised judicial offices for Pedrarias. All this was negotiated by the governor's wife and by that Francisco de Lizaur previously mentioned.[2]

At this time, I captured certain spies of Chief Guaturo, who was in service to a Darién resident. This chief had rebelled and made an agreement to join Chief Bea (the murderer of Captain Murga and other Christians) to kill all of us in Darién and burn the city. Aware of the deadly peril to the city, I went out in person with forty men in search of the chief, leaving the city as well protected as possible. I did not dare entrust this expedition to any other captain because of the suspicions planted by Bachelor Corral and his now executed Chief Corobari. I feared that the citizen whom Guaturo served would deceive me in the same manner because he vehemently defended his chief, denying that he had rebelled. To satisfy us both, I took the citizen along, much to his disgust, for he said that I was going to too much trouble and that he would bring the chief to town, but I did not trust him. I left Darién and went to Guaturo's sierras eighteen leagues from Darién, where I found out that he was in rebellion, had fled to the mountains, and had destroyed his village. It pleased Our Lord that I gave a good account of myself, for I captured Guaturo, his wife, and two very young children as well as Gonzalo, one of his principal Indians who served as his captain and counselor. In all, some forty of his people were taken. They confessed their rebellion and that they were friends and allies of Cemaco, a chief of Darién who with all his friends and supporters had been declared slaves by the Catholic king. Guaturo confessed that he was going to join Chief Bea to attack us one night, kill all Christians, and burn the city. Guaturo and his captain were sentenced to death on the strength of their confessions of evil intent. I ordered all the captured rebel Indians distributed among the companions who went with me and the same for Corobari's Indians, once he was executed. On the way back from Guaturo on top of Buenavista Hill seven leagues from Darién overlooking the lagoons of Bea where they killed Captain Murga, a gallows taller than a lance was erected. There Captain Gonzalo was hanged so that Bea's Indians could see it from the lagoons one and a half to two leagues below. Later, as soon as I entered Darién, Guaturo was hanged in the plaza. With his death and that of Chief Corobari a few days before, that city and province were very secure.

Nevertheless, on my return from Guaturo I found in the city certain letters from Governor Pedrarias responding to what city officials had written him during my absence. From his reply I understood that Bachelor Corral as alderman, the justices, and a council clerk (those were my enemies, all that was left of the council) had written what they wished. The governor, not knowing I had sent Bachelor Corral to Spain and thinking I had not yet returned, thanked them for the many lies they wrote against me and among other things revoked the power I had from him, giving it to Bachelor Corral. At the first city council meeting after my return from Guaturo they showed me these letters. I said it was obvious from the governor's letters that he responded to lies and falsehoods of Bachelor Corral and his supporters when no other alderman was present but I would be pleased if the bachelor were present now as he would be welcome to the staff of office. Further, I said that the city certainly needed a judge like him who, when the city was on guard for fear of Chiefs Corobari and Bea and it was the bachelor's turn to keep watch, met with Corobari as the chief himself confessed at his trial. I said I was aware that I had debased myself by being the governor's lieutenant but had only accepted the position to keep him from depopulating the city as was his aim. With that, I took the staff and put it on the principal chair from which I had presided for the governor and went to a lower seat saying, "This is the seat that Caesar gave me and from here I will serve as their majesties' official and not as the lord governor's lieutenant. I will act as I have sworn and am obligated in every way I am able to please the governor and in the service of the king and for the benefit of the republic." I vowed never to take up the staff of justice for Pedrarias or for another without their majesties' or their royal council's express order, and all this I had formally written down and witnessed by those present.

See what thanks and remunerations there were for he who had just liberated the land from such great enemies that it had in Chiefs Guaturo and Corobari!

With Pedrarias's letters came his order for the city to elect a delegate to a general meeting in Panamá at which important affairs relating to the territory would be discussed as well as the election of delegates to send to the Cortes in Spain.[3] This invention was because Licentiate Espinosa wanted to go to Castile to negotiate his and the governor's desires and have the poor wretches and the community pay his expenses.

When this order was read, all the citizens present in the council chamber stood with caps in hand and asked me to please accept this appointment as I was their majesties' inspector, alderman, and citizen of the city. They said there was no one else who could do it nor did the city have funds to pay expenses. They begged me for the love of God and so that the city would not be lost to accept the city's proxy for the meeting in Panamá as well as for the Cortes in Spain. They said that they considered me the city's father, who had always known how to sustain it and would not abandon it in time of need. In truth, although some of the supplicants possessed little credibility to move me, there were others of good intentions. Seeing the necessity and the tears of some and considering I was one of the richest and my investment would be lost with that of the rest, I accepted without any salary whatsoever. There and then they unanimously granted me the commission.

That night there was much tumult in Darién. The dean, his relatives, and Bachelor Corral's friends were very upset with this election, fearing that I could harm them and because they hated me. They were suspicious and afraid of me because of the bachelor's imprisonment and they set about to incite some of the townspeople to have the council revoke the commission the city had given me. The council met again and the procurator, the dean's cousin, announced in the city's name that many citizens requested the proxy's revocation as I was partisan. The procurator demanded the aldermen call a vote to choose with more deliberation and agreement the city's representative. After this petition was read in council in my presence, I replied that everything seemed the dean's fabrication. Nevertheless, even though their maliciousness was not a reason to give up the commission, I was content to revisit the matter and to put the naming of the representative to a majority vote of the town. So it was done and the entire town voted. Those who were behind this were few and of little credit and I received many more votes than anyone, and so, against the will of my enemies, the bachelor's supporters, and the dean, they had to give me the commission to go to Panamá to the governor's meeting. I was authorized to go in person to Spain or send any substitute I deemed suitable. I began to prepare my departure and chartered a boat to Nombre de Dios. The rest of the journey would be overland to Panamá, where Governor Pedrarias resided.

CHAPTER XVII—CONCERNING THE RESIDENCIES OF
PEDRARIAS AND HIS CHIEF JUSTICE, THE LICENTIATE
ESPINOSA; AND HOW THE ENEMIES OF THE AUTHOR OF
THESE HISTORIES TIRELESS IN THEIR PERSECUTION,
CONNIVED TO MURDER HIM AND HE WAS VERY BADLY
WOUNDED.

Each man's strengths are only made manifest by adversity, according to Saint Gregory.[1] I confess that the strength with which I resisted my adversities and which saved me from them was not mine but rather that of omnipotent God's.

Some friends of mine to whom I have communicated my writings have wished to stop me from mentioning my personal troubles in these histories. I, however, am of different opinion for the following reasons: First, because I did my duty and upheld justice, those who hated justice combined against me to have me treacherously murdered; second, even though Saint Paul was incomparably better than I, he did not deny his stripes—A Judaeis quinquies, quadragenas, una minus accepi;[2] third, because Christ, Our Redeemer, is God yet He did not disdain His Passion. (Of course, these comparisons are very highly disproportionate, as Christ could not sin and was blameless and was teaching us to bear suffering, and Saint Paul was the vessel of election and illuminated by God and suffered for His love while I am and have been a sinner.) However, Divine Grace did not allow my enemies to accomplish their intentions. I will never forget these words of the glorious doctor of the Church Saint Gregory concerning Saint Job: "If ever by silence he allowed men to do unjust things and did not contradict them with justice he certainly would not have had adversaries but because he held to the path of life he always found those desiring his death."[3] Another reason I include these things in my histories is that those who wished me dead were friends of that Bachelor Corral, who was behind it all. Corral was among Vasco Núñez's envoys to Diego de Nicuesa when they led him to the pitiless death they prepared for him. Yet another of Corral's friends was the notary I suspended from office and fined four times the excessive fees he defrauded the city. Another became my enemy because I refused to use my office against his wife, who he said was cuckolding him. Nevertheless, I saw them all come to bad ends because God is careful to make up for the defects of man's justice by punishing each one appropriately from heaven when it pleases Him.

Returning to the subject matter: as I was about ready to depart Darién there came to that city a notary, Pedro de Barreda. By order of Licentiate Alarconcillo, the residency judge, he came to proclaim in Acla and in Darién that all those wishing to register complaints against Governor Pedrarias or against Licentiate Espinosa, his chief justice, should appear in Panamá by a certain date and they would be heard and justice done. The wisest grumbled and joked about such an accounting. As everyone knew that the residency was manipulated by Pedrarias and once over he would still be in office, it seemed best to dissimulate their complaints rather than make the useless, difficult, and expensive journey to Panamá. They had no faith in the judicial process nor was anyone willing to antagonize and risk destruction from the person who would remain in control of the territory. So, there was no one foolish enough to waste time on the journey.

Nevertheless, in the king's name and that of the royal exchequer, as alderman of Darién, which had given me its commission, and in my own interests, I resolved to go and present claims against the governor and chief justice. On Friday, September 19, 1522, as I was at home preparing my departure, the bells rang for the Mass of the Confraternity of Saint Sebastian, of which I, like everyone in town, was a member. One of the city's justices of the peace entered and said to me: "Sir, will Your Grace attend the confraternity mass?" I responded: "Yes, certainly." So he and I and others went to the church, which was on the outskirts of the city. The majority of the townspeople were gathered at the church door awaiting the priest and when he arrived they entered after him.

Note, reader, and see what happened to me after this justice of the peace invited me to go to mass. He was a special friend of Bachelor Corral, who had told him that I had tried to block the council's nomination of him for that office. That was true, for he was a low-born ex-shoemaker and for that and other reasons I did not think he was fit to be an official simply because he was now rich.

When I was about to enter the church with the others he said to me: "Your Grace, please let me have a few words while the priest is dressing." I remained with him and while we strolled on the street in front of the church, a young apothecary named Simón Bernal approached. He was the son of that Luis de Córdoba whom I sent under arrest to Spain with

Bachelor Corral. Simón Bernal had been the dean's retainer and a few days earlier, having left his service, with some others communicated with me, begging me to take him on in my household. He said he wished to enter my service, seeing how well I treated and helped my servants and those who came to me. As I knew that young man had been my enemy's servant, I had no wish to include such a suspect person in my house and even more so considering I had sent his father under arrest to Spain. I sent word to thank him for the good regard he said he had for me and responded that I also had regard for him and would try to do what I could for him in the future.

When this young man came up to where the justice and I were strolling in front of the church, he took off his cap in greeting and I nodded as if to say "good morning" and he took up a position next to a wall in front of the church. At that time, the justice was importuning me to give a bailiff's staff to a worthy man as I had the power to appoint that office in the absence in Spain of the chief bailiff, my friend Bachelor Enciso.[4] I replied that I would be happy to grant his request because the man was a good person worthy of the position. At that moment, Simón Bernal came up behind me with a long, sharp dagger (although he was also wearing a sword) and inflicted a wound to my head that descended below my left ear, cut off a large piece of my jaw bone and entered my cheek. The long, deep wound hurled me to the ground and, as I fell, he stabbed me twice in the left shoulder. All this happened so fast the justice scarcely saw it and I did not realize what had happened. The criminal ran down the street, not daring to take sanctuary at that church. He knew that he would be arrested entering it and instead made for the cathedral, where the dean and other priests, his friends and supporters, waited to aid him, which they did.

As I fell stunned to the ground, I cried out loudly: "Mother of God, help me." Looking back I saw him with the dagger raised in his hand, and, hurrying to get up, I said: "Oh traitor, why have you killed me?" I reached automatically for my sword, which I was wearing underneath my gown, grabbing the hilt through the material, but I was half unconscious and could scarcely see him. Many persons ran out of the church and gave chase, as well as did the justice, who was young and fast, but the criminal reached the cathedral. Later the magistrates demanded that the dean and priests hand over the criminal, but they paid little attention to their writs and proclamations.

They carried me home, where I urgently sent for a confessor, well aware of the danger I was facing. A barber-surgeon arrived but when he saw me he said that it was useless to waste time on a dead man. However, all present begged him to try and he treated me, although no one thought I would last three hours. I did not feel the surgery nor speak until four hours later in bed when I began to regain consciousness. Again I asked for a confessor and made confession. I made a sworn statement before a notary pardoning the man who killed me and his accomplices so that God would pardon me as He had mounted His cross for my redemption and that of all sinners. I made this pardon with complete sincerity and would have abided by it always had they let me. From then on I turned my attention to my recovery, which in everyone's estimation was due to All-Powerful God because none of those who saw me thought I would see another day. It seems that God had reserved me for other tribulations.

In short, soon I was out of danger and healed with only some scarring from the wound. Eight or nine days later, to protect the dean, the clerics forcibly and secretly expelled from the church that poorly advised young man who stabbed me.

I was not unaware that my trials came from God's hand for my betterment, since as Saint Gregory says: "When in this life we suffer what we do not wish, it is necessary that we incline our will to that of Him who cannot wish any unjust thing."[5] It is a great consolation in adversity to think that everything happens by the disposition of God to whom nothing but justice is pleasing. However, the glorious doctor's authority I cited not withstanding, I suspected Pedrarias's hand in the accumulation of my troubles. And so, to fulfill my duty, two or three days after I was stabbed, I called that notary Pedro de Barreda, who had proclaimed Pedrarias's residency, and requested him to attest to my condition. Further, if I could not participate in the residency, I formally protested that my absence could not be considered prejudicial to his majesty's exchequer nor to mine so that later I would be able to claim ten thousand gold pesos from the governor and chief justice on the commissions I held from their majesties and on my own behalf. When the governor and chief justice were informed of this declaration, they became even more angry with me, saying I wished to make life difficult for them even in death.

While I was recuperating, their residencies were taken much to their taste. To ensure that no one made any complaints against them they came up with a scheme that I will now relate, for with such tricks, the king being so far away, these and other similar things are common in the Indies. In the port where the residency was publicly announced, two or three days later, the governor and the chief justice declared a redistribution of Indians. Of course, there was no one who did not want to be given more Indians nor those with none who did not hope for some. Others wanted to exchange the Indians they had and still others wanted to sell theirs. Since all this passed through the governor's and chief justice's hands, so as not to anger them in the redistribution, no one came forth with any complaints or claims for damages, and the residency was concluded. However, in the redistribution, the governor and chief justice did as they pleased anyway.

After his residency, Licentiate Espinosa went to Spain with ten thousand gold pesos, according to rumor. But here I want to relate briefly a singular event that happened in Acla concerning the proclamation of the residency of Governor Pedrarias and of his chief justice, Licentiate Espinosa.

CHAPTER XVIII—OF THE PROCLAMATION MADE IN
ACLA FOR THE RESIDENCY OF GOVERNOR PEDRARIAS
AND HIS OFFICIALS; HOW THE PROCLAMATION WAS
AFFIXED TO A POST IN THE PLAZA AND A HORSE THAT
BELONGED TO ADELANTADO VASCO NÚÑEZ DE BALBOA
TORE IT UP; AND HOW THE JUDGE CONDUCTED THE
RESIDENCY OF THE AUTHOR OF THESE HISTORIES AND
CONDEMNED THE PERSON WHO STABBED HIM TO BE
HANGED AND SUFFER OTHER PENALTIES.

The proclamation made in the town of Acla inviting those who wished to make complaints against the governor and chief justice to come to the residency in the city of Panamá was affixed to a post in the plaza. It happened that one Sunday after mass many townspeople accompanied Captain Andrés Garabito, Pedrarias's lieutenant there, to the door of his lodging, which was also on the plaza. While they were conversing and waiting for dinnertime, fifteen or twenty nags or mares entered the other end of the plaza to graze on the vegetation abundantly growing there. (In these recently established towns grass grows quickly in the humid soil of the streets and plazas if it is not constantly cleared away.) One of the horses that had belonged to Adelantado Vasco Núñez de Balboa left the herd with his head up and at a deliberate pace, not stopping to graze nor seeming to pay attention to where he was headed. After about one hundred paces he came to the post with the proclamation and ripped it to shreds with his teeth. Then slowly, again not stopping, he returned to the herd and began to graze with them.

Captain Garabito and the others who saw all this considered it a mystery and began to mutter about the residency, saying if that was what the old horse thought of it, what should men think. The lesson from that incident was that one could only trust in God, for a real residency would have to come from heaven. Truly, the incident set everyone talking, for that horse, as I said, belonged to Adelantado Vasco Núñez de Balboa, whose head was cut off ten or twelve steps from where the proclamation was torn up. This incident was remarked upon by all who saw it or heard of it and later in Spain was cited by some against Pedrarias and his chief justice before the gentlemen of the Council of the Indies.

After I recovered, I took on more retainers at considerable expense, fearing that there would be other attempts against me. Before he left

Acla, Licentiate Alarconcillo, the residency judge, sent his lieutenant, Juan Carballo, to Darién to keep watch on me so that I would not leave the territory without a residency. Pedrarias wrote me that no one had been found who would be a better friend to me in the residency than Carballo and that if I were asked to post bond or I were placed under house arrest I should be patient and everything would turn out well. This was Pedrarias's attempt to frighten me into fleeing. He knew that Carballo had a grudge against me because I had fined him for some infraction to pay twenty pesos to buy an Indian or slave to be the executioner for Darién. Pedrarias gave him the staff of office to harass me, as he in fact did. Carballo demanded of me a ten-thousand-peso bond to guarantee I would remain in the city for my residency and pay whatever would be adjudicated against me. If I did not post bond he said he would have to detain me. Having no reason to fear justice and not possessing such a sum, I told him that I had neither so much wealth nor knew anyone to guarantee it, nor did I have any reason to flee and therefore he could do as he wished. He put leg irons on me in my own house but after two or three days said he would remove them since I was still weak and ill, but only if I put up one thousand gold pesos and signed a declaration to pay another five thousand if I did not observe house arrest. I did as he wished. As my enemy and a petty, ill-bred man, he did me many discourtesies, thinking by them to ingratiate himself with Pedrarias.

In the midst of these tribulations the residency judge arrived and proclaimed my investigation. A thirty-day period was established for anyone to come forward with any civil or criminal complaints against me. I did not miss a single day of the hearings. The judge absolved me of all the complaints except one for sixty gold marks made in the name of Bachelor Corral (whom I sent under detention to Spain) for my having denied his two appeals to Pedrarias.[1] The judge referred the claim for the sixty gold marks to their majesties for final decision. Also, I was accused by a woman whom I had ordered flogged and to lose some teeth because she falsely accused her husband of murder. The judge also referred this to the Royal Council of the Indies. I was fined twenty gold pesos for whatever other claims might be presented—ten to make a fair copy of the residency (the innocent have to pay for their innocence!) and ten to the tribunal so that it did not appear I got off scot-free. In everything else I was absolved, my house arrest was ended, and the one-thousand-peso bond Carballo had demanded was returned, although he did not stop claiming from me those twenty pesos for the executioner. However, I was absolved of that as of the other claims. Note, reader, what a good friend of mine was this Carballo to whom Pedrarias had given the staff of office, writing me that he was the best friend he could find.

Finally, I guaranteed payment for whatever the Royal Council of the Indies might determine in the aforementioned referrals and in the matter of Bachelor Corral's detention. Inasmuch as the justices of the peace in Darién had only condemned the fugitive traitor who wounded me to the loss of his right hand and left foot and confiscation of half his assets to the tribunal, I complained to the judge that this was much too lenient considering my rank and his premeditated treachery. As I was their majesties' judge and official as well as holder of other high positions I demanded that the judge order proper justice done to give satisfaction for my affront. The judge received my complaint and proceeded against the fugitive, sentencing him to be hanged with the confiscation of all his assets and court costs while he was at large.

That done, the judge went to Acla to take residency of Lieutenant Andrés Garabito and Lieutenant Gabriel de Rojas. I remained in Darién convalescing and putting in order the accounts of my various offices and also keeping watch on my enemies, the dean and his supporters.

CHAPTER XIX—HOW THE TREACHEROUS SIMÓN
BERNAL WAS ARRESTED AND WAS BROUGHT TO JUSTICE.

Even though these things are not pleasant for the reader, they are appropriate for their singular litigation as well as necessary to understand what
one endures from those who govern in these parts because of the absence
of superior officials, who are vast distances away from the Indies, and the
huge expenses required to be heard by the sovereign. But this is the author's personal matter and I will not go into all the particulars so as not
to seem to boast of the victory that God was pleased to give me over
my enemies nor detail the circuitous manner in which the traitor who
wounded me was punished, because his flight did little to save him from
the punishment decreed by the court. It happened like this:

After undergoing my residency, I sold part of my belongings to raise a
large amount of cash. In due course I intended to go to Spain to seek
justice against Pedrarias and Chief Justice Licentiate Espinosa, who had
left for Castile. I also wished to report the state of the territory and work
for the preservation of the city so as not to lose my assets entirely. One
feast day, returning from mass (guarded constantly by five or six of my
armed men), some friends and honorable townspeople accompanied me
to my home. One of them dropped a small sealed letter addressed "To
Inspector Gonzalo Fernández de Oviedo." One of my servants picked it
up and gave it to me but did not see who dropped it. When I asked him
who had sent it he responded that he found it on the ground. I opened it
and read: "Sir, because I am your friend I warn you to be on guard and
watch out for yourself for you are in great danger."

The letter was unsigned and the handwriting was disguised. After I
read it I was alarmed, given that I had been wounded shortly before;
nevertheless, I dissimulated my concern with a smiling face and had
everyone sit down. Believing one of those present dropped the letter, I
said: "Gentlemen, do me the honor of being seated and see what someone has written me in this anonymous letter." (Shortly before that I told
the servant who found the letter to retire to another room and write
down the names of all present.) Astonished, they sat down and I read
them the letter. There was considerable difference of opinion: some said
that the author was not entirely a friend as he did not specify the danger
threatening me; others thought the warning was simply to keep me upset,
ever suspicious, and on guard; others said that the writer concealed his

identity for fear of antagonizing my enemies; and there were other opinions. And so it went back and forth concerning the message, all of which the writer listened to without saying a word.

After all had given their opinions I responded:

Gentlemen, I believe the author is a friend who is disturbed by my tribulations. He knows that this city would have been abandoned if I had left it like the other aldermen and royal officials. He knows what this republic owes me for the Indian trading enterprise and the other things I have done for everyone and he has seen the evils that have been my repayment and must have knowledge of others being planned and it pains him as a Christian and man of good conscience. Probably he is also a friend of some of my enemies and does not dare to speak plainly so as not to alienate anyone or for other reasons. But, however it may be, I thank the writer and truly count him a good friend. I know well this handwriting and know that he will tell me the rest. For that I will never forget him nor be ungrateful to him.

But, the truth was I did not recognize the handwriting nor did I know who wrote the letter; it was a stratagem that worked well. With this, the conversation ceased and everyone went home to eat. I remained at my house with my people, anxious, uneasy, and fearful, as any man would be. Nevertheless, I constantly kept in mind the words of that glorious doctor of the Church: "Jesus Christ made Himself our sole remedy; if you suffer fevers, He is the cooling source; if you are wounded, He is the doctor; if you fear death, He is the life; if you find yourself set upon, He is the fortress; if you hunger, he is the sustenance."[1]

From then on I rarely left the house except even more accompanied and on guard because, while I was almost free of the residency, my enemies were more and more dissatisfied and fearful of me.

As it happened, early that very night a good man came to my house to speak to me privately. He said: "Sir, you were closer to the truth than any of those who said the writer was not your friend for not speaking more plainly in the letter. I was the writer and if you want proof, here is another I wrote in case the first message did not get to your hands. I decided to let you know what is happening so that you can be on guard." I replied:

"Friend, I recognized your handwriting, guessed the truth, and waited for nightfall to call you here or to seek you out. I am well aware that you would not say anything but the truth for, as a perfect friend and gentleman, it would be beneath you to do otherwise. You have well seen that, as far as possible, I have been happy to honor and favor you and I want you to know that you have a good friend in me. Knowing that, tell me precisely what danger I am in, for in addition to serving God, you will repay the goodwill I have always had toward you. All this will be held in the strict secrecy your honor and life require." In this manner, I spoke to him with all the sweet talk I could muster. This man was a citizen of Santa María for whom I had done good things and who was pained at my tribulations.

After I made my exhortation he replied:

Sir, if justice here were not so perverted I would not worry if it were known that I warned you. But, the times being what they are, you must keep this secret, as from what I will tell you, you will see how important it is for you. What I know is that three nights ago Simón Bernal, who stabbed you, and Julián Guitérrez, a servant of Bachelor Corral, came to town from the country and about midnight near the Church of Saint Sebastián Bernal spoke to Juan Rodríguez Ortolano who, because of the heat, was at the door of the jail where he is prisoner. Simón Bernal carried a crossbow loaded with a heavy dart and Julián had a sword in his hand. Juan Rodríguez said to Simón Bernal: "Watch your step; you are sentenced to death for what you did and the minute they capture you, you will be hanged. Remember you are standing not twenty paces from where you wounded the inspector." To this Julián Guitérrez responded: "God knows I have told him that many times and that he should consider it and get away from here." Then Simón Bernal said: "I know that I am sentenced to death but I swear to God that I will shoot the dart in this crossbow or another into the inspector's chest one night while he stands at that window of his house." Saying this, he pointed to a window that could be seen from there. (It was the window of my bedroom where many nights I stood undressed to cool off because of the heat.) Juan Rodríguez said to Simón: "That is crazy and you had

better mend your ways. Consider that your arrogance tempts
God's punishment. I see that you have not repented of your mis-
deed and that you do not realize where your sins will lead you,
especially when you are dealing with a man who has the money
to pursue you. Consider what you are doing and your danger."
Simón responded: "Let come what may; if I kill him everything
will turn out well." Then he and Julián turned and entered the
city, leaving Juan Rodríguez. A little while later, I came by and
Juan Rodríguez related what I told you and said: "I would not tell
you anything of what Simón Bernal said to me except that I see
him determined to do evil to the inspector and to continue his
treacherous ways." Then he added: "If I were not in jail, I would
warn the inspector to ease my conscience because from here
many nights I see him standing at that window and that traitor
could easily kill him with a crossbow shot. It would weigh heavily
on my conscience not to warn him." So, sir, learning of this plot
and seeing Bernal's connection to the dean and your enemies and
since it is public knowledge that the governor dislikes you I dissimulated and told Juan Rodríguez that if Simón Bernal were
about surely he would pay for his sins. This, sir, is what you need
to be warned about. Take care not to stand at that window at
night and do whatever else you think necessary to ensure your
safety.

Then I said to him:

Well, you have done the best thing. Since good people are
obliged to aid their friends, for my sake do one thing for me: tell
Juan Rodríguez that you warned me and that he should know
that I have always regarded him as a friend. I know that he is in
jail for a claim against him for two hundred gold pesos by Diego
Rodríguez de Huelva, who is also my friend. I want to mediate
their differences and pay whatever default or balance is due to
make peace between them. If he wishes, I will place at his dis-
posal free and clear a gold bar from the mines worth two hundred castellanos, provided he lets me know the next time he sees
Simón Bernal or lets me know of his whereabouts.

My friend promised to tell him that and did, returning with his answer. Juan Rodríguez said he would do everything he could for friendship alone because he was sorry for my troubles and owed me that much.

From then on, I was on constant guard and determined to make every effort to find this man so desirous of my death. Each day or every third night after everyone had retired, I left the city to search for Bernal at my enemies' ranches (especially those of Bachelor Corral, the dean, and his band) within a radius of one to two leagues. Another night, my intimate friend Captain Juan de Ezcaray went out to search with other friends and some faithful servants of mine. That could not be kept secret and Simón, having seen us looking for him, withdrew to the city to take refuge in houses of the dean, his friends, and relatives. And so, for several days his whereabouts were unknown.

At this time, a caravel from Jamaica was in the harbor of Darién making ready to sail. When it was ready to depart, with a warrant that I had from the residency judge, I arranged for the caravel to be searched by a justice of the peace, Captain Juan de Ezcaray, some friends, and my servants. By chance they discovered Simón inside one of a pile of barrels covered over with hawsers and other things. The barrel had several small holes in it through which, from time to time, Simón would drip water so as to make it appear that the barrel contained liquid. By chance one of my servants knocked on it and, as it sounded hollow, he said: "The rogue could be in here." The captain and the justice had it opened and found the criminal, who was bound and brought to the prison. That day was seven and one-half months after I was wounded. Simón's arrest caused the dean as much grief as death itself.

The court ordered the prisoner guarded by Captain Juan de Ezcaray at my expense and then I notified the residency judge, who ordered Simón brought to Acla. The dean and his band, thinking to free him or at least tie up the matter, came up with all manner of objections to removing Simón from the city, alleging it was against the city's privileges. However, they had little success. Although several times they gathered in the dean's house to discuss saving him by force of arms, it came to nothing because without doubt they would have been fiercely resisted by the law and my friends. And so, in a brigantine I chartered, the justice of the peace and Captain Juan de Ezcaray with the necessary guard took Bernal to Acla. I sailed with them to procure justice. In the end, Simón confessed his crime and that it was premeditated. Further, he said that when he had requested to enter my household it was to kill me as I slept or in some other manner. He implicated a cleric who had put him up to the assault because as judge I arrested the cleric for thievery and would have punished this man had he not fled to the church.

The judge revoked the death sentence he had imposed in absentia, ordering instead the loss of Bernal's right hand and left foot, perpetual exile from the Indies, the confiscation of his assets to the royal treasury, and payment of costs. Both Simón and I accepted the sentence; it was carried out, and he was returned to jail for the costs. They nailed his foot and hand to the same stake in the plaza where Adelantado Vasco Núñez de Balboa's head had been placed.

The sentence was carried out on Saturday and the following day, Sunday, after mass, the judge, another person with him, and I were walking through the plaza. As we came to that stake Pedrarias's messenger came galloping up and announced in a loud voice: "Gentlemen and all present, bear witness that I present this order of Governor Pedrarias Dávila, Lieutenant General, to Licentiate Juan Rodríguez de Alarconcillo, Judge of Residency." The messenger requested the delivery be formally witnessed by a notary who was present. The licentiate, in view of the messenger's vehemence and formality stopped in the plaza and read the order. Then he said to the messenger: "Calm down, you must have slept en route for you arrive too late." His reply was, "Whether or not I slept, your honor, order an affidavit stating what time I arrived here. I left Panamá after vespers and it must now be three or four hours after dawn." So it seems that in two days or a little more than one and a half days he had covered forty leagues of bad road.

The judge turned to me and said: "Inspector, did you hear what this young man said and have you read the order?" I was at his side and read it as he did. I responded:

Sir, I have seen what it says. Take note where this order reached you, four or five paces from the stake where yesterday you had placed the hand and foot of the traitor Simón Bernal. This happened so that you and we may recognize the superiority of the Sovereign Judge on high over those of earth. It was no more in your power to fail to do justice than it was in Pedrarias's to try to prevent it and reveal his constant and notorious enmity against me by trying to remove this affair from your hands to let the traitor escape. Tomorrow or soon thereafter I will depart for Panamá to officially protest to him in no uncertain terms before all his gentlemen of what he has done and continues to do to me.

Then the licentiate ordered the notary to publicly read the order. In effect, Pedrarias's order said that, inasmuch as he was informed that Simón had stabbed me and was arrested, he ordered Licentiate Alarconcillo, his lieutenant, and whatever other judge might be involved in the case on receipt of his order not to proceed further but to refer the matter to him for review and decision. The governor took over the case and suspended the licentiate and any other judge from proceeding under pain of certain penalties. The licentiate drew up an official declaration recusing himself, stating that he would not have passed sentence if the governor's order had arrived earlier and referring to the governor anything else pertaining to the criminal and the case.

I then requested an official statement of the referral and the licentiate's response and declared that I had not proceeded against that traitor and his band as the governor's lieutenant but in my capacity as residency judge and their majesties' royal magistrate and as such it was not within the governor's purview. Further, I declared that because of that traitor I had spent two thousand gold pesos, which I would claim from the governor and Licentiate Alarconcillo if the criminal were not securely detained until I recovered my costs and losses. Further, I made it known that if justice had not been executed on the person of that traitor and the suspension order had been effected I would have been notoriously aggrieved by the delay. Further, since the judge had recused himself and presently there was no judge, and as such it was impossible for me to seek justice against other guilty parties, I considered myself aggrieved. I formally declared that if the guilty parties left, absented themselves, transported, or sold their assets in such a way that I could not recover losses from them, I would demand reimbursement from the governor, Licentiate Alarconcillo, and their assets, and from whomever the law allowed at the time, place, and manner before whomever was competent to hear the case. All this was written down and notarized.

CHAPTER XX—HOW THE AUTHOR LEFT ACLA PRE-
TENDING TO GO TO PANAMÁ TO COMPLAIN TO THE
GOVERNOR AND WENT INSTEAD TO SPAIN TO CLAIM
JUSTICE AGAINST PEDRARIAS; HOW OUR LORD EM-
PEROR ORDERED HIM HEARD AND A CORDOVAN
KNIGHT, PEDRO DE LOS RÍOS, WAS APPOINTED NEW
GOVERNOR OF CASTILLA DEL ORO; AND OF OTHER
ITEMS PERTINENT TO THE HISTORY.

On July 3, 1523, I embarked on the brigantine in which I had taken the traitor Simón Bernal from Darién to Acla. I pretended to be going to Panamá to complain to the governor of how notoriously he had acted against me in his order that denied me justice. The day after I left the port of Acla I secretly arranged with the ship's master to change course to that of the island route to Cuba, Jamaica, and Hispaniola. On the voyage I came down with constant fevers and other symptoms that weakened me so much that I did not think I would arrive alive. But it pleased God that on July 17 I landed at Santiago, Cuba, where I was warmly received by Adelantado Diego Velázquez.[1] My fevers ceased and, feeling better, after eight days in Cuba I sailed to the port of Yaguana in Hispaniola. From Yaguana I traveled overland eighty leagues to Santo Domingo, where I rested for fifteen or twenty days. There I found Admiral Don Diego Columbus with three ships ready to sail to Spain because our lord emperor had ordered him to come to court. The admiral treated me very kindly and took me with him on his ship. We set sail on September 16 and arrived at Sanlúcar de Barrameda, Spain, on November 5 of the same year.

In Seville I found out through letters from Tierra Firme that the traitor Simón Bernal had died of tetanus three or four days after I left Acla. Pray God that his death was such as to allow him time to save his soul, for he did as much evil to himself as to me.

I stayed in Seville a few days and then left for court. In Burgos I found the Royal Council of the Indies, which soon moved to Vitoria, where the emperor was. At that time his constable, Don Iñigo de Velasco, was besieging Fuenterrabia, occupied by the French since 1521 or 1522 during the Comunero Revolt.

There I informed his Caesarean majesty and the gentlemen of the

Royal Council of the Indies of my tribulations, entered a complaint against Pedrarias, and reported on the affairs of Tierra Firme. By virtue of the commission I had from the city of Darién, I procured from his majesty a new governor for that land. The latter mission took some time because Bachelor Corral, whom I had sent under arrest to Spain, was there representing Pedrarias and entered a complaint against me saying that I should not have deported him and that I had refused the appeal of his case to the governor. Finally I was ordered to pay one hundred thousand maravedís for costs (which I paid him in Spain) and to pay him damages for losses he might have suffered to his assets. For the determination of damages we were remitted to Tierra Firme to the new residency judge who was being sent there. Nevertheless, the bachelor was not absolved of the crimes for which I deported him. My litigation lasted more than two years because Doña Isabel de Bobadilla, Pedrarias's wife, his agents, and Bachelor Corral were all at court obstructing me and seeking to block Pedrarias's removal. During that time, Pedrarias, angered by the commission the city of Darién had given me, went there and effectively depopulated it so that it is now abandoned, being once the finest Christian settlement that there was in Tierra Firme. He defamed the city, writing falsely that it was unhealthy in order to destroy it because he hated it, as my history has related. Pedrarias acted as he did as much because Adelantado Vasco Núñez founded it as he did to destroy me. Thus, I lost my home and a good part of my assets.

In the end, in spite of the opposition I encountered and the influence of Pedrarias and his wife, they were not able to stop our lord emperor from replacing him as governor of Tierra Firme with a Cordovan knight named Pedro de los Ríos. His majesty named Licentiate Juan de Salmerón to go as the new governor's chief justice and residency judge. And so, in 1526 in Seville this governor was dispatched along with his wife, Doña Catalina de Saavedra, to help him establish his household. He departed in two ships and a caravel with about two hundred men and I went with him to pursue my complaints against Pedrarias as well as those other complaints in my charge. By chance Bachelor Corral and I were on the same ship. Since we had become friends (or at least we were speaking to each other), from Spain to Tierra Firme we ate at the same table. I thought the litigation between us was over with the one hundred thousand maravedís I paid him (even though I should not have had to) and from the moment I spoke to him I determined not to dwell on his crimes and excesses as long as he did not bring up past matters to curry favor with Pedrarias.

The bachelor was as pained as I was over the loss of our houses and assets in Darién. Doubtless, if we had combined forces to recoup our losses from Pedrarias he would have had to pay great sums to us and as much to the king, more money than he was worth. But Bachelor Corral thought he could collect more easily from me and five or six days after landing in Nombre de Dios he sued me for eight thousand pesos before the residency judge, claiming that because I sent him prisoner to Spain he had lost his assets. Moreover, he incited and helped the mother of the woman I had ordered flogged and her teeth removed because she falsely accused her husband. Her complaint was concluded in Spain by the gentlemen of the council and referred to the residency judge Juan de Salmerón for decision and sentence. It seems that the bachelor was after me on his own behalf as well as that of others. The woman's suit was dismissed and I was absolved. I responded to the bachelor that he seek his damages from Pedrarias, who depopulated Darién. Then I countersued Corral for the twenty thousand pesos I had lost because he and the dean were responsible for my tribulations and because he incited the mutiny among the people I was sending against Chief Bea, the murderer of Captain Martín de Murga and the other Christians. Further, I declared that when the city was on guard against Corral's Chief Corobari, the bachelor was negotiating with the chief at his ranch, as he freely admitted before I had him burned at the stake. As a result, the bachelor had been an accomplice in the same treachery and ought to be punished as was the chief. I charged that Darién was depopulated because the bachelor's concubine, Elvira, mother of his son and close relative of Chiefs Bea and Corobari, was there. His house was full of Indians who served as spies of Corobari, with whom the bachelor had dealings, friendship, and conversation. Fearing the Indians, many citizens had abandoned the city because of the notorious danger related to the bachelor's household. They had lost their properties and I mine, which were much greater and better than Bachelor Corral's.

As this litigation dragged on, by means of some good persons who intervened to mediate, we agreed to put his suit and my countersuit before the same residency judge for determination, whatever his finding might be. The judge denied both claims and ordered the litigation halted from that time forth under threat of heavy penalties. So, it all came to an end, each party much the poorer and each thinking himself aggrieved. It all ended in silence, with much loss for both parties.

In truth, neither in Bachelor Corral nor in me was the prudence of which Saint Antonio, Archbishop of Florence, writes concerning two soldiers named Guillermo de Brindiz and Raimundo Guasco.[2] Both were prisoners of the Tartars, who ordered them to fight each other to the death to entertain their cruel spectators, telling them that the victor would earn much praise. But, as those knights were good Christians and knew that the victor would be killed (because Tartars never tell the truth), these Catholic knights talked it over and decided that their combat would be directed toward the infidel Tartars. And so, both of them fell on the onlookers, killing fifteen and gravely wounding thirty others. Thus it is related by the above-named Holy Doctor.

So if Bachelor Corral and I had united against Pedrarias and his schemes, he would not have destroyed Darién while we were absent at court engaged in our litigation. Had he known we were in conformity, he would not have dared it, and our and others' assets would not have been lost. I thought that the bachelor, seeing the loss of his house, sought my friendship entirely because of his own interest, but he imagined it easier to collect from me what he lost than from the governor and, in the end, it was left to me alone to fight Pedrarias, my fight with the bachelor winding up as I have said.

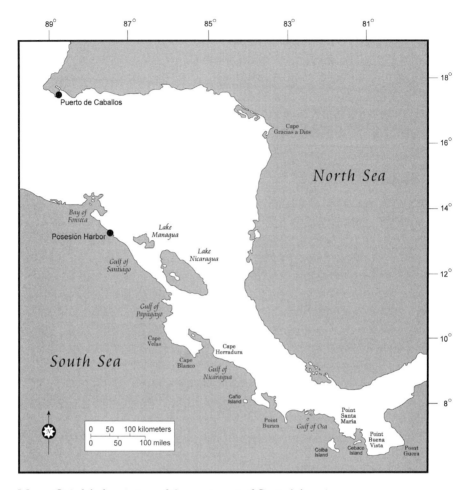

Map 5. Oviedo's description of the west coast of Central America.

CHAPTER XXI—WHICH TREATS OF SOME NOTABLE
THINGS THAT TRANSPIRED IN TIERRA FIRME BE-
TWEEN GOVERNOR PEDRARIAS DÁVILA AND CAPTAIN
GIL GONZÁLEZ DE AVILA AND OTHER CAPTAINS
WHILE I WAS IN SPAIN NEGOTIATING THE ARRIVAL
OF THE NEW GOVERNOR, PEDRO DE LOS RÍOS, TO
REPLACE PEDRARIAS; THE REPORT OF CAPTAIN GIL
GONZÁLEZ'S DISCOVERIES IN THE SOUTH SEA AND
ALONG ITS COAST; AND BECAUSE THE NARRATIVE IS
LENGTHY, THIS CHAPTER IS DIVIDED INTO EIGHT
SECTIONS.

Reader, you should recall, if you have followed the narrative, how Pedrarias, having been removed from the governorship of Castilla del Oro or,
at least, Lope de Sosa having been appointed in his place, was very angry
with me. Also you will have seen by what schemes he plotted my tribulations, how I was treacherously wounded, and how, with just cause, I
determined to spend all that I had seeking justice in Spain and requesting
a new governor. You will remember how, at last, that very just prince, his
Caesarean majesty, gave the office and governorship of Castilla del Oro
to Pedro de los Ríos. As I have said, in 1526 the latter went to Tierra
Firme and I accompanied him to demand justice in what remained to be
determined. But before I proceed further with that, it is important to the
history to recount certain notable and pertinent things that transpired
during my absence in Tierra Firme from 1523 to 1526 concerning Pedrarias
and Captain Gil González de Avila and other captains.

I.

In Chapter XIV I reported how Gil González had gone off to explore the
South Sea with a fleet piloted by Andrés Niño. About the time I left Acla
for Spain, Captain Gil González returned from his journey to Panamá
with gold and the report of his discoveries. He had found a very large lake
thought to be a freshwater sea in the province of Nicaragua, where he had
converted and baptized many thousands of Indians. After his return to
Panamá, some ninety thousand pesos of the gold he brought were melted
down and the King's Fifth subtracted to send to Spain. Pedrarias tried to
obstruct him, saying that Gil González wanted to bring the king's gold

to this city of Santo Domingo but if there were any disaster or loss the governor would be accountable if he did not take charge of the more than fifteen thousand pesos comprising the Fifth. Gil González said that he had won it with great effort on his expedition with men under his command, taking it, lance in hand, from the infidel enemies, so that transporting it through friendly lands and seas already subject to his majesty was nothing in comparison. He said that he would safeguard and be responsible for the gold and, if necessary, would go in person to court to take it to his majesty and give a report of his expedition.

Pedrarias rejected this and put up all sorts of obstructions to keep control of the gold or place it in control of whomever he would send but, in the end, Gil González departed with the gold and went to the port city of Nombre de Dios. Pedrarias greatly regretted having let him go and set out to arrest him and take the gold; however, when Pedrarias arrived at Nombre de Dios, he found that Gil González had already set sail. Thus, Gil González came to this city of Santo Domingo on the Island of Hispaniola and from here he sent Treasurer Andrés de Cereceda to Spain to deliver the King's Fifth and report his discoveries because Cereceda had been present at them. I will now recount as briefly as possible Gil González's discoveries, as they are integral to the history.

II.

I have said that Adelantado Vasco Núñez de Balboa was the first to reveal the South Sea to the Christians. Likewise, I have written of how, after his execution, Licentiate Espinosa, chief justice and Pedrarias's lieutenant, was sent in Vasco Núñez's ships to explore the South Sea and its coast. In Chapter XIII, I reported the latitudes of what Espinosa saw of that sea, its coasts, and islands on that voyage piloted by Juan de Castañeda. The third Spaniard to sail the South Sea was Captain Ferdinand Magellan when in 1520 he discovered the eastern entrance of the great strait that he passed through to the South Sea and then went on to the Moluccas and Spice Islands (also reported in Book XX). The fourth captain and explorer of the South Sea coast was Captain Gil González de Avila, along with his pilot Andrés Niño. I will report what was added to modern cosmography by his efforts, which I have seen in the emended chart of the famous cosmographer Alonso de Chaves.[1] I do not fault Chaves for the discrepancies in the degrees because he did not actually see the area. But,

I am obliged to believe or rather testify to what my own eyes saw rather than what others, who did not sail there, pretend to show me.

Previously, I reported that the furthest Licentiate Espinosa and Juan de Castañeda explored was to see the mouth of the Gulf of Sanlúcar (more exactly called the Gulf of Orotiña), which they did not enter.[2] They did not go beyond that inlet, which lies between the promontories of Herradura and Cape Blanco. To that gulf from point to point along the coast is more or less one hundred eighty leagues, although our pilots say two hundred. The exploration from there on is credited to another fleet under Captain Gil González de Avila. Andrés Niño went on at least one hundred leagues or a maximum of one hundred twenty farther than Licentiate Espinosa to Fonseca Bay, since point to point along the coast it would be a little more, but certainly not the six hundred fifty leagues from Panamá of which Gil González and Andrés Niño boasted. Gil González said that he had marched three hundred twenty leagues by land, from which point he returned with one hundred and twelve thousand pesos the chiefs gave him, more than half of it gold of very poor quality. He wrote me that, at the Indians' voluntary request, thirty-two thousand or more souls had been baptized. However, it seems to me that those newly converted to the faith misunderstood it, for, in the end, Gil González and his men had to leave the land in some hurry. They found large settlements and discovered a huge lake they thought was a freshwater sea along whose shores there are a great multitude of towns and Indians. When I went to that land later I examined the area better and know it in some detail. Farther on when the territory of Nicaragua is discussed, much more information will be given than what these expeditioners saw, though they should not be denied praise for their labors. Now let us return to their expedition, which, in truth, was a good deal less than how Andrés Niño and Gil González painted it and not less than that which I will attribute to them.

III.

Gil González built four ships in the Balsa River, which were not seaworthy and were all lost. In this endeavor he spent much time, money, and effort. Later he built four more on the Perlas Islands in the Gulf of San Miguel, from which this fleet sailed on January 21, 1522. After sailing about one hundred leagues west the sailors reported that all the water casks leaked so badly they had to be replaced; moreover, the vessels were badly infested with shipworms. They were obliged to careen the ships in the best location they could find and to off-load all they contained to repair the damage. Some years later the chief of Burica had reason to lament this visit because these repairs were made in his territory and greatly to his and his people's cost as Andrés Niño and his sailors committed many outrages there.[3] Later, Andrés Niño paid with his head when the Indians killed him, as will be reported in the appropriate place.

From that point they sent a brigantine to Panamá for pitch and other supplies. The company did not have enough provisions to sustain itself where the ships were beached. So to conserve supplies needed for the voyage, it was necessary for Gil González and one hundred men to move inland and live off the land while new water casks were made, the pitch arrived, and repairs were made. Also, they went to begin the search for gold, which was their principal objective, since, for a fleet financed by many purses, not surprisingly the greedy desire to fill them was not incidental but rather the main intent of the backers. Gil González proceeded west into the interior and several times found himself so far from the coast that he repented of his decision. He left instructions with Andrés Niño, who remained with the ships, that once the repairs were made he should sail along the coast to the west and after eighty or one hundred leagues, if Niño arrived first he was to wait for the expedition at the best harbor he found. Gil González would do likewise if he arrived first.

As Gil González moved inland foraging and baptizing many chiefs and Indians, it happened that from fording many rivers on foot and sweating, his leg became suddenly paralyzed. The pain was such that he could neither walk a step nor ride nor sleep day or night. For many days they carried him in a litter made from a blanket tied to a pole, sometimes shouldered by Indians, sometimes by Christians. Because of the constant rains, carrying the litter became too difficult and they stopped at the house of a principal chief, taking great care to post watch. The chief's village was on an island ten leagues long and six wide formed by two branches of a powerful river. Gil González lodged in the chief's house, which was as tall as a medium-size tower made like a pavilion set up on posts and covered with thatch. In the middle of the house they constructed a hut for Gil González, on posts ten feet high because of the damp.

During the fifteen days they were there, it rained so much and the river rose so high the entire island was inundated. The water rose chest high in the house on the highest part of the island where the captain was. Some Spaniards asked and received the captain's permission to leave the village and seek shelter in the trees. He, however, remained in the big house with some more faithful men awaiting God's will and thinking that the water would not pull the house down, all the while fearfully watching the water rise without any end in sight. In this peril, they had placed an image of Our Lady illuminated by an oil lamp in the highest part of the house. Every hour came more comrades who found no better shelter outside or in other parts. At midnight all the support posts gave way and the house collapsed on those in it. The captain's hut fell down, and he was left standing on top of it on two crutches up to his thighs in water. The roof beams settled to the floor, where the soldiers were chest deep in water.

It pleased God that, in spite of the impact of hitting the water, the house settled so slowly to the ground that the Virgin's lamp was not put out. It was a great help to have some light to find their way out of there without drowning, as they were like birds or mice in a trap. The companions who stayed with the captain escaped by cutting a hole in the roof with a hatchet and took out the captain on their shoulders because the others with Gil González's permission and the Indian servants had previously managed to attain the safety of the trees. Carrying the captain on their shoulders, they shouted for their companions to come help. After they regrouped with great effort, they put the captain in a hammock or blanket stretched between two trees and awaited daybreak in the rain, thunder, and lightning. This was their state until the rain stopped and the rivers subsided to their normal channels. Fearing that the rains would return, they constructed small huts in the trees of sticks and branches in which they could light fires. They used these huts during two more floods when they had to leave the houses closer to the ground. Afterward the ground was so covered with slime, mud, and trees washed down by the river that they could walk there only with the greatest difficulty.

In these tribulations, they suffered great losses; they lost some swords, bucklers, and clothing. To replace the lost bucklers they made others of padded cotton. Because the waters carried off their food supplies, they were forced to seek food toward the coast some ten leagues off. Since they could not go by land, they floated downriver to the sea on a fleet of rafts they made of trees tied together on which they loaded their baggage, themselves, and the Indian servants, more than five hundred souls in all. Some of the companions reached the mouth of the river at midnight and the current swept them out to sea, the outgoing tide many times pulling the rafts under the water. The next day those on shore saw them two leagues offshore, and as the ebb tide took them out the flood tide was bringing them back. Seeing them in such danger, the captain sent out small rafts with strong swimmers to bring them in. The rescuers found them totally exhausted, demoralized, and resigned to death, but it pleased God that no one was lost. Surely they must have thought many times of how much less dangerous it was when they earned their bread in their own country. However, these are things men are wont to do; not all men, of course, only the most courageous.

Once the captain and his men were reunited, they marched west along the coast to a small gulf called San Vicente, where they found Andrés Niño, who had just arrived with the ships repaired and with new water casks. Captain Gil González's first thought was to continue his exploration by sea, as his legs did not permit walking or riding, and to send a lieutenant to lead the land exploration. But when the men learned of the plan, they began to grumble and complain that he was abandoning his company. The expeditioners had begun to come upon greater chiefs than previous ones, increasing their expectations of finding gold, which could be better accomplished by land than by sea. To please the soldiers and because matters of war and peace would be better managed in person, he agreed to stay on land and go forward with one hundred men and four horses. He ordered one of his lieutenants with Andrés Niño and two other pilots to measure and record the leagues covered on the expedition. And so they would continue on a westerly course by land and sea with the intention of establishing peaceful relations through good treatment with all the chiefs they came upon and waging war on those who did not wish peace. Two ships remained at the Gulf of San Vicente with some men to guard the forty thousand gold pesos already collected. Andrés Niño went ahead to explore with the other ships while Gil González proceeded by land. They agreed to meet back at the same harbor.

This Gulf of San Vicente, if I am not mistaken, is at the point or promontory near Caño Island. The promontory is at eight and one-half degrees north and marks the entrance to the gulf or inlet whose northernmost point is nine degrees north. Within this inlet are several small islands.[4]

IV.

Along the sea and land routes they followed, many chiefs and Indians were baptized of their own volition. Gil González came to the lands of a chief called Nicoya, who gave him fourteen thousand pesos worth of gold.[5] Nicoya and six thousand or more persons were baptized and became such good friends of the Christians, our Spaniards, in the ten days they were there that when Gil González was preparing to leave the chief told him that since they no longer had to talk with their idols he should take them with him. He freely gave the captain all he wished to take, six gold statues a hand-span high and a few others somewhat larger. Nicoya begged Gil González to leave one of our Christians behind to tell them about God, but Gil González did not want to risk a man's life, besides which he had few enough men as it was.

Gil González told me that from that Gulf of San Vicente to Nicoya they marched fifty leagues. In truth, there are many fewer leagues than that but I am not surprised by the error as then those lands were unexplored.

At Nicoya, Gil González heard of Chief Nicaragua and the many principal Indians he had. The Indians of Nicoya advised him not to go there because Nicaragua was very powerful and even the Spaniards advised the same, but the captain refused to be afraid without seeing for himself and so continued on. A day's journey from Nicaragua's settlement, he sent ahead his interpreters and six principal Indians who accompanied him to tell the chief what was usually said to other chiefs, which was that he was a captain of the great king of the Christians sent by him to those parts to inform all principal Indians and their masters that in the sky far beyond the sun is a Lord who made the sun, moon, heavens, and stars; men, animals, and birds; seas, rivers, and fish; and all other things. Those who believe and acknowledge Him as Lord are the Christians, who when they die ascend to where He is and delight in His glory. Those not Christians when they die descend to a fiery place below the earth to suffer forever. All the lords, chiefs, or principals (called *calachuni* in that language), whom the Spaniards encountered previously in the lands of the rising sun, informed of these truths by him and other captains, believed and accepted the king of Castile as their lord, as did the captain and his Christians. The other Indians had become Christians and declared themselves the king of Castile's vassals, and Gil González was coming to inform the *calachunis* and princes in the direction of the setting sun of these truths because God so ordered it. Gil González requested Nicaragua to attend him in his town with all his people and not be afraid. He would tell him many other great things of this very God that he would take much pleasure in knowing. If he refused these beliefs or to become a vassal of the great king of the Christians, he should prepare to do battle, for the captain would be there the next day.

The afternoon of that same day, three musketeers were badly burned when the gunpowder they were testing set fire to their lodging and that of the captain. This accident happening on the eve of their departure for Nicaragua caused great anxiety among all the others.[6] The captain, as the spirited knight he was, addressed them, telling them not to be afraid nor show weakness as they were Spaniards and from a nation that produces valiant hearts. He reminded them that when Count Fernán González was about to do battle with King Almanzor and his Moors the earth suddenly opened up and swallowed a Christian knight, but in spite of this the count did not fail to conquer and was more victorious than ever.[7] He said that he expected them to be victorious as well, if it came to a battle. Moreover, he reminded them that such accidents happened every day to those who deal with gunpowder, but fortunately their companions would live. And so, with his courageous speech, their confidence was restored and their spirits readied for anything that might happen.

The captain left behind the three musketeers to convalesce with another man to look after them, and the next day marched to within a league of Nicaragua's village, where he came upon four principal Indians with the others the captain had sent ahead. The four Indians told him that the chief awaited him in his village in peace and friendship. Upon arrival, the captain and his men were lodged in houses around a plaza. The chief presented Gil González part of the fifteen thousand pesos total he was to give him. The captain reciprocated with a silk garment, a scarlet cap, a shirt of fine Dutch linen, and other Castilian items. After two or three days of evangelization, the chief said that he wished to become Christian along with his wives and Indians. And so, in one day more than nine thousand were baptized, all displaying such willingness that some of our soldiers wept out of pleasure and devotion and thanked God for what they were seeing.

The captain and his men were there eight days and, as they were accustomed to do in other towns, put up two crosses. They set up a big one on a large, stepped, earthen platform. These structures were in all the plazas as if begging for a cross. The chief wished the other cross placed in their temple and he carried it there himself. Neither Gil González nor the Christians understood then what these platforms were for, but they were for human sacrifice, as will be explained later when the territory of Nicaragua is addressed. (The Nicaraguans speak the same language as that of Mexico and New Spain.)

Eight days later, Gil González went on to another province six leagues away, where he found six villages one to one and a half or two leagues apart, each of about two thousand persons. After he sent out his messengers to them, he lodged in one of the villages, and the Indian lords came to see him presenting gold, slaves, and food for the Christians. As they knew that Nicaragua and his Indians had been baptized, they said that they also wished to be Christians and each lord with his people came to receive baptism. Every day all the other villages then requested Gil González to send them the chaplain to baptize them and tell them about God, each village competing to receive the chaplain first.

In the midst of this good work, it seems that other great chiefs farther away had news of our Spaniards and how they were presented *taguizte* ("gold" in their language). One of them called Diriajen came to see Gil González with almost five hundred men, each with one or two turkeys in hand. Behind them came ten pennant bearers with small white flags on poles and behind them seventeen women almost covered with gold plaques and two hundred some small hatchets of low-grade gold, all together worth eighteen thousand pesos. Behind them came the chief and his principal Indians surrounded by five trumpeters (more like fifers actually) who played a while near Captain Gil González's lodging. After they finished playing, everyone with the women and the gold entered to see the captain. The captain ordered that they be asked their purpose in coming and they responded they wanted to see who the Spanish were. They had been told that the Spanish were armed men who went about on top of four-footed animals and came to see who they were and what they wanted. After putting the gold in safekeeping, Gil González had the interpreters give them the same speech made to Nicaragua, the usual one he made to the Indians, and they responded that they wished to be Christians. They were asked when they wished baptism and replied that they would return for it in three days.

One presumes these Spaniards who preached our Catholic faith to the

Indians did not speak of the Christ's and his apostles' disdain for gold and temporal wealth, their principal intent being the salvation of souls; nor did the apostles bear knives, powder, horses, or other equipment for war and bloodletting. Take note of what the Apostle Saint Bartholomew did when he was selected to evangelize Laconia and the East Indies and later on the other apostles who only accepted food wherever they went, nothing else.[8] But our "converters" took their gold, even women, children, and other belongings, leaving the Indians nominally baptized and with no understanding of the sacrament they received. Pray God that of each thousand so baptized there were ten who understood what it was about.

Be it as it may, the devil is not pleased by the name Christian nor does he want to see men's salvation and one could imagine that he would seek to avert the Indians from the purpose of their baptisms. Likewise, one could imagine that the Indians noted the small number of our Spaniards. The third day, Saturday, April 17, when the Indians said they would come, was blisteringly hot. The priest had gone off on the best of the four horses with two brave companions to preach at some nearby villages and the remaining Spaniards had let down their guard. Suddenly at noon about four thousand Indians attacked Captain Gil González and his men. They were armed according to their fashion in sleeveless doublets, breastplates, and helmets of padded cotton; some bore strong wooden swords and bucklers, some bows and arrows (but not poisoned), and others javelins.[9] Thank God, when they were about a crossbow shot away, an Indian of the village where the Christians were saw them and gave the alarm. As fast as he could, the captain mounted one of the three horses and mustered the soldiers in the plaza in front of their quarters, putting a third of them facing the rear and flanks because there were so many enemy they feared being surrounded and burned out. The Indians vigorously attacked the Christians in the plaza, who responded in kind, fighting hand-to-hand as in a tournament with as much force as they were able. For a few minutes, the outcome of the battle was in doubt. Six or seven Spaniards were on the ground gravely wounded and the Indians carried off another alive, apparently not wishing to kill him there. Finally, the Indians were routed when the horsemen entered the melee, running them down and spearing them. This action encouraged the foot soldiers, who drove them from the village at lance point. The captain on the best of the remaining horses, although it was hastily and poorly saddled, was among the first to chase them into the countryside, all the while encouraging our soldiers and doing his duty as a good leader. He exhausted himself lancing the Indians he came upon here and there, but then, thinking it a mistake to leave his people so far behind, he turned back. He rode back through a hail of Indian spears, arrows, and stones, a situation more dangerous than when the Indians were driven from the plaza.

Returning to the first line of companions who were pursuing the Indians, the captain ordered them to fall back to the village. Because they were few in number the captain feared that the Indians would suspect all the Spaniards were in the field and would regroup and attack again. He was also concerned that the villagers, seeing them outside the town, would seize the opportunity to steal the gold stored in their lodging. And so, as fast as they could, they withdrew victorious, thanking God. Back in the village they regrouped against a possible second attack, which did not come because the Indians were occupied in gathering their dead and wounded from the fields.

Since the priest and his companions had not returned from the village, which was in the direction of the Indian attack, it was feared they had been killed. The captain sent a villager to them with a hastily written note relating what had happened and telling them to return as soon as possible. The chaplain and his two companions rushed back without encountering anyone who bothered them.

At that point, they decided to return to the ships. As much as the company had come that far unwillingly, the men, officers, and principal Spaniards urged a return to the coast, seeing that the captain that night had in mind the contrary. The captain recognized that he ought to concede to the men's wishes and he wished to safeguard what they had gained up to then. The company was worn out, some companions were wounded and others sick, and there was a desire not to risk the accumulated gold. Moreover, they did not trust the villagers. They thought that after they got back to Christian lands (although far away) they could return with more men and horses to punish and pacify those people as well as explore the land's secrets because no one could see it without thinking it very promising.

V.

When Chief Nicaragua found out that Gil González was returning after battling Chief Diriajen and his allies and that the Spaniards were carrying quantities of gold, he planned to take the gold and kill the Spaniards as they passed through his village. Captain Gil González suspected as much and formed his about sixty able-bodied men into a squadron, in the center of which he placed the gold, the sick, and the supplies. He then stationed a horseman and a musketeer at each of the four corners of the squadron. In this manner they passed through the village at eleven o'clock, but once through it the Indians began to follow them, telling the Indian porters to drop their bundles or run off with them. The Spanish marched on, not wishing to start a fight, but some of the Nicaraguans boldly mixed in with our porters to separate them and their cargo from the squadron. At this provocation, the captain ordered the crossbowmen to fire on them, and when a few were wounded, suddenly many Indian warriors started running out of the village to attack. Gil González saw that he could not avoid a battle and ordered Treasurer Andrés de Cereceda, those guarding the supplies, and the Indians carrying the goods and clothing to march on as fast as possible. The captain, three other horsemen, some good foot soldiers, crossbowmen, shieldmen, and musketeers, about sixteen men in all, guarded the rear. Innumerable people, many with bows and arrows, sallied from the town, fiercely attacking with much shouting and discharging of a volley of arrows. The horsemen, musketeers, and crossbowmen made several charges and succeeded in wounding the nearest Indians. When the horsemen charged again, the Indians turned and fled as rapidly as the peasants in my part of Spain flee from the wild bulls of the banks of the Jarama River.[10] The horsemen, greatly amused at their fear of the horses, speared some of them. Men on horseback seemed to the Indians a great novelty; they had never seen such animals. Certainly for them there was no less shock than that of the centaurs at the wedding of Peirithous when they battled Hercules.[11] But, not withstanding their fear of the horses, there were so many Indians they seemed like swarms of bees.

Our men were completely worn out, but a combination of fear, effort, and their captain's prudent diligence kept them going until the sun set over a beautiful plain. The most fatiguing part was getting the wounded and the rearguard across several ravines and regrouping the Indian porters who abandoned their bundles.

Finally, as the enemy saw their losses and the uselessness of following the Christians, at sunset they sued for peace and Captain Gil González accepted. Laying aside their weapons, three principal Indians ordered the

rest to stay behind and came to parley with our men. They made excuses
for Nicaragua and his men, saying that the attack was the work of another
chief called Zoatega, who was in the town that day and whom the Spaniards had not seen when they went through there the first time. Gil González said for them to tell their *teite* (*calachuni* or chief) that he had recognized some of the principal Indians that day in battle. Further, they
should inform Nicaragua that all the Christians were *tapaligues*. (In those
lands, *tapaligue* means a veteran soldier, one who has killed an enemy in
hand-to-hand combat.) Nevertheless, Gil González said that he was content to make peace, but if the Indians wished otherwise he would continue the battle because Christians do not tire nor do they need *yaat*,
which is a certain plant the Indians chew, which they say is incomparable
in fighting fatigue. The Indians did not know how to respond to this and
walked away saying: "*teba, teba, teba, xuya.*" *Teba* means "good" and *xuya*
means "go away." So, all together it meant something like "You speak
the truth and are valiant, go with God." Speaking to the other Indians,
the three principals said over and over: "*Toya, toya,*" meaning "depart,"
"leave," and so they all did, returning to their village. It pleased God that
no man and none of the gold was lost and no one was injured except for
one horse slightly wounded by an arrow.

That night the company rested on a hill along their route after posting
heavy guard. They had lost a good deal of their clothing because most of
the Indian porters Nicaragua had lent them on their first visit, when they
saw that they were being taken away from their land, either abandoned
their bundles or ran off with them. Some of the company lost their clothing and others their provisions when they were occupied in guarding the
gold and the wounded, as ordered. The Indians who remained with them
were mostly Cuevan speakers from the eastern region who did not understand the western Indians and, because they were returning to their
land, they did not run away. In fact, many of them fought bravely alongside the Christians.

After five or six hours' rest, after midnight, the moon came out and
they resumed their march in order to cross a dangerous pass before daybreak. The enemy could reach it by another route so that if the Indians
got there first the passage would be difficult. Nevertheless, they were able
to go through unmolested. After several days' journey they came to the
Gulf of San Vicente, from which they had set out. Andrés Niño had
returned eight days earlier from his voyage of discovery. He reported that

he had sailed on from there three hundred fifty leagues to the west (although he was much mistaken in the distance). Niño had not gone farther than that because of his ships' conditions and lack of water.

In a letter he wrote me, Gil González reported that Chief Nicaragua's village three leagues inland from the South Sea is on another sea of fresh water that rises and falls.[12] He reported that he rode into the sea on horseback and took possession in the emperor's name. In the distance he saw a populated island two leagues from shore but time did not permit a closer examination.[13] Even though the north shore could not be seen, at first he thought it a river and had his men paddle out half a league to see which way the current ran. However, they found no indication of any current. His pilots insisted that there was an outlet to the North Sea but that was only a conjecture.

I am reminded of Pliny writing about the Scythians. He says that Alexander the Great wrote that the sea there was of fresh water.[14] Marcus Varro writes that the same was shown to Pompey when he was near there during the war with Mithridates. This sea is of fresh water, which is due to the large number of rivers that empty into it and dilute the salt water. I have previously reported how at low tide the water of the Gulf of Urabá is fresh and this could be what Alexander and Pompey saw. For the same reason Lake Nicaragua is fresh because its site is low and infinite rivers flow into it. In another section, I have already said that after Gil González was in Nicaragua I went there and saw this and other great lakes as well as many other things I will save for the appropriate place.[15]

Returning to Gil González: after he came to the Gulf of San Vicente he found the largest ship unseaworthy and embarked for Panamá in the others and in canoes. But now I will describe the geography of the coast, Andrés Niño's journey to the farthest point he sailed, and the inlet of the Gulf of Sanlúcar, which others call the Gulf of Nicaragua, others the Gulf of Orotiña, and still others the Gulf of Los Güetares (either of these last two is correct). I will describe what I saw and not what I find in our cosmographers' charts up to the present year of 1548. I will speak of the principal islands in this inlet, which Andrés Niño did not see, even though it was on his route. Nor did he enter the Gulf of Orotiña or Los Güetares, which Licentiate Espinosa and Pilot Juan de Castañeda called the Gulf of Sanlúcar but which they did not enter. Later a portion of that territory was populated with Christians by Captain Francisco Hernández, Pedrarias's lieutenant. Also, I will speak of the coast and the latitudes from there to the west, according to the modern chart and its corrections.

Licentiate Espinosa and Pilot Juan de Castañeda sailed twenty more leagues west from the Islands of San Lázaro. From those islands to Herradura harbor is twenty leagues along the coast west by north.[16] At that point commences the mouth of the Gulf of Los Güetares (which Espinosa called Sanlúcar), which forms an inlet eighteen or twenty leagues long and nine wide, more or less. This inlet contains beautiful, fertile, and populated islands. On the other side of this gulf, across from the Herradura harbor, is Cape Blanco (so called because the terrain is white and because of a nearby tall, white-tipped rock in the sea). Between the rock and Cape Blanco an eighty- to one-hundred-ton caravel can safely enter. Herradura harbor is at eight degrees north and Cape Blanco at seven and one-half, according to cosmographer Alonso de Chaves or whoever informed him.[17] To better understand the geography of the gulf I include a drawing as I remember it to be and encourage its emendation by anyone who knows it better.[18]

VI.

Now that I have described the Gulf of Orotiña (or Los Güetares), commonly called the Gulf of Nicaragua on the navigational charts by uninformed cosmographers who have not seen it, I wish to pass on to the rest of this gulf, which these discoverers did not report and which I saw. The Island of Chira has a circumference of seven or eight leagues and is very populous and fertile. When Gil González passed that way it had a population of more than five hundred warriors, not counting the elderly, women, and children. The island that the Spanish call Ciervos (deer) Island, the Indians call Cachoa because there and in the other islands are innumerable deer and pigs. Cachoa is smaller and lies between the islands of Chira and Chara off the northern coast of Tierra Firme.[19]

Facing Cachoa Island are the people and province of Orotiña and to the east the people and province of Chorotega. Behind to the north and northeast are the sierras and people called the Güetares. Between Cachoa Island and the coast toward the south is another small island called Irra, and more easterly another small island called Urco, and still farther east another small island named Pocosi near land in the southern part of the gulf. These three small islands lie between Tierra Firme and Ciervos Island (called Cachoa). From this gulf the tides penetrate three leagues up the Zapandi River, which enters the bottom of the gulf and where there lives a chief called Zapandi, the same as the river. Northwest of him is another chief called Corobici.[20]

The Güetares are very numerous. They live on the sierras above Herradura harbor extending west along the gulf coast in the northern zone to the territory of the Chorotegas. On the opposite gulf coast, the southern side, the closest river to the Zapandi is the Cange and farther east is the Paro River. In the lands of the chiefs of Cange, Niquia, and Nicoya (all residing along the gulf) there are many brazil trees. On Chara Island I found some of this wood, which the Indian women use to dye cotton or whatever they wish. I and the other Spaniards with me assumed the wood to be from the brazil tree; however, Chief Nari of Chara Island said they were trees about three feet high, which they call *nanci* and which abound in Nicoya, Masaya, Tecoatega, and much of Nicaragua. More particulars of this tree and its fruit are found in Book IX, Chapter XX. On Chira Island they make fine black clay pottery that looks like jet. The vessels are very beautiful to see and I brought some lovely pieces of it back to this city of Santo Domingo.

Chara Island the Christians call Sanlúcar. There and in Chira and other gulf islands the Indian women wear colored loin cloths, pieces of cotton cloth dyed and embroidered in many colors held in place by a string around their waist. This cloth is about two hand-spans wide. It hangs down from the string in back, then is pulled through the legs and up to be tucked into the string in front, covering the navel. In this way they cover their genital area but all the rest they leave bare.

The women part their long hair in the middle and then each side is tightly braided, falling over the ears. Sometimes it happens that the women for some problem or need observe that vow of Semiramis who, when Babylonia rebelled against her, refused to finish dressing her hair until the city was subjugated and returned to her obedience.[21] In the same way these Indian women when some need or service to their lord or husband comes up, first see to it before they braid their hair. And so I saw some of them with one side braided and the other loose like Semiramis. A tercet of Francisco Petrarca's *Triumph of Fame* recalls the story from that chronicle of the world: "Then I saw the magnificent queen, who with hair half braided and half loose rushed off to the ruin of Babylonia."[22] Justinus details this story at greater length, recounting that one day as Semiramis's hair was being dressed and only half of it was braided, she received the news of the Babylonian rebellion and immediately rushed off to arm herself against the rebels, refusing to finish the other half until the city was reduced.[23]

Returning to our history: these men and women of the Gulf of Nicoya and surrounding areas are very handsome and well-formed. The men tie up their hair with a cotton ribbon to form a braid down their back about a hand span in length or at least to the base of their skull. Others pull the hair straight up from the top of the head. The men wrap their foreskins in cotton twine so that their members are compressed to the point that on some you can only see the wrappings.[24] I asked them why they did this and they said that it was their custom and it was better to do this than let it hang loose like the Indians of Chira Island or like our horses.

On Chira Island I saw a two-year-old girl who was still nursing. Crying for her mother, who was occupied in household tasks, she said *mama* over and over. When I asked the chief what she was saying he replied that she was calling for her mother. The Charan Indians speak a different language but understand some Cuevan, which they have learned through the Christians. Chara Island probably has a circumference of four leagues.

There are pearls in all these islands. I saw some in Chara, Chira, and Pocosi and even found some in the oysters the Indians brought us to eat. Pocosi is a small island of about one league in circumference; I have walked around it. It has a deep and singular harbor about a musket shot from Tierra Firme. There is a small Indian village there and abundant supplies of fish.

In these islands there are shellfish the Christians call burro's foot, which are like very large and thick oysters, some containing pearls. The fishermen say that they are the best tasting of all. From its shell they make beautiful coral-like beads called *chuquira* for necklaces and bracelets. Some of the beads are purple and some white but, whatever the color, they are beautiful and fairly hard. The largest burro's feet are as big as a man's head.

There are also pearl-bearing shellfish called *nacarones*, which I reported in Book XIX, Chapter IX.[25] With this shell they make spades and also oars for their canoes or rafts. In Chara and Pocosi they do not have canoes, rather they use rafts made of four, five, or six tree trunks tied together at the ends with smaller trunks placed crosswise in the middle.

The ropes they use are of esparto grass similar to that of Castile, except that it is longer but not as strong. Nevertheless, it is strong enough to tie thatch to the roofs of their dwellings.

I examined these shellfish and pearls, especially those of Pocosi, while I was detained several days while a leaky caravel that was about to sink was repaired. There I experienced for the first time the very annoying winged bedbugs that infest the native dwellings. They come out at night in large numbers and are more troublesome and swift than those in Spain. They bite more and are larger than flying ants. If they excrete on the hammock or sheets, as they frequently do, or if you squash them as they surround you in bed they leave a stain the size of a fingernail as black as ink but worse because it cannot be removed with soap or bleach without wearing away a hole in the cloth the size of the stain. Nevertheless, these bugs do not stink. These insects infest the entire province and islands of Nicaragua.

In these islands the Indians eat many deer and wild pigs, which are extremely numerous, as well as diverse kinds of corn and beans, excellent seafood, and also toads. I have found the toads tied up in their houses and seen them roasted and eaten. There is nothing alive they do not eat, however filthy it may be. They have many fruits that I will not stop now to describe because I will speak of them later when I detail other things about Nicaragua, especially that fruit they call *paco,* which is a very singular thing.[26]

The Indians of Nicoya and Oroci speak the Chorotega language. Like the Indians of New Spain, they pierce their lower lips and insert round white bones about the size of a half-real coin. They use bows and arrows and are very brave. Since Gil González passed through there, they call themselves Christians but I believe that few of them really are. They worship many idols made of clay and sticks in very small, low houses, which they build for them in the villages in addition to their principal prayer houses called *teyopa* in Chorotega and, in Nicaraguan, *archilobo.* Nicoya is a land of much honey and beeswax. The bees there are as small as the flies in Spain but are black and stingless. However, there are small wasps whose stings are very painful.

All the Nicoyan Indians, especially the principal ones and their wives, tattoo their arms. The black ink they use is made of their own blood and charcoal, which they cut into the skin with flint knives. The designs are of tigers, which the Chorotegas call *nambue,* the Nicaraguans *teguam,* and the Cuevans *ochi.*

VII.

From Cape Blanco twenty leagues along the coast to the west, near the mainland, is an island called Moya but before that is a harbor called De las Velas.[27] From Cape Blanco west to Posesión harbor by sea is a distance of one hundred leagues, more or less.[28] All this is the Gulf of Papagayo, not an inappropriate name as, because of the navigational perils there, men cross it crying or praying.[29] Moya Island is at seven and one-half degrees north latitude near Point Catalina, another small island, eight and one-third degrees north and sixteen to twenty leagues from Moya. From Point Catalina to Point Nicaragua is thirty leagues and halfway between them is an inlet called the Gulf of Santiago.[30] Point Nicaragua is at nine and one-half degrees north. From Cape Blanco on to the west, little by little the coast curves toward the North Pole.

From Point Nicaragua to Posesión River harbor is a distance of ten leagues. The river is at ten and one-half degrees north, according to the recent charts of cosmographer Alonso de Chaves. At the entrance of the river into the harbor is a tall, flat-topped island one-fourth to one-half leagues around that divides the river into two mouths. Small ships can enter the eastern mouth and larger ones the western. For two days my ship was anchored in this river mouth and during that time we caught many fish called *roncadores* because they make a sound like snoring.[31] They are well armed with teeth and are good to eat. The harbor and river are called Posesión, because on his voyage of discovery, Pilot Andrés Niño performed there certain acts of possession. However Niño and Gil González may have measured the six hundred fifty leagues they claimed to have explored by sea, they were mistaken by more than half, because from Posesión harbor to Panamá there are only three hundred leagues more or less by current reckoning. I have sailed that distance twice with expert pilots.

Between Posesión River and Point Nicaragua, mentioned above, there is another river called the Mesa. It is true that Andrés Niño sailed on twenty leagues to Fonseca Bay by a more westerly route. Fonseca Bay was named in honor of Gil González de Avila's patron, the president of the

Royal Council of the Indies, at that time Juan Rodríguez de Fonseca, bishop of Palencia and later of Burgos. On a whim the flatterer Niño named an island in the bay Petronila for I cannot say what reason. Since these explorers are not able to give appropriate names to harbors, rivers, gulfs, or promontories, I wish they would try to find out the names the natives have for these places. The mouth of Fonseca Bay is at a little less than eleven degrees north, according to cosmographer Chaves but in this and all he says of this coast from Panamá I believe he received erroneous information.[32] Therefore, so that Chaves and the emperor's other cosmographers can emend their maps and navigational charts, if they wish to believe me, I will report what I wrote in my notes of my own sightings with the astrolabe carefully taken on land several times:[33] Panamá is at eight and one-half degrees north; Chira Island in the Gulf of Orotiña (or Nicaragua), ten; and Chara Island (also called Sanlúcar), nine degrees, thirty-eight minutes, which is two-thirds of a degree minus two minutes; Pocosi Island, two leagues east and a little to the south, is at a little more than nine and one-half degrees; Cape Blanco, which is the mouth of the said gulf at the southern end, is a little to the west at seven and one-half degrees; the mouth of the river and harbor of Posesión without doubt is at thirteen degrees.[34] So, what Andrés Niño saw and explored farther than Pilot Juan de Castañeda was from Orotiña Gulf and Cape Blanco to Fonseca Bay, which could be more or less one hundred twenty leagues but to explore it one would seem to sail more because, as the popular saying has it, "the unfamiliar road seems longer to he who never saw it." Between Posesión River and Fonseca Bay is another river, the San Pedro.[35] The westernmost point of Fonseca Bay is called Cape Hermoso.[36] Here I will stop with the cosmography of this coast and return to it later.

It seems to me that it is time to return to the story of Gil González and Pedrarias Dávila and what happened to the gold and the discovered territory when Gil González returned to Panamá on June 25, 1523. The gold was melted down and found to be worth much less than it appeared by quantity because it was generally very low grade, mostly pure copper. Once Gil González escaped from Castilla del Oro and Pedrarias Dávila's impediments, as was reported, he came to this city of Santo Domingo in our island of Hispaniola. Here he formed another expedition with very good men and ships and returned to Tierra Firme but more to the west at a site they thought parallel to the great freshwater lake that he and Pilot Andrés Niño believed flowed into the North Sea. They disembarked at the harbor at Cape Higüeras, which Gil González named Puerto de Caballos (horses).

VIII.

One of their horses died there, but this was not sufficient reason to change the name of the harbor that others had discovered much before them. Gil González had the horse buried secretly but not to honor it as Bucephalus was by Alexander the Great or as did Emperor Octavius Agustus his horse and as the Cid Ruy Díaz did for Babieca. Gil González did it so that the Indians would not find out that the horses they had never before seen and greatly feared were mortal. Further on at another harbor called Honduras he established a town and named it San Gil de Buena Vista. Leaving some Spaniards there, he took the majority of the men ten to twelve leagues inland to a place he thought more appropriate for his exploration and conquest.

When Gil González came to this city of Santo Domingo to outfit his second expedition, Hernando Cortez, who was in New Spain, learned of it and put together two counter-expeditions so that Gil González would not take Higüeras harbor, which was said to be a rich prize. Cortez sent one expedition by land under Captain Pedro de Alvarado and another by sea under Captain Cristóbal de Olit, both men of great military experience.[37] Cristóbal de Olit sailed to Cuba and as soon as he landed, he rebelled, declaring that he did not sail for Cortez but for himself, saying he wanted his own piece of Tierra Firme just as Cortez had. From Cuba he crossed over to Higüeras and landed his expedition there on the coast, settling close to the town of San Gil, where Gil González was. When each became aware of the other's presence, through an exchange of letters and messengers they became confederates, promising each other friendship and aid. It appears that their mutual aim was to disarm their enemies and secure themselves against their competitors. Gil González had Pedrarias at his back, who had sent his lieutenant Francisco Hernández and other captains and men to settle Nicaragua, and Cristóbal de Olit feared Hernando Cortez. In these, they had enough powerful competitors without having to contend against each other. I will wait until the section on Honduras to report what Cortez did.

Returning to Pedrarias: after Gil González left Panamá and while he was outfitting an expedition in Santo Domingo to return to Tierra Firme, Pedrarias, greedy to add Gil González's discoveries west of Panamá in Nicaragua Province to his own territory, sent out his expedition to occupy it under his lieutenant-general, Francisco Hernández, along with Captains Gabriel de Rojas, Francisco Campañón, Hernando de Soto, and others. Pedrarias's expedition settled in Nagrando Province near the great lake, establishing themselves at the site of the present city of León, which was founded by the ill-fated Francisco Hernández. From there, Hernández sent out Captain Gabriel de Rojas with some men who by chance came upon Gil González's settlement. Gil González told him that neither he nor Pedrarias had any business in those lands and that he should return immediately to Francisco Hernández. Further, he told Captain Rojas that for himself he could have there all that he wished, but, as Pedrarias's captain, Gil González would not permit him or any other to be present in that land. Captain Rojas retired with many expressions of courtesy because he did not have sufficient men to do otherwise and even promised not to return.

Rojas returned to Captain Francisco Hernández and told him about Gil González, and so Hernández sent out Captain Hernando de Soto with more men in search of Gil González. However, the latter was on guard, suspecting that Captain Rojas and other captains of Pedrarias would return. From the Indians of the area he had notice that Captain Hernando de Soto and many Christians were coming and so, stealing a march on them, he attacked their camp at night. In the battle there were some casualties and Captain de Soto and his men were disarmed and taken prisoner and were despoiled of the good sum of the low-grade gold they had with them. After two or three days Gil González set them free upon certain promises and pledges, returned their gold and arms, and they then returned to their captain Francisco Hernández.

After Gil González's victory over de Soto he went to where his "friend" Cristóbal de Olit was and the latter promptly arrested him. What happened then would be part of the history of Nicaragua and since here I only wish to deal with Governor Pedrarias I will return to his story.[38] As I said previously, Pedrarias did not arrive in time at Port Nombre de Dios to detain Gil González and seize the Nicaraguan gold. But at Nombre de Dios Pedrarias found out that the new bishop of Tierra Firme, Friar Vicente Peraza of the Dominican order, successor to

Bishop Friar Juan de Quevedo, had disembarked in the city of Santa María del Antigua del Darién. To keep the new bishop from staying there and to finish the destruction and depopulation of that city, Pedrarias embarked for Darién to see the bishop. What resulted from that meeting will be revealed in the following chapter.

CHAPTER XXII—OF THE TOTAL DEPOPULATION OF
THE CITY OF DARIÉN AND THE DIFFERENCES BISHOP
FRIAR VICENTE PEDRAZA AND LICENTIATE SALAYA,
CHIEF JUSTICE, HAD WITH PEDRARIAS; OF THE ORIGIN
AND BEGINNING OF THE DISCOVERY OF PERU BY CAP-
TAINS FRANCISCO PIZARRO AND DIEGO DE ALMAGRO
AT THEIR OWN COST AND IN COMPANY WITH SCHOOL-
MASTER FERNANDO DE LUQUE;[1] AND OF WHAT HAP-
PENED TO GOVERNOR PEDRO DE LOS RÍOS ON THE
ISLAND OF DOMINICA WHEN HE WAS COMING TO
UNDERTAKE THE GOVERNANCE OF CASTILLA DEL ORO;
AND OF OTHER THINGS.

After Pedrarias arrived at the city of Darién he met with the new bishop
and, speaking poorly of that city while praising Panamá to the skies, he
induced the bishop to leave with him for Panamá. Both publicly and
privately Pedrarias convinced the residents of Darién to go to Panamá
and Acla, saying they were wasting their time in Darién as there were no
Indians he could give them there but that in other settlements there were
Indians available and all were rich and he would make them even richer.
Then he and the bishop returned to Panamá.

Two or three months later in September 1524, Darién was abandoned.
One of the last remaining residents in Darién was Diego Rivero (of
whom I spoke in Book XXV, Chapter II, when he rebelled against Governor Diego de Nicuesa and abandoned him on Escudo Island). Rivero's
own Indians together with some others killed him. They hanged his
eight- or ten-year-old son from the rafters of his house and murdered the
child's mother as well as three or four sick Christians who remained behind in Darién. Then they burned most of the city, including my house
(which I described earlier). My losses totaled more than six thousand
castellanos.

The principal reason for Darién's abandonment was the differences
and troubles among Pedrarias, Bachelor Diego de Corral, and me. Truly,
that city would have survived if I were not first destroyed and persecuted,
as I have detailed. That settlement lasted from 1509 to 1524 and Pedrarias,
in allowing it to be lost, did no less disservice to God and King than to
Enciso and to the others whose service in founding it was very great. It
would not be a bad thing to rebuild the city because of the richness and

fertility of its setting and surrounding territory. But, let us return to the friendship between the new prelate and the governor.

In Panamá, the governor and bishop got along for a while but then they fought over a certain card game. The bishop said some very harsh things to him and died soon after. It was said that they had given him something that killed him. The same opinion was held concerning the death of Licentiate Salaya, Pedrarias's chief justice. One day Salaya publicly said some harsh things to the governor, who responded that he should temper his words or he would lose his head. The licentiate responded: "The man who cuts off my head will be smarter, abler, and better than I am; and you are not that man, nor is anyone in this land. You have cut off enough heads for no just cause and have not had to account for any. So, *you* watch what *you* say, for the only reason the emperor sent me here was to keep an eye on you and not allow you to commit more unjust deaths than what you have." And with these and other words they took leave of each other. However, a few days later they were good friends again and the governor gave him Indians and other things to make up with him. Soon after, the licentiate fell sick and died. It was said that they had given him so much scammony in a purge that it finished him off.[2] Although Pedrarias might have had nothing to do with his death, as it came so soon after their confrontation, some said that the licentiate's disrespectful words to the governor led to Salaya's death.

After this, certain captains came from Nicaragua to Pedrarias to denounce Lieutenant Francisco Hernández. They convinced Pedrarias that Hernández was rebelling against him. Pedrarias determined to go there, taking with him the majority of the people. He left behind very few men in the north coast towns of Acla and Nombre de Dios. In the south coast towns of Panamá and Natá there were already few men because Pedrarias had allowed two hundred men and some ships to leave to explore the South Sea. The leaders of that expedition were Captains Francisco Pizarro and Diego de Almagro, companions of Schoolmaster Fernando de Luque. A share of the expedition was allotted to Governor Pedrarias to obtain his license even though he invested no money toward the expenses as the capitulations required. This was the origin and beginning of the discovery of Peru, from which has flowed so much treasure. (This discovery will be related in the appropriate place.)[3] In January 1526 Pedrarias left Panamá for Nicaragua, all but abandoning those four towns (even though he called them cities, none of the four was more than a mediocre village).[4]

That same year on the last day of April Governor Pedro de los Ríos left Spain from Seville. On May 31 he arrived at Gomera to take on supplies before continuing on to the Island of Dominica. There he stayed three and a half days while they resupplied with water and firewood and repaired a ship, which a huge wave had dismasted at sea and which miraculously made it to port only by constant operation of its pumps. At the harbor of Angla del Aguada, while they repaired the ship, some of the company wandered off to gather hearts of palm from the many trees along that island's coast. Suddenly, Carib Indians attacked them with bows and arrows and killed two Christians—one named Cogollos; the other, Vargas. Emboldened by this victory, many Indian warriors gathered on the beach, displaying their war paint, bows, and arrows and sounding their shell trumpets. There another Spaniard escaped with two arrow wounds. Right away our men formed ranks to protect the embarkation of the women, children, and other folks not useful in battle, all of whom had come ashore to stretch their legs and wash clothes. The governor returned to his ship with them while the rest of us remained ashore to resist the enemy—Licentiate Juan de Salmerón, the chief justice; Diego Guitiérrez de los Ríos, the governor's nephew; the governor's bastard brother named Egas; and I; as well as other knights and gentlemen. In truth, the governor wanted to stay behind with us but, as he was very stout and heavy, we made him and Bachelor Diego de Corral return to the ship and had them send back the launches for us as soon as possible.

I was returning bearing the appointment as governor and captain-general of the province of Cartagena with its islands and appurtenances (as reported in Book XXVI, Chapter III, dealing with that province).[5] Also, I was coming to collect for their majesties' exchequer the assets of Adelantado Vasco Núñez de Balboa and his confederates (whom Pedrarias and his chief justice, Licentiate Espinosa, had executed) and to settle my claim against Pedrarias in order to go off to serve their majesties in the governance of Cartagena.

Even though the Indians were much more numerous than we who stayed behind to guard the embarkation of the others, they did not dare come close enough for us to engage them. As the sun was setting, there was no time for battle and we returned to the ships.

The next day we continued our voyage and arrived at the harbor of Nombre de Dios on Monday, July 30, 1526. The following day, Governor Pedro de los Ríos and Chief Justice Licentiate Juan de Salmerón took up their staffs and possession of office. In Nombre de Dios, we learned that Governor Pedrarias had departed for Nicaragua seven months previously to punish his lieutenant, Francisco Hernández, who they said was in rebellion. As I reported, Pedrarias had taken with him the majority of the Christians as well as many pacified Cuevan Indian laborers.

Twenty-five days after Governor Pedro de los Ríos arrived in Nombre de Dios he went overland to Panamá to await Pedrarias's return for residency and to attend to the state of the land and affairs of governance.

CHAPTER XXIII—HOW THE NEW GOVERNOR, PEDRO
DE LOS RÍOS, SENT SOME MEN TO PACIFY CHIEF TROTA
AND HOW THE CHRISTIANS WERE DEFEATED AND
SCATTERED; HOW NEWS ARRIVED THAT IN NICARA-
GUA PEDRARIAS HAD EXECUTED HIS LIEUTENANT,
FRANCISCO HERNÁNDEZ; HOW CAPTAIN DIEGO DE
ALMAGRO CAME TO PANAMÁ WITH NEWS OF THE
DISCOVERY OF PERU; AND HOW AND AT WHAT PRICE
DIEGO DE ALMAGRO SEPARATED PEDRARIAS DÁVILA
FROM THE PERUVIAN EXPEDITION COMPANY.

A few days after coming to Panamá, in January 1527, the new governor, Pedro de los Ríos, because of a lack of supplies in Panamá, decided
to send some of the newly arrived soldiers to the town of Natá, thirty
leagues along the coast from Panamá. He did so because in Natá there
was more provision for food and to occupy the soldiers in good exercise
against some rebellious chiefs in that region, especially the one called
Trota. Once in Natá, a gentleman named Captain Alonso de Vargas was
given the order to find and pacify that chief. Vargas took about ten veteran Spaniards and thirty others who had come from Castile with the
governor, some forty men in all. The expedition took along a pacified
chief in service to Pedro de Plasencia, a resident of Natá. This chief, as a
friend of the Christians, was to be a mediator so that Chief Trota would
feel secure and come to terms with the Spanish without recourse to battle.

One or two days' march inland, they captured two Indians sent to spy
on them, but they were not well guarded and made their escape within
two days. Later, some principal Indians of Chief Trota and other regional
chiefs came saying that they wished to be friends. Feigning humbleness
and peacefulness, they carefully observed the disposition and small number of the Spaniards as well as the poor state of the Christians' arms. They
noted that Captain Alonso de Vargas was ill and, even though they knew
him to be a valiant man, it did not appear that he was in a condition to
fight. Ostensibly to talk peace, there came to the camp a principal Indian
of Pedro de Plasencia's Chief Pocoa and with him another from Chief
Trota. The captain and the Christians thought it good that Chief Pocoa
intervene in the peace parley and left the negotiations in his hands, which
he was pleased to accept. Pocoa was trusted because his master Pedro de
Plasencia praised him as a good and loyal man, saying that he would stake

his head that Pocoa would serve them well and not be false. In truth, however, Pocoa saw to it that Pedro de Plasencia's head was not the only one lost.

Two or three days after the Christians sent out Chief Pocoa with those two Indians to make peace with Trota and the other chiefs, suddenly, during the fourth watch, five hundred or more warriors attacked the Christians.[1] In the vanguard was Chief Pocoa, a gold disk on his chest and throwing spears in his hands. It is customary in those parts that the chiefs and principal Indians wear into battle some gold ornament on their chest, head, or arms to identify themselves to the other Indians and even to the enemy. Chief Trota was there as well and with great force and war cries resounding through the valleys, they attacked, hurling such a multitude of spears that they fell like rain. The Spaniards, not expecting their friend Pocoa would bring such a response, nevertheless fought bravely at first, killing twenty-five to thirty Indians. Finally, however, their efforts were not sufficient against such a force and they were broken and defeated. Captain Alonso de Vargas was killed along with four or five of the most valiant veterans and twelve to thirteen of those soldiers newly arrived with Governor Pedro de los Ríos. In total, nineteen Spaniards died with their captain in that skirmish. The rest escaped by fleeing into the forests and after some days returned one by one to Natá. Among those killed was Pedro de Plasencia. He fled from the battle, but Chief Pocoa followed him for a long distance and finally caught up with him and killed him, thus repaying Plasencia's (good or bad) treatment when the chief lived in his household in peacetime.

A good three months after this incident, Captain Diego de Almagro returned by ship to Panamá. For nine months he and Captain Francisco Pizarro had been exploring the southern coast to Peru by order of Governor Pedrarias Dávila. Governor Pedro de los Ríos and everyone were very pleased by his arrival as they had had no word of these two captains. Almagro brought about three thousand pesos worth of sixteen- to seventeen-karat gold, some small amounts of silver, and other things. He reported much gold in that land, saying he could have brought one hundred thousand pesos worth but left it behind thinking that it was of lower quality than the gold he brought.

Captain Diego de Almagro spent some days in Panamá resting and visiting his properties and farms (his and Captain Francisco Pizarro's possessions in that city and the surrounding area were very good ones).

Then he returned to look for Pizarro with the forty or fifty men Governor Pedro de los Ríos gave him. He also took along six horses, which the Indians of those parts and of the entire Peruvian coast feared greatly. Captain Almagro said they had word of a very rich and powerful chief named Coco and that Captain Pizarro and his men were on the coast of a large and beautiful river called the San Juan above Peru, the mouth of which was at two degrees north. He had many things to say about that land, which will be reported in more detail in the third part of these histories.

Nevertheless, there is an amusing anecdote I will recount here about Pedrarias and Captain Almagro concerning how Pedrarias left the company that was formed to finance the Peruvian exploration. Pedrarias's share was a third or fourth part of the expedition, which would have brought him or his heirs more than a million gold pesos, according to a widely held opinion. But it pleased God that as he had invested only words in the financing of the expedition, that is what he got in return and he only received what Diego de Almagro gave him to get him out of such a great enterprise. It happened as follows:

In December 1526, a ship arrived at Panamá from Nicaragua with the news that Pedrarias would soon return, after having executed Captain Francisco Hernández, his lieutenant in Nicaragua. Pedrarias had intruded into that territory, stretching the limits of his governance for his own interests after seeing the gold that Captain Gil González took from there and wishing to do him harm. The ship arrived not expecting to find a new governor in the land, believing that Pedrarias was not yet removed from office. This ship brought many Nicaraguan Indians to be put to work or to be sold by the citizens of Panamá to whomever would buy them. A few days later Pedrarias landed near Natá in another ship and learned of the new governor, to whom he sent a letter by messenger. On February 3, 1527, Pedrarias came to Panamá and on the sixth of that month his residency was proclaimed, which will be addressed in the following chapter.

At that time, I had some accounts to settle with Pedrarias, and one day while I was negotiating with him in his house Captain Diego de Almagro entered and said to him:

Sir, Your Excellency is aware that in this Peruvian expedition you have a share along with Captain Francisco Pizarro, School-

master Don Fernando de Luque, my companions, and me. While
you have not invested anything, we have spent all our money and
that of other friends amounting to date to more than fifteen thousand gold castellanos. Now Captain Francisco Pizarro and the
Christians with him are in great need of provisions, men, horses,
and many other items. This is a very promising venture and, so
that such a good beginning is not lost, we beg Your Excellency
to aid us with some cattle for jerky, some money for horses and
other necessary items such as rigging, sails, and pitch for the
ships. All that has been spent will bring a good return according
to the share that has been contributed. As you participated in the
contract for this expedition, do not be the cause of its failure and
our ruin as well. If you do not wish to wait until the end of this
business, pay off what you owe on your share to date and let us
drop the matter.

After Pedrarias heard what Almagro had to say, he responded angrily:
"Obviously, such disrespectful speech is because I am leaving office. What
I would 'pay you' if I had not been removed from the governorship would
be to hold you accountable for the Christians killed because of Pizarro's
and your fault and for the destruction of the king's land. But you will
soon have to account for all those disorders and deaths before you leave
Panamá." To which Captain Almagro replied, "Sir, enough of that. There
is justice and judge that will see to us all, and it is fitting that everyone
give accounting for the living and the dead. You will be called into account, I will, and Pizarro will in order that our lord emperor grant us
many great rewards for our services. Pay up if you wish to profit from this
enterprise that has cost you no sweat, no effort, nor anything but a calf
you gave us on departure worth perhaps two or three gold pesos. And, if
not, remove yourself from the enterprise and we will forgive you half of
what you owe in the expenses to date." Pedrarias responded with a grudg-
ing laugh, "You will not lose anything and you will give me four thousand
pesos." Almagro said, "We will let you out without paying any of what
you owe and leave it to God whether we win or lose."
When Pedrarias saw that they were excusing him from what he owed
the expedition, which was by all accounts four or five thousand pesos, he
asked, "What will you give me in addition to that?" Almagro responded,
"I will give you three hundred pesos." He was very angry and swore to

God that, although he did not have that sum, he would find it to get rid of Pedrarias and not have to ask him for anything. Pedrarias replied, "No, you will give me two thousand." Almagro said, "I will give you five hundred." "No, you will give me more than a thousand," replied Pedrarias. Still angry, Almagro said, "I will pay one thousand but I do not have it at present. I promise to pay within the time you determine." With that, Pedrarias said he was content. Then a document was drawn up by which Almagro agreed to pay one thousand gold pesos, provided Pedrarias would withdraw from the company and he did, washing his hands of the entire business. I was one of the witnesses who signed the agreement by which Pedrarias renounced all rights in the company. In this manner, he retired from the business and by his miserliness he did not wait to enjoy the huge treasure that was well known to have been taken from those parts.[2]

Let us go on to Pedrarias's residency.

CHAPTER XXIV—OF PEDRARIAS'S RESIDENCY BY
LICENTIATE JUAN DE SALMERÓN, CHIEF JUSTICE OF
THE NEW GOVERNOR OF CASTILLA DEL ORO, PEDRO
DE LOS RÍOS; AND HOW PEDRARIAS AND THE AUTHOR
OF THESE HISTORIES CAME TO AN AGREEMENT AND
WITH WHAT PROVISIONS.

After Pedrarias's residency was proclaimed, Licentiate Espinosa, who had gone to Spain some time before, sent back a royal warrant barring consideration of anything that had happened before Pedrarias's previous residency taken by Juan Rodríguez de Alarconcillo. That residency was nothing but a joke as that judge was Pedrarias's principal officer, requested by and paid by the governor.

Such are the tricks and schemes by which justice is defrauded and the king loses his vassals. There is another way these residencies result in the governors' being left blameless and those aggrieved by them left with their damages and offenses received: it is that in these parts men do not put down roots, they only pass through with the intention of leaving the territory and returning to their homelands to buy estates as soon as they make some money. Others who are newly arrived die because of weak constitutions or other reasons, others move on, and others are unjustly forced to leave by the governors. And so, when it is time for the governor's reckoning, the majority of the aggrieved parties are absent, especially those who desire to settle in the land. The latter are the ones most upset that the governor does not do as he ought and the ones he fears most. In addition, many of the judges who come here to give remedy to the victims arrive poor and debt ridden. They do not sail so many leagues for the good of their souls but rather to pull themselves out of poverty as quickly as possible and that cannot happen except at the outgoing governor's expense and the latter only makes what restitution he is required and not to the judge but to the person he robbed.[1]

I am not saying that Pedrarias did anything of this sort, nor do I believe that Licentiate Salmerón took money from him. However, I do know that Pedrarias employed a very subtle stratagem, which was that, under the pretext of populating Nicaragua and punishing his lieutenant, Francisco Hernández, he almost depopulated Castilla del Oro, taking the people to Nicaragua and thus removing the majority of those likely to bother him in a residency. But, for all this, there were still some presenting many civil and criminal claims against him, the majority of which were excluded and dismissed, including the crown claims, under the provisions of the previously mentioned royal warrant. I did not see the warrant, but Licentiate Salmerón himself told me that he had and would not consider any claim of mine prior to Pedrarias's residency conducted by Licentiate Alarconcillo, nor would he hear anything except my personal claims, leaving aside those made on behalf of the king and the republic.

At the time of the residency, I had fourteen or fifteen claims against Pedrarias and believed that, if justice were done, I would have a judgment against him for more than eight thousand gold pesos. After the majority of the suits were concluded, my litigation continued and there were many persons mediating to bring us to peace and accord. Their efforts failed because I was resentful, believing that Pedrarias had been behind the attempt on my life. Nevertheless, I suspected that the judge was favorable to Pedrarias and that I would not receive justice. Even if I did, I recalled how more than four years previously I had to go to Spain for redress and how I suffered many costly delays and other vexations what with the death of one king, the time it took for another one to come to Spain from so far away, the Comunero Revolt, and other events of those days. Seeing that any judgment in my or Pedrarias's favor would be appealed by him or by me, forcing a return to Spain in a desperate search for remedy, I had to come to an agreement with Pedrarias. He gave me seven hundred gold pesos and two marks worth of pearls for the two thousand gold pesos of mine he had embargoed three years ago and retained until that residency.

This settlement and our peacemaking was contracted under one condition—that Pedrarias sign a sworn declaration that neither by word, deed, or counsel had he anything to do with the offense against me. And he so swore and attested that he knew nothing of it, nor assented, nor gave any opinion regarding such a deed but, to the contrary, he was deeply saddened by it. So, I have his signed and sworn statement and I was satisfied in this matter. However, left pending was my suit against the dean for which I had brought a provision allowing the case to be heard in a civil court, but just as I was ready to pursue the matter he died, God determining that the reckoning I intended to have from him would be made before His Divine Majesty (for which may he be pardoned). Truly the dean did me much harm, but, as an unlettered idiot, he was the pawn of Bachelor Corral in the plot to murder me, as I have previously said.

Without my deserving it, God in His absolute power and by His goodness and mercy has seen fit to liberate me from all these travails and has let me see all my enemies removed from this miserable life. I pray God that in the other life He has pity on their souls and pardons them.

And so, with Pedrarias's residency finished and Bachelor Corral's departure for Spain to tend to some business in which he was involved, I left for the province of Nicaragua to see Governor Diego López de Salcedo and visit that land, as I will later report when that region is dealt with. Pedro de los Ríos remained as governor of Castilla del Oro, and later Pedrarias Dávila was granted the governorship of Nicaragua even before his residency was seen or known in Spain.

Notes

Complete bibliographical information on works cited is provided in the bibliography.

Introduction

Unless otherwise noted, the biographical information on Oviedo relies primarily on two studies: that of Juan Pérez de Tudela Bueso's lengthy introduction to the *General and Natural History of the Indies,* unfortunately not yet translated to English, and Antonello Gerbi's *Nature in the New World,* available in an excellent translation by Jeremy Moyle.

1. Antonello Gerbi's study is especially informative for Oviedo's Italian days, which Gerbi describes with some nationalistic pride as "the decisive years from the twenty-first to the twenty-fourth of [Oviedo's] life coinciding with the peak of the Italian Renaissance, the period of its most mature and triumphant achievements" (*Nature in the New World,* 138).

2. Years later Oviedo had the heartbreaking task of recording in his *History* the death of this son at age twenty-seven (Oviedo, *Historia general y natural de las Indias,* edited by J. Pérez de Tudela Bueso, 121:151). He drowned fording a river in Arequipa returning with Diego de Almagro's ill-fated expedition to Chile, leaving his young son and daughter with Oviedo in Santo Domingo. To compound the loss, Oviedo writes, his five-year-old grandson died a few days after news was received of his father's death.

3. The multiple functions of the House of Trade for the Indies are summarized by K. Romoli: "It was a clearing house for goods and treasure, both public and private. It collected royalties and revenues . . . and managed Crown properties in the Indies. It controlled . . . letters patent and contract, inspection, registry, insurance policies, emigration. It was a custom house, a bureau of records and a hydrographic office. It procured arms, stores and ships for government service . . . served as custodian and executor of estates, received all confiscated or embargoed goods. It main-

tained a school of navigation, filed and collated charts and licensed pilots for the Indies" (Romoli, *Balboa of Darién*, 8).

4. Tierra Firme (The Spanish Main): "At the time of discovery this name was given to the entire coast of the mainland south and west of Hispaniola. In 1509 Ferdinand divided Tierra Firme into two parts: Nueva Andalucía, the region extending from the middle of the Gulf of Urabá east to Cape Vela; and Castilla del Oro, the region extending west from the middle of the Gulf of Urabá to Cape Gracias a Dios. Castilla del Oro was divided into Darién (east), Panamá (center), and Veragua (west)" (Stoudemire, *The Natural History of the West Indies by Gonzalo Fernández de Oviedo*, 127). Darién, Panamá, and Veragua (now Veraguas) remain to this day the names of governmental divisions of the Republic of Panamá.

5. Santa María del Antigua del Darién: often referred to as Santa María de la Antigua del Darién, Santa María la Antigua, Santa María, or simply Darién.

6. The 1953 biography of K. Romoli (*Balboa of Darién*) continues to be cited as the best and most complete source on Balboa's life and deeds. Also useful are the earlier *Life and Letters of Vasco Núñez de Balboa* and *Old Panama and Castilla del Oro*, both by C. L. G. Anderson.

7. The recent and beautifully illustrated work by María del Carmen Mena García (*Sevilla y las flotas de Indias*) is a study of the records of the "Splendid Armada" conserved in the Archives of the Indies offering a wealth of valuable information concerning every aspect of the outfitting of this transatlantic fleet in 1513–14. Pedrarias Dávila (primarily because of the writings of Oviedo and Las Casas) has come down through history as the worst of the Spanish despoilers of the New World. The most complete study of Pedrarias is that of Alvarez Rubiano (*Pedrarias Dávila*), which is valuable in spite of its out-of-date imperialism. More recent and more balanced (but less detailed) is Mena García's *Pedrarias Dávila o "la ira de Dios."*

8. Seeking to impress King Ferdinand in order to obtain royal confirmation of his de facto governorship, Balboa exaggerated the abundance of alluvial gold to be had in Darién. Here, for example, is a sample of his description of the province of Abanumaqué: "[it] has great deposits of gold: I have very reliable information that in it are very rich rivers of gold" (Fernández de Navarrete, *Colección de viajes y descubrimientos*, 218). Balboa succeeded in getting the king's attention, but his strategy backfired when Pedrarias was appointed to replace him. Navarrete also reproduces Pedrarias's commission and detailed instructions from King Ferdinand (*Colección de viajes y descubrimientos*, 205–15).

9. One of the disillusioned newcomers to abandon Darién was the future chronicler of Mexico, Bernal Díaz del Castillo.

10. From Oviedo's prologue to his *Claribalte* (Valencia: Juan Viñao, 1519; facsimile edition, Madrid: Real Academia Española, 1956, 2 recto).

11. The recent book by Hugh Thomas, *Rivers of Gold*, includes a great deal of information on the personalities and events of this transitional period.

12. A well-known summary of the long and spirited debate on the "just war" is that of Lewis Hanke, *Aristotle and the American Indians* (see also Pagdan's *The Fall of*

Natural Man). The *encomienda* system that distributed Indians to conquistadores was first established in the Antilles and was viewed by the crown as a disaster. Ferdinand's instructions to Pedrarias were ambivalent regarding the extension of the system to Darién unless there was strict adherence to the Laws of Burgos (or Valladolid) of 1512, which governed the correct treatment of the Native Americans. Nevertheless, it was one thing to legislate in Spain but quite another to implement reforms in the Indies, where there were a variety of opposing interests and conditions. See Mena García, "La autonomía legislativa en Indias," for an analysis of the Panamanian encomienda.

13. Pérez de Tudela Bueso characterizes Oviedo as a "glib and lively conversationalist, an astute observer, ingratiating, by turns ironic and courtly, a flatterer, and possessed of a highly opportune and reverential sense for authority" (Pérez de Tudela Bueso, "Vida y escritos de Gonzalo Fernández de Oviedo," xix). Even Oviedo's greatest detractor, Las Casas, grudgingly acknowledged his personal magnetism, writing "he was a good talker, a chatterer, who knew how to be very persuasive concerning what he wanted" (Las Casas, *Historia de las Indias,* edited by Agustín Millares Carlo, 3:311). Certainly, Las Casas as well was very persuasive concerning what he wanted. In terms of tenaciousness, ego, drive, and expressive talents, Las Casas and Oviedo had much in common; no wonder they came into conflict.

14. For the foundation of the city of Panamá and its importance see Mena García's *La ciudad en un cruce de caminos* and *La sociedad de Panamá en el siglo XVI.*

15. Two months prior to receiving his appointment as official chronicler, Oviedo presented to the Empress Isabel his completed *Royal Catalog of Castile,* which was his first declared writing project begun in Toro in 1505. See "Un autógrafo inédito de Gonzalo Fernández de Oviedo y Valdés: la historia de España escrita desde el Nuevo Mundo," by E. A. Romano de Thuesen, who has also edited the manuscript in an unpublished dissertation.

16. According to Daymond Turner in *Gonzalo Fernández de Oviedo y Valdés: An Annotated Bibliography,* 1533 also marks Oviedo's *Report on the Imprisonment of the King of France . . . (Relación de lo sucedido en la prisión del rey de Francia . . .)* concerning King Francis's defeat by Emperor Charles at the battle of Pavia.

17. *Quincuagena:* a group of fifty, from the Latin *quinguaginta.* The *Batallas y quincuagenas,* begun about 1544, is a series of dialogues between an old warden (Oviedo) and his friend, Sereno, on the lives of illustrious personages from the reigns of the Catholic Monarchs and Charles V. Oviedo's typically grandiose plan was for three "*batallas*" (parts), each with four quincuagenas or groups of dialogues on fifty individuals. Fewer than the projected six hundred dialogues were written. Pérez de Tudela Bueso has found three hundred forty and estimates about one hundred lost. The *Quincuagenas,* finished in 1556, is another huge and rambling Oviedo project. There were to be four quincuagenas of fifty "*estancias*" (chapters) each. The subjects of the estancias are best described as whatever popped into Oviedo's head at the time. Both these final Oviedo works offer a wealth of information on people and topics of his time.

18. Pérez de Tudela Bueso, "Vida y escritos," clxvi.

19. Peña y Cámara, "Contribuciones documentales y críticas para una biografía de Gonzalo Fernández de Oviedo," 655.

20. Oviedo, *Historia,* 117:8.

21. *Ibid.,* 9.

22. The great historical mission of the Emperor Charles to be a new Charlemagne, the universal monarch to unite all of Europe, was promoted by Mercurino Gattinara, grand chancellor after the death of Jean le Sauvage in 1518 (M. Fernández Alvarez, *Carlos V, el César y el Hombre,* 112). R. Padrón writes: "In the unity of the world's geography, Oviedo finds the geographical counterpart of a providentialist historiography, one that saw in Charles V the divinely ordained successor to the emperors of Rome, and in his monarchy, the new empire that would serve as God's instrument in the spread of Christianity throughout the globe" (Padrón, *The Spacious World,* 148–49).

23. "Whether Oviedo realized it or not, the publication of the *Summary* marked a new direction in his life. A direction . . . which would lead to the winning of the highest sovereignty—the intellectual—over the New World" (Pérez de Tudela Bueso, "Vida y escritos," c).

24. Translation from Stoudemire, *Natural History,* 4–5.

25. See Turner's "Forgotten Treasure from the Indies: The Illustrations and Drawings of Fernández de Oviedo" and the more recent "Taming the Visible" by J. Carrillo on Oviedo's drawings, their evolution in subsequent Italian and Spanish texts, and their significance.

26. Turner's bibliography is helpful in untangling all this. See also his "The Aborted First Printing of the Second Part of Oviedo's *General and Natural History of the Indies.*" However, J. Carrillo's more recent article, "The *Historia General y Natural de las Indias* by Gonzalo Fernández de Oviedo," is now the most complete guide to the multiple manuscripts of the *History.*

27. Turner, *Gonzalo Fernández de Oviedo y Valdés: An Annotated Bibliography,* 8.

28. For many years it was thought that the failure to finish the printing of the entire *General and Natural History* was the result of machinations of Las Casas. However, it appears that the reason was more prosaic—Oviedo was unable to secure financial backing for such a costly project. J. Carrillo translates a portion of a letter from Oviedo to the bishop of Hispaniola in which the author reports that he has left the completed manuscript in Spain. It was Oviedo's hope that the emperor would finance the publication upon Charles's return to Spain. Nevertheless, Carrillo does not discard Las Casas's influence in the failure to publish (J. Carrillo, "The *Historia General,*" 328).

29. Turner is critical of the Amador de los Ríos text, noting that it is far from a "complete" edition of Oviedo's *History* by some sixty chapters. See his analysis in Note 4 of "The Aborted First Printing," 21.

30. One thinks especially of the miscellany that is Book VI, "The Book of Deposits," modeled on Pedro Mexía's popular *Silva de varia lección.* See Isaías Lerner's "La visión humanística de América: Gonzalo Fernández de Oviedo."

31. Oviedo, *Historia*, 121:305.

32. In his essential and exhaustive study, "Panegírico y libelo del primer cronista de Indias: Gonzalo Fernández de Oviedo," A. F. Bolaños details the polarized critical reception of Oviedo and his work from its inception in the sixteenth century to the present day, concluding that "the tendency of many other critics today to reproduce these excesses in the interpretation of the [personality and work] of Oviedo is an obstacle for a just comprehension of its historic, literary, and testimonial value" (643).

33. In addition to casting doubt on Columbus's status as the first discoverer of the Indies and thus damaging the family suit, if the Indies were prior possessions of Spain then a "just war" to recover them would be licit.

34. Las Casas tacitly acknowledged Oviedo's authoritative status, writing "now his *History* has taken flight, deceiving everyone who reads it, poisoning their minds against all the Indians" (Las Casas, *Historia*, 3:321).

35. Las Casas, *Historia*, 3:323. One notes that Las Casas, who generally wrote in Latin, produced his own *History* in Spanish.

36. Oviedo, *Historia*, 117:10.

37. Oviedo, *Historia*, 121:415.

38. Las Casas, *Historia*, 3:321.

39. Translation by Richard Eden (1577) with spelling modernized, in Alexander VI, *Inter caetera*, 40–41.

40. R. Mojica has written an interesting article on what he terms Oviedo's "historical antinomy": "Oviedo worked under the influence of a double impulse. On the one hand, he saw the enterprise and historical destiny of Spain as something that approached the unambiguous dignity of a theological given. On the other hand, exposed as he was to the clutter of historical events, he was bound to withstand the moral misgivings and the uncertainty that attended the lives and destiny of many of his contemporaries in the Indies. . . . Oviedo's uncertainties and moral anxieties in face of the excesses and crimes committed in the Indies, together with the ideology of empire . . . commit him to an optimistic view of history . . . [these are] the two powerful forces behind Oviedo's discursive strategy" (Mojica, "FORTUNA AURI: The Dialectics of Gold in Gonzalo Fernández de Oviedo's Imperial Discourse," 126, 127).

41. For example, Bolaños cites Salas and Gerbi to that effect and writes that an Oviedo anti-indigenist is a distortion fabricated by Las Casas and that "Oviedo defends the Indian with the same vehemence as the friar [Las Casas], although under different conceptions" ("Panegírico y libelo," 602–3).

42. Padrón, *The Spacious World*, 43.

43. Pérez de Tudela Bueso, "Rasgos del semblante espiritual de Gonzalo Fernández de Oviedo: La hidalguía caballeresca ante el nuevo mundo," 391.

44. T. R. Walton's *The Spanish Treasure Fleets* is a valuable and readable sourcebook on the silver and gold trade, especially chapter 1 on the period of conquest from 1492–1544, pp. 3–35. A photograph of one of the silver ingots of approximately 1,000 pesos is included on pp. 40–41.

45. Mena García, *Sevilla y las flotas de Indias*, 386–407.
46. Pérez-Mallaína, *Spain's Men of the Sea*, 116–20.
47. *Ibid.*, 115.
48. Pérez de Tudela Bueso, "Vida y escritos," xlv.
49. Las Casas, *Historia*, 3:314.
50. Carande, *Carlos V y sus banqueros*, 1:240.
51. Walton, 37.
52. Ibid., 82.
53. Carande, 1:245. For example, the price of hardtack rose from 190.5 maravedís per quintal in 1513 to 750 in 1563 (Mena García, *Sevilla y las flotas de Indias*, 390).

Chapter VI

1. Gonzalo de Ayora from Cordova was a friend and compatriot of the Great Captain, with whom he served in the Italian campaigns. In Spain he was the commander of the Royal Guard and introduced important military reforms. Because of his support of Philip I he was dismissed from command when that prince died and Ferdinand was recalled as regent of Castile. Ayora authored numerous letters and reports concerning events of the times as well as a chronicle of Queen Isabella.

2. Pedrarias's royal commission as governor and captain-general and his instructions are reprinted in Fernández de Navarrete (66:205–14).

3. This Island of Hispaniola: after Oviedo left Tierra Firme about 1530, he established himself in Santo Domingo, then the capital of the Indies. Most of his history was shaped there on the basis of the copious notes and papers he had collected from the first moment of his involvement in the expedition.

4. Seville, with its House of Trade, was the official center for navigation to and from the Indies. The Guadalquivir River there would not accommodate larger ships and Sanlúcar de Barrameda, the port situated at the mouth of the river, was where, according to Pérez-Mallaína, "all the convoys gathered to finish loading and to undergo final inspections before departure" (*Spain's Men of the Sea*, 4).

5. Ships (*naos*): "The standard full-rigged ship of the day" (S. E. Morison in Christopher Columbus, *Journals and Other Documents*, 48). Pérez-Mallaína (*Spain's Men of the Sea*, 130) describes a *nao* as having around a hundred tons of capacity and caravels of between sixty and eighty tons. Mena García (*Sevilla y las flotas de Indias*) reports 1,250 men (76) on sixteen ships (158).

6. Ferdinand Magellan discovered the straits named for him in 1520.

7. Shrovetide: the three days before Ash Wednesday was once a time of confession and absolution. Shrove Tuesday (Mardi Gras, carnival) was the last day of Shrovetide, long observed as a season of merrymaking before Lent.

8. The treacherous sand bar obstructing the entrance to the Guadalquivir River "converted the zone into one of the most important ships' graveyards known . . . all ships were consigned to the care of the bar pilots, experienced in finding the channel that led into the gulf of Cádiz" (Pérez-Mallaína, *Spain's Men of the Sea*, 9).

9. Gomera: the third of the Canary Islands, the last Spanish outpost to take on supplies before the long passage to the Indies.

10. Dominica: one of the windward islands of the Lesser Antilles.

11. El Aguada: a place where water (*agua*) is available. Throughout the text, position is indicated solely by latitude, which was determined by astrolabes and other instruments. The determination of longitude at sea required precise measurements of time that were not available until John Harrison invented the chronometer in eighteenth-century England. See D. Sobel and W. J. H. Andrews's *The Illustrated Longitude.*

12. The Caribs (*caribes*): the dominant indigenous peoples of the Lesser Antilles, hence the Caribbean Sea.

13. Santa Marta: a town and province now in northwest Colombia.

14. Indian dwelling: Oviedo consistently uses the indigenous term *buhío* (modern spelling, *bohío*), which is a cabin, hut, or dwelling constructed of reeds and branches.

15. The formal act of taking possession is described more fully in Michele de Cuneo's "Letter" on the second voyage of Columbus (1495). On this voyage Columbus gave the Island of Saona to Cuneo, as he was the first to sight it. Cuneo reports: "I took possession of it according to the appropriate modes and forms, as the Lord Admiral was doing of the other islands in the name of His Majesty the King, that is by virtue of a document signed by a notary. On the above-mentioned island I uprooted grass and cut trees and planted the cross and also the gallows, and in the name of God I baptized it with the name *La Bella Saonese*" (Columbus, *Journals and Other Documents,* 224–25).

16. The Ocean Sea: that is, the Atlantic Ocean.

Chapter VII

1. The reference is to the donation of America to Spain by Pope Alexander VI in 1493 by the bull *Inter caetera.*

2. These eight signatories are identified by Las Casas in his *Historia:* the Episcopus Palentinus was Bishop Fonseca of Palencia, Friar Tomás de Matienzo was the king's confessor, Friar Alonso de Bustillo was a theologian, Licenciate Santiago was one of the king's councilors, Doctor Palacios Rubios was a famous jurist, Licenciate de Sosa was a jurist and later bishop of Almería, and Licenciate Gregorio and Fray Bernardus (Bernardo de Mesa) were both preachers to the king. Palacios, Santiago, and Sosa were also members of the royal council.

3. The account of Arroyo's death referred to in another chapter (Book XXVI, Chapter X) is more detailed: "[S]tanding next to me he was struck by an arrow on the shin. The blow was very weak and the wound very slight. As soon as the arrow struck him breaking the skin and drawing a little blood it fell on the ground. The arrow tip was a bone of a fish we call *raya*. But the poison was such that in the instant he was struck it was obvious that the wound was fatal and, although he was acknowledged a man of great strength and spirit, he fainted and died raving three days later"

(119:79–80). Years later, Sir Walter Raleigh writes of this poison in his *Discoverie of Guiana* (1596): The victim "abideth a most ugly and lamentable death, some times dying stark mad, sometimes their bowels breaking out of their bellies, and are presently discoloured as black as pitch, and so unsavoury as no man can endure to cure or attend them" (quoted from C. Nicholl's *The Creature in the Map*, 291).

4. Emerald-colored agates (*plasmas de esmeralda*). In Book XXVI, Chapter X Oviedo writes in more detail: "There I found a sapphire as large as a chicken egg, almost as large as a goose egg, not a perfect blue but something between crystal and sapphire-colored—a white sapphire. That day they found a mantel, six or seven yards long and half as wide, with many pictures woven in it and inset with many carnelians, emerald-colored agates, chalcedonies, jaspers, and other gems; there were also many pieces of wrought gold of diverse kinds and quality: seven thousand castellanos, more or less" (119:80). This booty was given to Treasurer Alonso de la Puente, who was to take out the royal share and return the remainder to its discoverers. However, that was the last they saw of the treasure, provoking Oviedo's comment: "Let's not speak more of this, for not only is the king cheated in these things but we all were as well and I, moreover, was sorry that I had not kept that sapphire" (119:80).

5. Cenú: the coastal region between Cartagena and the Gulf of Urabá, now in the Republic of Colombia.

Chapter VIII

1. Staffs (*varas*): municipal and other officers carried staffs—long, heavy rods or wands—as a symbol of their authority.

2. Oviedo consistently uses the term *cacique* for chief, an Arawak word the Spanish picked up in the Caribbean and employed throughout the New World and that is still used to describe a regional political boss.

3. Isla Rica (now called Isla del Rey) is the largest of the Pearl Islands, lying between the Gulf of San Miguel and the Bay of Panamá.

4. Las Casas writes of Arbolancha's activity at court on behalf of Balboa in his *Historia* (3:11–12, 22). With him Balboa sent to King Ferdinand the best of the pearls he had found. Arbolancha arrived at court in May 1514 and was well received by Bishop Fonseca, Secretary Conchillos, and the king. However, unfortunately for Balboa, a new governor, Pedrarias, had already sailed for Tierra Firme.

Chapter IX

1. *Adelantado:* a military and political governor of a frontier region, originating in medieval Spain during the wars between Christians and Spanish Muslims.

2. Oviedo had a financial interest in promoting the area and the town. Romoli, who visited the area during her research on the life of Balboa, was more objective: "Darién had no decent harbor, no large rivers, and little arable land. It dominated no trade routes. . . . Ships had a hard time reaching it and a worse one getting away. . . .

Its climate was unhealthy and . . . its mineral resources were insignificant . . . Santa María de la Antigua was tucked away in a narrow, rather marshy valley five miles from the sea—a strategically inapt location where it was impossible to produce food for more than a few hundred people" (Romoli, *Balboa of Darién*, 2–3).

3. The King's Fifth was the fifth part of the profits from gold, pearls, and slaves that was set aside for the royal treasury.

4. In the *Historia*, Oviedo several times calls attention to the fate of the bearers of this title. For example, in Book XLI, Chapter III, he writes: "In my opinion this title of adelantado in these Indies is ill-starred as we see in the case of many adelantados the same misfortune of their bad ends, some drowned at sea, others treacherously murdered, and others meeting diverse and pitiless deaths seeking these riches so many centuries hidden from the Christians and which were to cost dearly the majority of those who sought them and found them" (120:355).

Chapter X

1. Oviedo seems to imply here that all two million perished, an outrageous number that even exceeds Las Casas's exaggerated figure of eight hundred thousand casualties reported in his famous *A Short Account of the Destruction of the Indies* (34). Modern estimates of the indigenous population of the isthmus at the arrival of the Spaniards place it between one hundred fifty thousand and two hundred fifty thousand (Muñoz Delgado, "Santa María de la Antigua del Darién," 644; Araúz and Pizzurno, *El Panamá hispano*, 97).

2. Frequently throughout the text, territorial chiefs are referred to by the names of the provinces or rivers.

3. Oviedo in Book XII, Chapter X writes a lengthy description of the New World "tigers," called *ochi* by the native peoples of Darién, and concludes that they are not the animal known as the tiger in the Old World but rather a type of panther.

4. In Book XII, Chapter XI, Oviedo reports, "The Spaniards in Tierra Firme call *danta* an animal that the Indians of Cueva province call *beorí*. The Spaniards give them this name because their hide is very thick: but they are not dantas. . . . The largest of these beorís are the size of a year-old calf. Their coat is dark brown somewhat thicker than the buffalo. They do not have horns even though some people call them cows" (118:42–43). Oviedo apparently thinks of a danta as a type of buffalo, although it is, in fact, a tapir.

5. Saint Gregory (the Great), ca. A.D. 540–604, Pope Gregory I, 590–604, is one of Oviedo's favorite sources for support. A note to the Spanish text edited by José Amador de los Ríos identifies this citation as being from his *Moralia*, Book XXIX, commenting on Chapter 28 of the Book of Job.

6. Lope de Olano figures prominently in Chapters I through III of Book XXVIII. According to Oviedo, Captain Lope de Olano deserted Governor Nicuesa's ill-fated expedition along the coast of Panamá and returned to the main party reporting that the governor had died. However, after suffering extreme hardships, Nicuesa

was rescued. Instead of hanging Olano, Nicuesa had him put in chains and condemned to grind corn like the native women. Later in Santa María, Olano (who was Basque) conspired with other Basques in the events leading to Nicuesa's pitiless death. Ahead in Chapter XII and again in Book XXIX, Chapter XXXIII, Oviedo is pleased to report Olano's end at the hands of Chief Careta: "Some years later God called him to account for his treachery: Chief Careta killed him and other Christians at the site of present-day Acla, a well-earned end for what he and others in his company did" (119:344).

7. Amador de los Ríos references this with Saint Gregory's *Moralia*, Book VII, concerning Chapter 6 of the Book of Job.

8. Book XIX, Chapter VIII: "In which the chronicler treats of some opinions of the ancient historians concerning pearls, and of some particularities of them, and of some great pearls that have been found in these Indies" (118:202). This famous pearl, called *la peregrina* ("the wanderer," but also, in those days "wonderful," "unique") passed through many princely hands and is now in the collection of the actress Elizabeth Taylor. Several beautiful photos of it are in her book *My Love Affair with Jewels* (pp. 83–92) and it illustrates the back of the dust jacket. Mena García (*Pedrarias Dávila*, 87) traces its history, noting that, like the Hope diamond, the peregrina supposedly carries with it a curse.

9. Valderrábano's end is recounted in Chapter XII of this book. He was executed along with his friend Balboa.

10. At the end of Book XXIX, Chapter XXXIII, there is a summary of the lives of forty-five captains of Castilla del Oro, most of them, in Oviedo's estimation, coming to untimely ends for their sins.

Chapter XI

1. Cassia (*cañafístula*): used medicinally and as flavoring.

2. This would be Oviedo's second wife, Isabel de Aguilar, whom he married sometime before 1512.

3. Both ports and La Coruña, mentioned two sentences later, are on the northern coast of Spain on the Bay of Biscay.

4. Ushant (*Ouessant*): an island off the northwest coast of France.

5. The shrine is at Santiago de Compostela.

6. Scilly Islands: a group of about 140 small islands southwest of England. Oviedo writes "Sorlinga Islands," which Gerbi (*Nature in the New World*, 210) feels are the Scilly.

7. The grand chancellor of Burgundy: Jean le Sauvage, Lord of Escanbeque (Flanders). Until his death in 1518 he replaced Fonseca as director of the affairs of the Indies. Sauvage was a supporter of Las Casas who, almost alone of the Spaniards, had good things to say about the chancellor. Although Las Casas wrote often of the corruption of Fonseca, he is silent about the fifty thousand ducats that Sauvage is generally thought to have accumulated in his four months in Spain. H. Keniston

writes that "[Sauvage's] passing helped to ease the anti-Burgundian attitude of the Spaniards, for he was regarded as one of the most rapacious of the foreigners" (*Francisco de los Cobos,* 49).

8. Ugo de Urríes y Ruiz de Calcena, Lord of Ayerbe had been secretary for Aragón to King Ferdinand and then managed to make the transition to the new administration of King Charles.

9. Oviedo had two children by Isabel and an older son by his first wife, Margarita de Vergara. His older son apparently came to the Indies later.

Chapter XII

1. This was Pedrarias's oldest daughter, María de Peñalosa (Mena García, *Pedrarias Dávila,* 100).

2. Oviedo's text here is rather confusing: he writes that the death occurred "at the beginning of the year, or, more precisely, the last day of the year 1519, which was the eve of the Nativity of Christ, 24 December."

3. In the section cited, Argüello is called a secretary and noted as "a special friend of Vasco Núñez."

4. Acla, founded by Gabriel de Rojas in 1514 at the mouth of the Gulf of Urabá, was abandoned in 1532.

5. Garabito is said to have betrayed Balboa because he was jealous of Balboa's relationship with the daughter of Chief Careta (Alvarez Rubiano, *Pedrarias Dávila,* 128).

6. Specifically, this activity was the medieval "juego de cañas," a type of mock battle in which the opposing sides fought on horseback with light canes or reeds.

Chapter XIII

1. The ensuing itinerary is difficult to follow on modern maps except in a general fashion, as many of the place names have changed over the centuries. Also, the latitudes of the places that conserve their sixteenth-century names—for instance, Chame, Caño, Cebaco, Burica—have been determined with greater precision and usually differ by one to two degrees from Oviedo's reports.

2. Codro: Micer Codro, the Venetian, is mentioned in no fewer than six chapters from Part I to Part III in which he is variously referred to as philosopher, doctor, and botanist. Oviedo, who knew him personally and regarded him highly, reports that he came to Panamá in 1515. Twice Oviedo tells the anecdote of his death and his celebrated confrontation with Captain Valenzuela. The most extensive and affecting version is in Part III, Book XXXIX, Chapter II (120:343). In brief, the dying Codro accused Captain Valenzuela of causing his death and summoned him to appear before God to answer for his mistreatment within a year. Valenzuela responded jocosely that he would give his power of attorney to his dead father to act in his stead. Nevertheless, Oviedo reports that Valenzuela died within a year. According to Las Casas, Codro told Balboa that when he saw a certain star in a certain position in the sky "he

would be in great danger, but if he escaped that peril he would be the greatest and richest lord there ever was in all the Indies." Balboa saw the star shortly before falling into Pedrarias's fatal trap and joked with his comrades, "A man would be a fool to believe in soothsayers, especially Micer Codro . . . and here I see the star when I possess four ships and three hundred men about to sail the South Sea" (Las Casas, *Historia,* 3:85). Gerbi was unable to discover the real name of this Venetian traveler but reports that after his death "an aura of magic and legend quickly grew up around his name" (*Nature in the New World,* 198–99).

Chapter XIV

1. The Niños were a well-known seafaring family from Moguer. According to Morison, at least three Niños went on Columbus's first voyage and other members of the family accompanied him on the last three voyages as well as other voyages to the New World (*Admiral of the Ocean Sea,* 1:181).

2. Yaguana: "destroyed by Osorio in 1605 . . . Haitian historians now believe it was on the site of the present Port-au-Prince" (Stoudemire, *Natural History,* 127).

3. Although Oviedo was highly critical of Las Casas's failed plan to protect the indigenous peoples in settlements directed by clerics, his own proposal to establish secular protectorates in the jurisdiction of Santa Marta (under the hundred knights of Santiago referred to) was even less practical and came to nothing.

4. Nombre de Dios: the harbor was discovered by Christopher Columbus in 1502. In 1510, the town was founded by Diego de Albítez, but its city status was transferred five leagues away to the better harbor of Portobelo in 1585 (Alcedo, *Diccionario geográfico de las Indias Occidentales o América,* 207:36).

5. Very soon after Charles arrived in Spain, his grandfather Maximilian, the Holy Roman Emperor, died and Charles left Spain to campaign for the imperial crown. The turmoil of this period contributed to the Revolt of the Communes (*Comuneros*) of 1520–21. According to Karl Brandi, the rebellion was headed by certain Spanish cities mainly in Castile and León (Toledo, Valladolid, Segovia, and Avila, among the most important). These communities were unhappy with Charles's absence in pursuit of the imperial crown and disgusted by the rapacity of his Flemish officials appointed to high positions in Spain. Brandi adds that "social disagreements between Grandees and towns, the latter led for the most part by small nobility, sharpened the conflict" (*The Emperor Charles V,* 143). The revolt was crushed by the Constable of Castile, Don Iñigo Velasco, at the battle of Villalar, April 23, 1521.

Chapter XV

1. The details of this trade are given in Book XXVI, Chapter IV. In spite of Oviedo's self-proclaimed probity, he recounts with some satisfaction how he had made some worthless hatchets from scrap iron, which he traded with the Indians, netting some fifteen hundred pesos. Three months later when he calculated that the

inferior hatchets had lost their edge, he sent another trading mission with sharpening stones. When the Indians presented their dull hatchets, Oviedo's men sharpened them below deck out of sight and traded them again as new, this time netting seven thousand castellanos.

2. Peter Martyr, an intimate of Bishop Fonseca and member of the Council of the Indies, had supported Pedrarias's appointment but later was dismayed by the reports from Darién. In Martyr's fourth *Decade* he reported to Pope Leo X: "captains were sent out to diverse parts with companies of soldiers. I will relate it with few words because it is all horrible and nothing pleasant. Since I concluded my [previous] Decade, nothing has been done there other than kill and be killed, murder and be murdered" (Mártir de Anglería, *Décadas del nuevo mundo*, 285).

3. In general, the Castilian Oviedo did not have a high opinion of Basques, who with their impenetrable language he felt formed a subversive clan, as he noted in the case of the unfortunate Governor Nicuesa.

4. The Basque hatchets were heavy, first-class implements made of steel and much prized by the natives.

5. Oviedo described the *areito* in the *Summary* of his general history published in 1526 as follows: "When the Indians want to amuse themselves and sing, a great company of men and women get together and catch hands, alternately men and women. The leader, who is called *tequina*, man or woman, takes a few steps forward and then back, something like a contradance, and they go around in this fashion, and he sings in a low or medium voice anything that he cares to, making the measure of his voice keep time with the steps. And what he speaks is repeated by the multitude that takes part in the contradance or *areito*, and the same steps and order, but in a louder voice. This goes on for three or four hours or longer, or from one day to another . . . They drink so much that often they get so drunk that they appear to lose all senses" (translation by Stoudemire, *Natural History*, 38).

6. Previously Oviedo states that Corobari is the relative of Elvira. Later in the text, Bea is specifically mentioned as Elvira's cousin. It would seem that all three are related.

Chapter XVI

1. The plural here refers to Charles and his mother, Queen Juana, although she was not properly an empress. After Charles's election as Holy Roman Emperor upon the death of his grandfather, Emperor Maximilian (January 12, 1519), he was to be addressed as "majesty" and communications to him were to begin "S.C.C.R. Majestad" (*Sacra, Cesárea, Católica, Real Majestad:* Holy, Caesarean, Catholic, Royal Majesty) (Keniston, *Francisco de los Cobos*, 57). There was no empress until Charles married Isabel of Portugal in 1526.

2. Francisco de Lizaur: Oviedo reports in Chapter XIV that Lizaur, Pedrarias's agent, went with Doña Isabel to Spain.

3. The Cortes: "A general assembly in the ancient kingdoms of Castile, Aragon,

Valencia, Navarre and Catalonia in which delegates were authorized to intervene in affairs of state by their own right, or as representatives of classes or bodies in the cities and towns which had a vote in the assembly according to the laws, rights, customs and privileges of each kingdom" (*Diccionario de la lengua española*, hereinafter *DRAE*).

Chapter XVII

1. Amador de los Ríos (in his notes to Oviedo's *Historia*) indicates that this is from Saint Gregory's *Moralia*, Book XXIII, Chapter XXXI, commenting on chapters 31 and 32 of Job.

2. Amador de los Ríos finds this in Corinthians II, 10 and 24, where Saint Paul speaks of the sufferings he endured to spread Christ's word: "Of the Jews five times received I forty stripes save one."

3. From the *Moralia*, Book XXII, Chapter XIV, on Job 31 (Amador de los Ríos).

4. It is curious that Oviedo calls Enciso his friend. Martín Fernández de Enciso published the first work on America in Spanish, the *Suma de geografía* (Seville: Juan Cromberger, 1519; reprinted 1530 and 1546). Oviedo never once mentions this work even though he must have known of it. Gerbi conjectures that this deliberate silence is because Oviedo did not want to acknowledge any other work on America preceding his own (*Nature in the New World*, 76–91).

5. From the *Moralia*, Book II, Chapter XVIII, on Job 1 (Amador de los Ríos).

Chapter XVIII

1. Amador de los Ríos notes that in the original manuscript, Oviedo crossed out information on the two appeals. One was to have his arrest referred to Pedrarias; the other was against the confiscation and redistribution of Corobari's Indians to the company of soldiers who captured the chief.

Chapter XIX

1. Amador de los Ríos identifies this, without specifying work, chapter, or other locus, as being from Saint Ambrose: "Omnia nobis factus est Christus; si febribus aestuas, fons est; si vulnus habes, medicus est; si mortem times, vita est; si auxilio indiges, virtus est; si cibum quaeris, alimentum est." Saint Ambrose was bishop of Milan ca. A.D. 340–97.

Chapter XX

1. Diego Velázquez: the governor of Cuba, perhaps more famous for having the conquest of Mexico with its fabulous wealth stolen from him by the captain he sent to explore that coast—Hernando Cortez. In the synopsis heading of the first chapter of Book XXXIII of Oviedo's history dealing with New Spain (Mexico), he writes

"how by subtle ways [Cortez] separated himself from the obedience and friendship of the Adelantado Diego Velázquez, his superior under whose orders he had gone to that land" (120:8).

2. Amador de los Ríos finds this reference in Anthony of Florence, Title 19, Chapter VIII, Paragraph XIV.

Chapter XXI

1. Alonso de Chaves (?–1587): cosmographer major of the House of Trade for the Indies. He was the author of perhaps the first manual for seamen, *Quatri partitu en cosmographia practica,* otherwise known as *Espejo de navegantes.* Throughout his *History,* Oviedo notes corrections to Chaves's "modern" chart, dated 1536, stating "my intention is not to offend their authority, but rather supply more accurate accounts . . . for the correction of the official maps" (118:327).

2. This gulf in Costa Rica, later also called the Gulf of Los Güetares and still later the Gulf of Nicaragua, is now referred to as the Gulf of Nicoya.

3. On modern maps, the chief's name is immortalized in Burica Island, Point Burica, and the Burica Peninsula on the Pacific coast between Costa Rica and Panamá.

4. Caño Island retains its name today. It is in Coronado Bay off the Osa Peninsula of Costa Rica. The Gulf of San Vicente of which Oviedo writes could be present-day Playa San Josecito or perhaps Drake Bay a little to the north. Given the latitudes Oviedo supplies, Gulf of San Vicente corresponds to modern-day Coronado Bay.

5. The chief's name is preserved in the peninsula and gulf of Nicoya (called Orotiña or Sanlúcar by Oviedo) on the Pacific coast of Costa Rica.

6. Soldiers and especially sailors were a superstitious lot. Accidents like this at the start of an enterprise were taken as bad omens.

7. Count Fernán González, ca. A.D. 950, is credited with establishing Castile as an independent kingdom.

8. Laconia is "the southeastern district of the Peloponnese (Southern Greece)"; the chief city was Sparta (M. Grant, *A Guide to the Ancient World*). Amador de los Ríos references this incident from *Chronica, ab initio mundi, alius Theutonica.* Gerbi identifies the author of this chronicle as the German historian Johannes Carion and says that Oviedo appears to cite from a Latin translation of the original German (*Nature in the New World,* 258, n. 11).

9. These wooden swords were generally inset with sharpened pieces of stone or obsidian.

10. The Jarama River flows through the provinces of Guadalajara and Madrid.

11. The wedding of Peirithous (or Pirithous) and Hippodame and the battle with the centaurs are recounted in Book 13 of Ovid's *Metamorphoses.* Oviedo's memory here is faulty: the hero to the rescue was Theseus not Hercules. Still, the comparison seems a little forced.

12. Lake Nicaragua is 110 miles long and 36 miles wide. The water level fluctuates according to the season.

13. Probably Ometepe Island, sixteen miles long by eight miles wide, actually two islands connected by a short isthmus.

14. Amador de los Ríos notes this as being from Book VI, Chapter XIX of Pliny. The sea not named by Oviedo is the Caspian.

15. Oviedo returns to the subject of Nicaragua in Book XLII. The reference here is probably to Chapter IV, "Which treats of the lakes of Nicaragua" (120:385), and Chapter V, "Which treats of the horrible, burning mountain of Mayasa, which continually each night emits flames" (120:390).

16. West by north (*Oeste cuarta de noroeste*): Morison explains the sixteenth-century compass card in his *Admiral of the Ocean Sea* (1:246). The *cuarta* or quarter-winds represented a compass point of eleven and one-fourth degrees.

17. Both Herradura and Cape Blanco are a little more than nine degrees, thirty minutes north.

18. The drawing is reproduced at the end of the *Biblioteca de autores españoles* edition, vol. 121, plate 9.

19. There are numerous islands in this gulf, but only Chira has retained the same name. Cachoa (Ciervos) is probably the island called Venado (deer) today. Chara, also known as Sanlúcar, as Oviedo writes a few lines farther on, is now called San Lucas.

20. The Zapandi River is now called the Tempisque.

21. Amador de los Ríos references this as being from Johannes Carion's *Chronica theutonica:* "Nec prius decorem capillorum redegit in ordinem quem tantam urben in suam potestatem restituit."

22. Amador de los Ríos identifies this as being from *Triunfo de la Fama*, Chapter II: "poi vidi la magnanima reyna. / Che una treccia rivolta e l'atra sparsa / Corse a la babilonica rapina."

23. Amador de los Ríos identifies this as being from Justinus, *De bello ext.*, Book I. The *Epitome* of Marcus Junianus Justinus (fl. 3rd cent. A.D.) was an abridgment of the lost *Historiae Philippicae et totius mundi origines et terrae situs* of Pompeius Trogas.

24. This seems to be a type of infibulation.

25. *Nácar* is mother-of-pearl. The *DRAE* defines *nacarón* as mother-of-pearl of inferior quality.

26. The description is found in Book VIII, Chapter XXXI.

27. It is difficult to identify these places with certainty. De las Velas may be Cape Velas at about ten degrees, fifteen minutes. There are several islands beyond Cape Velas. Perhaps Moya is present-day Chocoyas Island.

28. Posesión: now Port Esparta, Corinto, Nicaragua, about twelve degrees, thirty minutes north.

29. *Papagayo* is a parrot. According to the *DRAE,* the phrase *hablar como el/un papagayo* has two figurative meanings rather similar to those found in English: "to

parrot, to imitate" and "to chatter like a parrot." Oviedo probably means the men chattered mechanically away at their prayers during this difficult crossing. Later in Part III, Book XXXIX Oviedo reviews New World geography and in Chapter II he returns to Tierra Firme to offer another explanation, writing that the Gulf of Papagayo comes by its name from the peculiar winds there that make a ship's rigging vibrate and chatter more than in other places (120:345).

30. Point Catalina is probably Cape Santa Elena (about eleven degrees). Point Nicaragua is perhaps now Point Consigüina (thirteen degrees).

31. These are small sea bass called cassells. The *DRAE* says they make this characteristic sound when they are caught and removed from the water.

32. The Gulf of Fonseca is actually at a little more than thirteen degrees north.

33. Sightings taken on land were more accurate than those taken on board a rolling ship.

34. Oviedo's results are close to modern figures except for Cape Blanco, which is at a little more than nine degrees, thirty minutes.

35. San Pedro: previously, according to Chaves (see note 1, this chapter), this river was called the Mesa.

36. The westernmost point of Fonseca Bay is now called Cape Amapala.

37. Olit, now generally spelled Olid.

38. A typical story of the perils of trusting anyone in those frontier times from Book XXI, Chapter I: Olid had also captured Captain Francisco de las Casas, Cortez's brother-in-law. Las Casas and Gil González were too well treated as prisoners by Olid—one night at dinner with him, the two stabbed Olid with table knives but Olid was able to escape. Las Casas and Gil González declared themselves governors and tracked down and executed Olid. Shortly afterward, Las Casas arrested Gil González and sent him in chains to New Spain (Mexico). Gil González was then sent to Spain, where he died soon after returning to his home town of Avila.

Chapter XXII

1. Schoolmaster (*maestrescuela*): a cathedral office, in ancient times held by a theologian. Fernando de Luque, according to Oviedo, was from Porcuna in Andalusia (121:124). After the conquest of Peru, Oviedo reports, "His majesty granted a bishopric to Father Luque, the companion of [Pizarro and Almagro] with whose money they accomplished their deeds, but both paid him back with ingratitude, according to a letter the bishop elect wrote to me in his own hand" (121:33).

2. Scammony is the twining Asian convolvulus, *Convolvulus scammonia* (*Webster's*).

3. Oviedo covers Peru in Book XLVI.

4. The four towns referred to are Acla, Nombre de Dios, Panamá, and Natá.

5. For lack of sufficient financing, Oviedo never took possession of this territory, now in Colombia.

Chapter XXIII

1. The fourth watch (*al cuarto de alba*): the last of the four watches of the night (*DRAE*).

2. Oviedo naturally takes much delight in Pedrarias's passing up the subsequent Peruvian bonanza. At about this time Oviedo, who had lost considerable money because of Pedrarias's depopulation of Darién, was forced to settle with the governor for a fraction of his claim.

Chapter XXIV

1. This passage is difficult to follow due to its obliqueness. Obviously, from the statements that follow, it appears that Oviedo is treading very carefully. It appears to mean that since the governor makes restitution to the aggrieved party, if the judge wishes to make some money he has to make a deal with the governor, perhaps take a bribe for a favorable judgment. Two paragraphs later Oviedo says that he suspected that the judge was favorable to Pedrarias.

Bibliography

Works by Oviedo

A comprehensive guide to Oviedo's known works is Daymond Turner's annotated bibliographical monograph written forty years ago, from which much of the following information is excerpted and amplified with editions published since Turner's study. The list of primary sources is arranged in order of composition as far as can be determined. Reprintings in full or in part are only indicated for Spanish and English editions.

Claribalte (1519)

Libro del muy esforzado y inuencible Caballero dela Fortuna propiamente llamado don claribalte. Valencia: Juan Viñao, 1519. (Facsimile edition, Madrid: Real Academia Española, 1956).

Claribalte: Gonzalo Fernández de Oviedo. Estudio preliminar, edición crítica, notas e índices por M. J. Rodilla León. México: Universidad Autónoma Metropolitana— Universidad Iztapalapa: Universidad Nacional Autónoma de México, 2002.

Claribalte. Edición de Alberto del Río Nogueras. Alcalá de Henares: Centro de Estudios Cervantinos, 2002.

Relación de . . . la prisión del rey de Francia (ca. 1525)

Relación de lo sucedido en la prisión de el rey de Francia desde que fue traydo en España por todo el tiempo que estuvo en ella, hasta que el Emperador le dio libertad y volvió en Francia casado con Madama Leonor, hermana del Emperador Carlos quinto, Rey de España. In *Colección de documentos inéditos para la historia de España.* Vol. 38. Madrid: Imprenta de la Viuda de Calero, 1861.

Relación de . . . la prisión del rey de Francia . . . In *Historia de la villa y Corte de Madrid.* Edited by J. Amador de los Ríos and Juan de Dios de la Rada y Delgado. Madrid: M. López de la Hoya, 1862. Appendix II, Vol. 2, 457–70.

La prisión de Francisco I en Madrid. In *Biblioteca Universal,* Vol 176. Edited by M. Pérez, Madrid, 1920.

Sumario (1526)

Oviedo de la natural hystoria de las Indias. Toledo: Remón de Petras, 1526.

The hystorie of the Weste Indies. In Richard Eden, *The Decades of the Newe World or West India.* London: Guilhelmi, 1555.

The hystorie of the Weste Indies. In *The History of Trauayle in the West and East Indies.* London: Richard Lugge, 1577.

Extracts of Gonzalo Ferdinando De Oviedo his Summarie and General Historie of the Indies. In Samuel Purchas, *Hakluytus Posthumus.* London: Samuel Purchas for Henry Fetherstone, 1625.

De la natural historia de las Indias. In Andrés González Barcia Carballido y Zúñiga, *Historiadores primitivos de las Indias.* Madrid, 1749.

De la natural historia de las Indias. In Enrique de Bedia, *Historiadores primitivos de Indias. Biblioteca de autores españoles,* vol. 22. Madrid: Rivadaneyra, 1852.

The Natural History of the West Indies, First Printed in 1526. In Edward Arber, *The First Three English Books on America.* Birmingham, 1885. Reissued, Westminster, 1895.

Extracts of Gonzalo Ferdinando De Oviedo his Summarie. In *Hakluytus Posthumus or Purchas His Pilgrimes.* Hakluyt Society, extra series, no. 15. Glasgow: James MacLehose and Sons, 1906.

De la natural historia de las Indias. Edited by A. López. Madrid: Editorial Summa, 1942.

Sumario de la natural historia de las Indias. Edición, introducción y notas de J. Miranda. In *Biblioteca Americana.* Serie Cronistas de Indias, 13. Mexico-Buenos Aires: Fondo de Cultura Económica, 1950.

Natural History of the West Indies by Gonzalo Fernández de Oviedo. Translated and edited by Sterling A. Stoudemire. University of North Carolina Studies in the Romance Languages and Literatures, No. 32. Chapel Hill: University of North Carolina Press, 1959.

De la natural hystoria de las Indias. A facsimile edition in honor of Sterling A. Stoudemire. Chapel Hill: University of North Carolina Press, 1969.

Sumario de la natural y general historia de las Indias. Madrid: Espasa-Calpe, 1978.

Sumario de la natural historia de las Indias. Edited by Manuel Ballesteros Gaibrois. Madrid: Historia 16, 1986.

Florilegio histórico de las Indias. Oviedo, Asturias, España: Grupo Editorial Asturiano; Madrid: Distribución general, Ediciones Istmo, 1992. (Chapters 1–10 from the *Sumario*).

Sumario de la natural historia de las Indias. Madrid: Confederación Española de Gremios y Asociaciones de Libreros, 1992.

Sumario de la natural historia de las Indias. Edited by N. del Castillo Mathieu. Santa

Fé de Bogotá, Instituto Caro y Cuervo: Universidad de Bogotá "Jorge Tadeo Lozano," 1995.

Sumario de la natural historia de las Indias. Edited by Manuel Ballesteros Gaibrois. Las Rozas (Madrid): Dastin, 2002.

Catálogo real de Castilla (1532)

Cathálogo Real de Castilla, y de todos los Reyes de las Españas e de Nápoles y Secilia, e de los Reyes y señores de las Casas de Françia, Austria, Holanda y Borgoña; de donde proceden los quatro abolorios de la Cesárea Magestad del Emperador don Carlos, nuestro Rey e señor de las Españas, con relación de todos los Emperadores y Summos Pontífices que han sucedido desde Jullio César, que fue el primero emperador, y desde el apóstol Sanct Pedro, que fue el primero Papa, hasta este año de Cristo de MDXXXII años. 1532. Biblioteca del Real Monasterio del Escorial, Ms. H-1-7.

"Transcripción y Edición del *Catálogo Real de Castilla*, autógrafo inédito de Gonzalo Fernández de Oviedo y Valdés." Evelia Ana Romano de Thuesen, Ph.D. diss., University of California, Santa Barbara, 1992.

Historia general y natural de las Indias (1535, 1547, 1557)

La historia general de las Indias. Seville: Juan Cromberger, 1535.

Cronica de las Indias. La hystoria de las Indias agora nueuament impressa corregida y emendada. Salamanca: Juan de Junta, 1547.

Libro XX, de la segunda parte de la general historia de las Indias. Valladolid: Francisco Fernández de Córdoba, 1557.

Historia general y natural de las Indias, islas y tierra firme del mar océano, por el capitán Gonzalo Fernández de Oviedo y Valdés, primer cronista del Nuevo Mundo. Edited by J. Amador de los Ríos. 4 vols. Madrid: Imprenta de la Real Academia de la Historia, 1851–55.

Historia general y natural de las Indias, islas y tierra-firme del mar océano. Prologue by J. N. González. Notes by J. Amador de los Ríos. 14 vols. Asunción del Paraguay: Editorial Guaranía, 1944–45.

Historia general y natural de las Indias. Edición y estudio preliminar de J. Pérez de Tudela Bueso. In *Biblioteca de autores españoles,* vols. 117–21. Madrid: Ediciones Atlas, 1959.

Selections from the Historia general

Libro XLVII, cap. 1–67. In *Colección de historiadores de Chile.* Vol. 22, pp. 1–254. Santiago de Chile, 1901.

Selecciones de la Historia general. In *Colección de historiadores de Chile.* Vols. 27, 29. Santiago de Chile, 1901–2.

"An Account Based on the Diary of Rodrigo Ranjel." In E. G. Bourne, *Narratives of the Career of Hernando de Soto.* New York: Allerton Book Company, 1922.

Historia de Indias (selecciones). Madrid: Bueno del Amo, 1927.

The Discovery of the Amazon According to the Account of Friar Gaspar de Carvajal. Introduction by J. T. Medina. Translated by B. T. Lee. New York: American Geographical Society, 1934.

"Selections from Oviedo's *Historia de Indias*." Appendix to Fr. Gaspar de Carvajal, *The Discovery of the Amazon*. New York: American Geographic Society, 1934.

"Almagro: episodios de su vida." *Boletín de la Academia chilena de la historia* 110 & 2do semestre (1936):25–78.

Relación del nuevo descubrimiento del famoso Río Grande . . . por el capitán Francisco de Orellana. Edited by T. Medina. Quito, Ecuador: Imprenta del Ministerio de Educación, 1942.

Los viajes de Colón. Edited by Jaime Delgado. Madrid: Atlas, 1944. (Books 1 and 2 of *Historia general y natural de las Indias*.)

Biblioteca histórica de Puerto-Rico, que contiene various documentos de los siglos XV, XVI, XVII y XVIII. Edited by A. Tapia y Rivera. San Juan de Puerto Rico: Instituto de Literatura Puertorriqueño, 1945.

Sucesos y diálogo de la Nueva España. Selected by and with a prologue by E. O'Gorman. México: Universidad Nacional Autónoma, 1946.

The Narrative of Alvar Cabeza de Vaca. Translated by F. Bandelier. Introduction by J. F. Bannon. Barre, MA: Printed for the Imprint Society, 1972.

The Journal of the Vaca Party: The Account of the Narváez Expedition 1528 1536. Translated by B.C. Hedrick and C. L. Riley. Carbondale: University Museum, Southern Illinois University, 1974.

The Conquest and Settlement of the Island of Boriquen or Puerto Rico. Translated and edited by Daymond Turner. Avon, CT: Limited Editions Club, 1975.

Costa Rica vista por Fernández de Oviedo. Edited by C. M. Meléndez Chavarri. San José, Costa Rica: Ministerio de Cultura, Juventud y Deportes, Departamento de Publicaciones, 1978.

Imponente complejo volcánico en Masaya, Nicaragua. Edited by A. Eskorcia Zuñiga. Masaya, Nicaragua: A. E. Zuñiga, 1978.

Escenario geográfico de Costa Rica según los informes de Gonzalo Fernández de Oviedo en la "Historia general y natural de las Indias." Edited by M. Molina Lunes and J. Piana de Cuestas. San José: Universidad de Costa Rica, 1979.

Historia general y natural de las Indias. Books 1–20. México: Centro de Estudios de Historia de México, 1979.

Historia general y natural de las Indias; la provincia de Venezuela. Colección Viajes y descripciones, 8. Caracas: Fundación de Promoción Cultural de Venezuela, 1986.

Crónicas escogidas: Oviedo las Casas. Biblioteca de Clásicos Dominicanos, Vol. IV. Preface and notes by J. R. Reyes. Santo Domingo: Ediciones de la Fundación Corripio, 1988.

The Hernando de Soto Expedition. Edited by J. T. Milanich. New York: Garland, 1991. (Reprints the Bourne translation of the Ranjel diary.)

Florilegio histórico de las Indias. Oviedo, Asturias, España: Grupo Editorial Asturiano; Madrid: Distribución general, Ediciones Istmo, 1992. (Includes *Historia general*, Book XXXIII, Prologue and Chapters 1–13.)

"Account of the Northern Conquest and Discovery of Hernando de Soto by Rodrigo Ranjel." In *The De Soto Chronicles*. Edited by Lawrence A. Clayton, Vernon James Knight, Jr., and Edward C. Moore. Vol. 1, pp. 247–307. Tuscaloosa: University of Alabama Press, 1993.

Historias de Indias: Selección de textos de América. Edited by Germán Arciniegas. Barcelona: Océano, 1995.

Oviedo on Columbus. Edited by J. Carrillo. Translated by D. Avalle-Arce. Preface by A. Pagden. Turnhout, Belgium: Brepols, 2000.

We Came Naked and Barefoot: The Journal of Cabeza de Vaca across North America. A. D. Krieger. Edited by M. H. Krieger. Foreword and afterword by T. R. Hester. Austin: University of Texas Press, 2002. (Book XXXV, Chapters 1–7 of the *General y natural historia de las Indias*.)

Regla de la vida espiritual (1548)

Regla de la vida espiritual y teología secreta. Seville: Domingo Robertis, 1548.

Libro de la cámara real del príncipe Don Juan (1547–48)

Libro de la cámara real del príncipe Don Juan. Edited by Escudero de la Peña. Madrid: Imprenta de la viuda e hijos de Galiano, 1870.

"Libro de la cámara real del príncipe don Juan e oficios de su casa e servicio ordinario de Gonzalo Fernández de Oviedo y Valdés según el manuscrito autógrafo Escorial E. IV.8. Estudio, Transcripción y notas." Jon Vincent Blake, Ph.D. diss. Chapel Hill: University of North Carolina Press, 1975.

Batallas y quincuagenas (begun ca. 1544)

Batallas y quincuagenas. Transcription by J. Amador de los Ríos. Edited and with a prologue by J. Pérez de Tudela y Bueso. 4 vols. Madrid: Real Academia de la Historia, 1983–2003.

Quincuagenas (1556)

Las quincuagenas de los generosos y no menos famosos reyes, príncipes, duques, marqueses, y condes e caballeros e personas notables de España. Edited by Vicente de la Fuente. Madrid: Imprenta y Fundición de Manuel Tello, 1880. (Only one volume of the three-volume manuscript was published.)

"Noticias de Madrid y de las familias madrileñas de su tiempo, por Gonzalo Fernández de Oviedo," extract by Julián Paz. *Revista de la Biblioteca, Archivo y Museo* (Ayuntamiento de Madrid) 16(1947):273–332.

"Elogio del Cardenal Tavera por G. Fernández de Oviedo: 1555," extract by P. Vicente Beltrán de Heredia. *Cartulario de la Universidad de Salamanca, La Universidad en el Siglo de Oro*, 2:640. Salamanca, 1970.

Las memorias de Gonzalo Fernández de Oviedo. Edited by Juan Bautista Avalle-Arce. North Carolina Studies in the Romance Languages and Literatures. Texts, Textual Studies, and Translations, Nos. 1–2. Chapel Hill, NC: Publications of the

Department of Romance Languages, 1974. (A selection of the *quincuagenas* from all three volumes of the manuscript.)

De las grandezas de Madrid: noticias de Madrid y sus familias. (1514–1556). Edited by F. Gutiérrez Carbajo. Madrid: Guillermo Blázquez, 2000.

Selected Sources

Alcedo, Antonio de. *Diccionario geográfico de las Indias Occidentales o América.* In *Biblioteca de autores españoles,* vols. 205–8. Madrid: Atlas, 1959.

Alcocer Martínez, Mariano. *D. Juan Rodríguez de Fonseca: estudio crítico-biográfico.* Valladolid: Imprenta de la Casa Social Católica, 1926.

Alexander VI (pope). *Inter caetera.* In *Hakluytus Posthumus or Purchas His Pilgrimes.* Translated by Richard Eden. Vol. 2, pp. 32–42. Glasgow: J. MacLehose, 1906.

Alvarez Rubiano, Pablo. *Pedrarias Dávila: contribución al estudio de la figura del "gran justador," gobernador de Castilla del Oro y Nicaragua.* Madrid: CSIC, 1944.

Anderson, Dr. C. L. G. *Life and Letters of Vasco Núñez de Balboa.* New York: Fleming H. Revell, 1941.

———. *Old Panama and Castilla del Oro.* New York: North River Press, 1944.

Araúz, Celestino Andrés, and Patricia Pizzurno. *El Panamá hispano (1501–1821).* Panamá: Diario La Prensa de Panamá, 1991.

Avalle-Arce, Juan B. "Oviedo a media luz." *Nueva Revista de Filología Hispánica* 29, no. 1(1980):138–51.

Belenguer, Ernest. *Fernando el Católico.* Barcelona: Ediciones Península, 2001.

Brandi, Karl. *The Emperor Charles V.* Translated by C. V. Wedgwood. London: J. Cape, 1939.

Bolaños, Alvaro F. "Panegírico y libelo del primer cronista de Indias: Gonzalo Fernández de Oviedo." *Thesaurus (Boletín del Instituto Caro y Cuervo)* 45, no. 3(1990):577–649.

Carande, Ramón. *Carlos V y sus banqueros.* 3 vols. Barcelona: Editorial Crítica, Junta de Castilla y León, 1987.

Carrillo, Jesús. "The *Historia General y Natural de las Indias* by Gonzalo Fernández de Oviedo." *Huntington Library Quarterly* 65(2002):321–44.

———. "Taming the Visible: Word and Image in Oviedo's *Historia General y Natural de las Indias.*" *Viator* (Belgium) 31(2000):399–431.

Columbus, Christopher. *Journals and Other Documents on the Life and Voyages of Christopher Columbus.* Translated and edited by Samuel E. Morison. New York: Heritage Press, 1963.

Columbus, Ferdinand. *The Life of the Admiral Christopher Columbus by His Son Ferdinand.* Translated and annotated by Benjamin Keen. New Brunswick, NJ: Rutgers University Press, 1959.

Diccionario de la lengua española (DRAE). Compiled by Real Academia Española. 21st ed. Madrid: Espasa-Calpe, 1992.

Fernández Alvarez, M. *Carlos V, el César y el Hombre.* Madrid: Espasa Calpe, 2000.

Fernández de Enciso, Martín. *Suma de geografía*. Translated and amplified by Roger Barlow. In *A brief summe of geographie*. Hakluyt Society, 2nd series, no. 69. London: Robert MacLehose, 1932.

Fernández de Navarrete, Martín. *Colección de viajes y descubrimientos que hicieron por mar los españoles desde fines del siglo XV*. In *Biblioteca de autores españoles*, vol. 76. Madrid: Atlas, 1964.

Gerbi, Antonello. *Nature in the New World: From Christopher Columbus to Gonzalo Fernández de Oviedo*. Translated by Jeremy Moyle. Pittsburgh: University of Pittsburgh Press, 1985.

Grant, Michael. *A Guide to the Ancient World: A Dictionary of Classical Place Names*. New York: Barnes and Noble, 1997.

Hanke, Lewis. *Aristotle and the American Indians: A Study in Race Prejudice in the Modern World*. Bloomington: Indiana University Press, 1970.

Keniston, Hayward. *Francisco de los Cobos: Secretary of the Emperor Charles V*. Pittsburgh: University of Pittsburgh Press, 1958.

Las Casas, Fray Bartolomé de. *Historia de las Indias*. 3 vols. Edited by Augustín Millares Carlo. Introduction by Lewis Hanke. México: Fondo de Cultura Económica, 1951.

———. *A Short Account of the Destruction of the Indies*. Edited and translated by Nigel Griffin. Introduction by Anthony Pagden. London: Penguin Books, 1992.

Lerner, Isaías. "La visión humanística de América: Gonzalo Fernández de Oviedo." In *Las Indias (América) en la literatura del Siglo de Oro: Homenaje a Jesús Cañedo*. Kassel: Edition Reichenberger, 1992.

Mártir de Anglería, Pedro. *Décadas del nuevo mundo*. Madrid: Ediciones Polifemo, 1989.

Mena García, María del Carmen. "La autonomía legislativa en Indias: las leyes de Burgos y su aplicación en Castilla del Oro por Pedrarias Dávila." *Revista de Indias* 49, no. 186(1989):283–353.

———. *La ciudad en un cruce de caminos (Panamá y sus orígenes urbanos)*. Sevilla: Escuela de Estudios Hispano-Americanos de Sevilla, 1992.

———. *Pedrarias Dávila o "la ira de Dios": una historia olvidada*. Sevilla: Universidad de Sevilla, 1992.

———. *Sevilla y las flotas de Indias: la gran armada de Castilla del Oro*. Sevilla: Universidad de Sevilla, 1998.

———. *La sociedad de Panamá en el siglo XVI*. Sevilla: Publicaciones de la Excma. Diputación de Sevilla, 1984.

Mojica, Rafael. "FORTUNA AURI: The Dialectics of Gold in Gonzalo Fernández de Oviedo's Imperial Discourse." *Revista de Estudios Hispánicos* 23(1966): 125–35.

Molina de Lines, María, and Josefina Piana de Cuestas. *El escenario geográfico de Costa Rica en el s. XVI según los informes de Gonzalo Fernández de Oviedo en "La Historia general y natural de las Indias."* Proyecto de Historia de Costa Rica, No. 2. San José: Universidad de Costa Rica, 1979.

Morison, Samuel E. *Admiral of the Ocean Sea: A Life of Christopher Columbus.* 2 vols. Boston: Little, Brown, 1942.

Muñoz Delgado, Juan Jacobs. "Santa María de la Antigua del Darién." *Boletín de Historia y Antigüedades* (Bogotá, Columbia) 83, no. 794(1996):639–55.

Nicholl, Charles. *The Creature in the Map: Sir Walter Raleigh's Quest for El Dorado.* London: Vintage, 1996.

Padrón, Ricardo. *The Spacious World: Cartography, Literature, and Empire in Early Modern Spain.* Chicago: University of Chicago Press, 2004.

Pagden, Anthony. *The Fall of Natural Man.* Cambridge: Cambridge University Press, 1982.

Peña y Cámara, José de la. "Contribuciones documentales y críticas para una biografía de Gonzalo Fernández de Oviedo." *Revista de Indias* 17, no. 69-70(1957): 603–705.

Pérez-Mallaína, Pablo E. *Spain's Men of the Sea: Daily Life on the Indies Fleets in the Sixteenth Century.* Translated by C. R. Phillips. Baltimore: Johns Hopkins University Press, 1998.

Pérez de Tudela Bueso, Juan. "Rasgos del semblante espiritual de Gonzalo Fernández de Oviedo: La hidalguía caballeresca ante el nuevo mundo." *Revista de Indias* 17, no. 69-70(1957):391–443.

———. "Vida y escritos de Gonzalo Fernández de Oviedo." Introduction to *Historia general y natural de las Indias.* In *Biblioteca de autores españoles,* vol. 117, pp. vii–clxxv. Madrid: Atlas, 1959.

Romano de Thuesen, Evelia. "Un autógrafo inédito de Gonzalo Fernández de Oviedo y Valdés: la historia de España escrita desde el Nuevo Mundo." In *Encuentros y desencuentros de culturas: desde la edad media al siglo XVIII. Actas de la Asociación Internacional de Hispanistas.* Vol. 3, pp. 93–101. Irvine: University of California, 1994.

Romoli, Kathleen. *Balboa of Darién: Discoverer of the Pacific.* Garden City, NY: Doubleday, 1953.

Rubin, Nancy. *Isabella of Castile.* New York, St. Martin's, 1991.

Sagarra Gamazo, Adelaida. *La otra versión de la historia Indiana: Colón y Fonseca.* Valladolid: Universidad de Valladolid, 1997.

Salas, Alberto M. *Tres cronistas de Indias: Pedro Mártir de Anglería, Gonzalo Fernández de Oviedo, Fray Bartolomé de las Casas.* Mexico City: Fondo de Cultura Económica, 1986.

Sobel, Dava, and William J. H. Andrews. *The Illustrated Longitude.* New York: Walker, 1998.

Taylor, Elizabeth. *My Love Affair with Jewels.* New York: Simon and Schuster, 2002.

Thomas, Hugh. *Rivers of Gold: The Rise of the Spanish Empire, from Columbus to Magellan.* New York: Random House, 2003.

Turner, Daymond. "The Aborted First Printing of the Second Part of Oviedo's *General and Natural History of the Indies.*" *Huntington Library Quarterly* 46(1983): 105–25.

———. "Forgotten Treasure from the Indies: The Illustrations and Drawings of Fernández de Oviedo." *Huntington Library Quarterly* 48(1985):1–46.

———. *Gonzalo Fernández de Oviedo y Valdés: An Annotated Bibliography.* University of North Carolina Studies in the Romance Languages and Literatures, No. 66. Chapel Hill: University of North Carolina Press, 1966.

Walton, Timothy R. *The Spanish Treasure Fleets.* Sarasota, FL: Pineapple Press, 1994.

Index

147; crops grown by, 55, 77, 99, 162; decimation of population, 74, 83–84, 93; defense of their land, 48–50, 54–57, 170, 154–55, 172–73; dress of, 160–61; dress for war, 48, 56, 154, 173; ethnographic remarks about, 77, 153, 157, 160–63; evangelization of, 17, 23, 151, 152, 153–154; living in Spanish communities, 60, 114, 172; material effects of, 49–50, 54, 57, 82, 148–49; retaliation against Spanish, 77, 80, 92, 113, 120–22; native religious practices of, 151, 153, 162; Spanish atrocities against, 67–68, 77, 79, 81, 98, 148; Spanish intentions toward, 51–54, 63–64, 150, 151, 153. *See also* Slavery

Indies, 5, 32, 35, 37, 89
Irra Island, 159
Isabella I (queen of Castile), 1, 2, 4; biography of, 30–31
Island of Madeira, 86
Island of Santa María, 99
Italy, 2

Jamaica, 140
Jarama River, 156
Jiménez de Cisneros, Francisco (cardinal), 10, 88, 89; biography of, 32
Juana (the Beltraneja), 1
Juana, Queen (the Mad), 2, 3, 31, 32
Juanaga, 107
Juanaga, Chief, 61
Juan, Prince, 2, 15, 31
Jumento, Chief, 75, 76
Junta, Juan de, 18
Justinus, 160

King's Fifth, 68, 70, 76, 92, 145
Knights of Santiago, 104

La Coruña, 87
Lake Nicaragua, 145, 147, 158

Language: barrier between Spanish and Indians, 48, 68; Indian, 157, 161, 162
Las Casas, Friar Bartolomé de, xi, 10; biography of, 36–37; criticism of *General and Natural History*, 21–22; enmity against Oviedo, 11, 21–22, 24; *History of the Indies*, 21, 37; *A Short Account of the Destruction of the Indies*, 24, 37
Lascasismo, 24
Ledesma, Juan de, 110
Ledesma, Pedro de, 57
León, Nicaragua, 166
Lizaur, Francisco de, 106, 121
Loaysa, García Jofre de (cardinal), 19
López de Llerena, Juan, 113
López de Salcedo, Diego, 14, 178
López de Talavera, Ruy, 113
Luque, Fernando de, 169, 175

Madrid, 88, 89
Magellan, Ferdinand, 45, 146
Mahe, Chief, 75
Maldonado, Diego, 103
Manzanedo, Bernaldino de, 89
Maravedí, value of, 26
Márquez, Diego, 43, 45, 72, 78, 95, 102, 106, 107
Martyr, Peter, xi, 16–17; biography of, 37–38; *Decades of the New World*, 37
Masaya, 160
Matienzo, Friar Tomás de, 54
Matinino Island, 87
Medellín, Juan de, 113
Mena García, María del Carmen, 27
Mercado, Luis de, 43
Mesa River, 163
Miguel, Pedro, 45
Mithridates, 158
Moluccas, 146
Money and purchasing power, 26–28
Morales, Gaspar de, 43, 47, 54, 76, 81, 96
Moya Island, 163